Michael J

*To Brian
with best wishes
Michael Bry*

THE ALHAMBRA REVEALED
The Remarkable Story of the Kingdom of Granada

Andalus Press

For Norah Hamilton Cleary

Published by Andalus Press
Dublin, Ireland.

info@andalus.ie
www.andalus.ie

ISBN 978-0-9933554-2-4
© Michael B. Barry 2017
Michael B. Barry asserts the moral right to be identified as the author of this work.

All rights reserved. No part of this publication may be reproduced, stored in a retrieval system, or transmitted in any form or by any means, mechanical, electronic, recording, photocopying or otherwise, without the prior permission of the publisher.

By the same author:
Across Deep Waters, Bridges of Ireland
Restoring a Victorian House
Through the Cities, the Revolution in Light Rail
Tales of the Permanent Way, Stories from the Heart of Ireland's Railways
Fifty Things to do in Dublin
Dublin's Strangest Tales (with Patrick Sammon)
Bridges of Dublin, the Remarkable Story of Dublin's Liffey Bridges (with Annette Black)
The Green Divide, an Illustrated History of the Irish Civil War
Courage Boys, We are Winning, an Illustrated History of the 1916 Rising
Victorian Dublin Revealed, the Remarkable Legacy of Nineteenth-Century Dublin
Beyond the Chaos, the Remarkable Heritage of Syria
Homage to al-Andalus, the Rise and Fall of Islamic Spain

Jacket design by Anú Design.
Book design by Michael B. Barry.

Printed by Białostockie Zakłady Graficzne SA, Poland.

Contents

Acknowledgements		4
Introduction		5
Chapter 1	Iliberris to Granada	7
Chapter 2	The Nasrid Kingdom of Granada	43
Chapter 3	Conquest and Decline	97
Chapter 4	The Alhambra	133
General Information		201
Chronology		202
Glossary		203
Illustration Credits		204
Bibliography		204
Index		206

The Iberian Peninsula

Acknowledgements

My sincere thanks are due to the following:

Mariano Bozo, of the Patronato de la Alhambra y Generalife, was most helpful and facilitated my early-morning entry to the Alhambra. Antonio de Linares, as always, supported me greatly in my quest for the essence of Granada and the Alhambra. José Morillas provided me with ideas for the book. Jim Gahan was a knowledgeable travelling companion on one of my trips to Granada. Tony Redmond kindly provided me with an image of the historic town of Galera.

The staff of the museums and institutions in Spain and elsewhere proved very kind in providing me with images of buildings and artefacts relating to the era of al-Andalus. These include:
Antonio Sáez Antón, Patrimonio Histórico-Artístico del Senado, Madrid; Antonio Salas Sola, Visita Arjona; Barbara Jimenez Serrano, Archivo y Biblioteca del Patronato de la Alhambra y Generalife; Encarnación Maldonado Maldonado, Museo de Almería; Esperanza Montero, Museo del Ejército, Toledo; Eva Schubert, Museum Without Frontiers; Francisca Hornos, Museo de Jaén; Francisca López Garrido, Museo Arqueológico de Córdoba; Inmaculada Cortés, Fundación El Legado Andalusí; Juan Ruiz, Cabildo Metropolitano de Zaragoza; Mar Beltrán Alandete, Fundación Bancaja; Mónica Martín Díaz, Museo Arqueológico Nacional, Madrid; Mónica Requelme Nicolas, Museo Arqueológico de Granada; Purificación Marinetto Sánchez, Museo de la Alhambra, Granada; Rocío Castillo, Museo Lázaro Galdiano, Madrid; Victorino Benlloch, Capilla Real de Granada.

Patrick Sammon, always clear of eye, checked out my chapters – I am privileged to have his generous help. As usual my most important thanks go to Veronica Barry. Muse, editor and much else – this book would not have come about without her.

Introduction

Visiting the Alhambra is an astonishing experience. Looking up from the downtown Granada one sees on the Sabika Hill an undulating collection of defensive walls, interspersed with towers. This view of rather plain honey-coloured walls does not prepare you for the shock when you enter the Alhambra complex itself. As you enter the Nasrid palaces, there is sensory overload. You will be overwhelmed by the magnificence of the patios, fountains and pools, combined with the sounds of gently trickling water. All around is the beauty of the inscribed stucco, the multi-coloured azulejos, and the exquisite stalactite-type mocárabe ceilings. This book is designed to enhance and sustain this experience, not just to describe the grandeur of the Alhambra, but also to explain the circumstances – a fascinating story – under which this all came about.

The genesis of this book goes back over a decade ago when my interest in Spanish history was sparked by a modest fortification, dating from the time of al-Andalus, which I came across in the hills of the Sierra Bermeja (near Estepona in Andalucía). Who were these people? How did they live? That sent me on a five-year quest, researching and travelling all across Spain to explore the vestiges of al-Andalus. That led to my book *'Homage to al-Andalus, the Rise and Fall of Islamic Spain'* in 2008. In this I set out the story of al-Andalus, from start to finish. The book was very well received and is now in its second edition.

Following feedback and specific requests, I decided to focus afresh on the Alhambra, the most magnificent example of a medieval Islamic palace-city in Western Europe. It definitely warrants a book which complements it, which gives a clear and detailed description as well as, importantly, fully exploring its past.

Indeed many books have been written about the Alhambra, although very few give comprehensive information on its background. So I have endeavoured to redress this situation with a book which would give a complete description of the Alhambra in its historical setting. The core of this book is made up of a guide to the Alhambra in Chapter 4. This is intended to provide the visitor with a clear and user-friendly description of the palace-city, presented in a logical sequence that follows the way visitors proceed through the various buildings. All of this is supported by a comprehensive set of maps and illustrations. Along with this I present the story of how all this came about and its historical context, again with, what is by now, my trademark style of providing many photographs with detailed and interesting captions.

This story is presented in a linear and, hopefully, understandable fashion. Chapter 1 tells how the Muslims seized the Iberian Peninsula from the Visigoths after the invasion of AD 711 and al-Andalus came into being. Next came the Umayyad dynasty leading to the glory of the Córdoba Caliphate. When the Caliphate fell apart the Zirids set up their taifa in *Madinat Gharnata*, the genesis of the present city of Granada. Fundamentalism from the south eventually resulted in a collapse which allowed the burgeoning Christian kingdoms to the north to seize most of the territory of al-Andalus. Chapter 2 tells the story of Ibn al-Ahmar, the last strong man standing, who established the Nasrid dynasty, with its headquarters high on the Sabika Hill over Granada. The great palace-city of the Alhambra was constructed, surprisingly achieving such magnificence against the background of ferocious dynastic intrigue within the Nasrid royal family. The coming to power of the Catholic Monarchs, Fernando and Isabel, in the fifteenth century led directly to the fall of the Nasrid kingdom, the last remnant of Islam on the Peninsula, culminating in the takeover of the Alhambra in 1492. Chapter 3 tells the poignant story of the breaking of the accords which guaranteed the rights of the conquered Muslims. Forced baptisms and oppression led to uprisings culminating in evictions from Granada and then the final expulsion of the *Moriscos* from Spain. There were many subsequent changes in Christian Granada: construction of a large number of churches and other new buildings as well as alterations to the Alhambra. Luckily attention was focussed elsewhere in the centuries that followed and the Alhambra became a neglected haunt of gypsies and sheep. Alterations to the city's fabric during the end of the nineteenth century further removed vestiges of the Islamic city.

Quite apart from the Alhambra, Granada has many fascinating seams of history related to the Kingdom of Granada, its rise and fall. The narrow streets of the Albaicín evoke the feel of an Islamic city suburb. There are the gates and walls of the Zirid and Nasrid cities. It is not just the Palacio of Carlos V which evokes the clash of civilisations. The rush to build Christian buildings after the conquest in 1492 resulted in the demolition of much of Islamic Granada but in consequence there is a swathe of impressive Renaissance buildings, from churches and monasteries to civil ones like the Hospital Real. The Capilla Real where the Catholic Monarchs are buried is worth visiting: the statues, sepulchres and exhibits provide a rich insight into the history of Granada and Spain after the conquest. And Granada today? It is a bright, energetic city, strengthened by its university and burnished by the ornament sitting on the Sabika Hill.

In the course of preparing this book I was lucky to encounter many kind people who helped me and it was a pleasure to meet them. I treasure the generous help of the Patronato de la Alhambra y Generalife who greatly facilitated me. I had many memorable experiences including: visiting the Alhambra early in the morning, before the tourists arrive, thus savouring its magnificence in a peaceful setting; and meeting an expert in restoration, within one of the Nasrid palaces, as she expertly and precisely rehabilitated the stucco calligraphy. In summary, the writing and researching of this book was a most enjoyable experience: spending time in Granada, particulary the Alhambra; exploring these in depth; and unpeeling the surface layers of history to reveal the interesting narratives hidden beneath. What follows is the result, which I hope is both informative and entertaining.

Michael Barry, Andalucía, December 2016

Chapter 1
Iliberris to Granada

The Iberian Peninsula is roughly shaped as a rectangle, with a distance from north to south of more than 800 kilometres. This Peninsula has a history that is richer and more varied than most other parts of the world – and it has a history that has been largely shaped by its geography. The Pyrenees mountain range forms the neck of the Peninsula, dividing it from France. The Meseta Central, covering most of the Peninsula, is a high central tableland. With an average height of around 700 metres, the Meseta is bounded by several mountain systems. The north is dominated by two rivers: the Duero which flows to the Atlantic and the Ebro which flows to the Mediterranean. To the south-east lie the mountains of the Baetic Cordillera which commence just beyond Gibraltar and run parallel to the Mediterranean coast towards Murcia and Valencia. Included here is the Peninsula's highest mountain (Mulhacén, at 3,481 metres in the Sierra Nevada – incidentally it is named after the penultimate ruler of Granada). The major river of the south, the Guadalquivir, flows south-west through fertile low-lying lands past Córdoba and Seville and on to the Atlantic. Much of the land is barren and unproductive. However, there are specific, and extensive, areas of rich land. From antiquity, the agricultural products of these rich areas (as well as the gold, silver, copper and other products of Iberia's mines) have attracted settlers.

Around 800 BC the Phoenicians settled in the Peninsula with colonies from Gadir (Cádiz), to Sexi (Almuñécar). The Greeks in turn founded colonies in the north. The term Iberia began to be used in classical writings and an Iberian civilization developed, with urban settlements incorporating aspects of Greek and Phoenician life. By the fourth century BC, the North African state of Carthage eclipsed the domain of the Phoenicians. The Carthaginians invaded the Iberian Peninsula, conquered its southern part and founded Carthago Nova (Cartagena) in 228 BC.

The Roman Era

The Second Punic War between Carthage and Rome was sparked by an attack by the Carthaginian general Hannibal on the Iberian town of Saguntum (present-day Sagunto) in 219 BC, then under Roman protection. To deny the supply of manpower and silver for the Carthaginian war effort, the Romans sent troops to Iberia in 218 BC and eventually defeated the Carthaginians in 202 BC. In Iberia, the Romans controlled the eastern coast and the hinterland of the river Baetis (Guadalquivir). The conquest continued and, by 19 BC, they captured Cantabria and now controlled the Peninsula.

Roman Hispania was divided into three provinces. Tarraconensis, with its capital in Tarraco (Tarragona), encompassed the north. Baetica (very roughly present-day Andalucía) had its capital in Corduba (Córdoba). Lusitania (roughly most of present-day Portugal and parts of Extremadura) had its capital at Augusta Emerita (Mérida). During the first 400 years after Christ, Hispania formed a flourishing and productive part of the Roman Empire. Settlements were founded across the Peninsula and planted with Roman citizens and soldiers. Hispania's mines were intensively worked and mineral exports such as gold, silver, copper and lead made a valuable contribution to the imperial economy. There was a strong agricultural sector, with exports of wool, olive oil and wine.

One of the more productive areas was at the eastern end of Baetica, near the border with Tarraconensis. This was by a plain, the *Vega*, to the west of the chain of high mountains (now known as the Sierra Nevada). Here was the Roman settlement of Iliberris (later known as Elvira). Its exact location has not been satisfactorily identified: some say it was located on the site of present-day Albaicín in Granada; others that it was about 13 kilometres to the west, near Atarfe. The people here were of Turdetanian (an ancient people living in the Guadalquivir valley) origin. As with the rest of Hispania, veterans of the Roman army settled here. The Romans built a vast network of

Below: acqueduct at Mérida. The Romans built extensive infrastructure, including roads, bridges and aqueducts in Hispania, a prosperous and productive part of the their empire.

Above: a nineteenth-century view of the bridge at Córdoba, originally built during the Roman era.

roads in Hispania. There were the main arterial roads such as the Via de Plata which linked Italica in the south to the mines of Asturias in the north. In addition, there was a dense network of secondary roads. Iliberris was on such a road between Anticaria (Antequera) and Acci (Guadix) to the east. Because of good land and the superior agricultural skills of the Romans (such as irrigation) this part of Hispania was a prosperous, productive part of the vast Roman Empire. Wine, olive oil, wheat and other products from large estates were shipped across the Mediterranean to the heart of the Empire in Rome. Christianity is thought to have reached Iberia at the end of the first century AD, and spread gradually over the following centuries. An ecclesiastical council was held at Iliberris in AD 313. Of the 19 bishops present, most came from dioceses in Baetica.

No empire lasts and by the end of the third century that of the Romans was in decline. In AD 395 the Emperor Theodosius split the Roman Empire. He assigned the eastern and the western sections to each of his sons respectively. The rivalry which developed between the two sections further weakened the Empire. On the borders, Germanic tribes were on the move and posed a danger. One such tribe, the Visigoths, wandered south and invaded Italy. They penetrated as far as Rome, which they sacked in 410. In the meantime, other Germanic tribes, under pressure from the Huns, crossed the Rhine frontier of the weakened Empire. They made their way southwards through Gaul and invaded the north-west of Hispania in 409. The invaders ranged far and wide across Iberia. The Hasding Vandals and the Suevi occupied Galicia. The Alans occupied part of Lusitania and extended across to Carthago Nova (Cartagena). The Siling Vandals continued southwards to Baetica.

Rise of the Visigoth Kingdom

Fresh from the sack of Rome, the Visigoths moved westwards towards southern Gaul. The Visigoths, who by now had absorbed Roman ways, alternated between being enemies and allies of the Romans. They settled in southern Gaul in 418. The other Germanic tribes continued their wanderings. The Hasding Vandals crossed from Baetica to North Africa in 429 and conquered the Roman province there. Another Germanic tribe, the Franks, moved on southern Gaul at the beginning of the sixth century and pushed the Visigoths southwards. These now set up a kingdom in Hispania. As they became established, the Visigoths continued as primarily military leaders – the underlying layers of the newly conquered society continued to be strongly Roman. Roman administrators still carried out their duties under the new rulers. Over at Iliberris the Visigoths minted no less than 13 different issues of coins bearing the inscription *Eliberri*. The coming to power of Leovigild, in 568, marked the rise of a strong ruler in the Visigothic kingdom. He began a process of consolidation of the kingdom. He based himself in Toledo and took on the trappings of Roman imperial rule, taking a crown, sceptre and throne. He moved against his enemies both external and internal. By Leovigild's death in 586, the Visigothic kingdom was well entrenched across the Peninsula. However, the economy under the Visigoths had significantly declined from the glory days of Hispania. Agricultural production was much lower and there was a move to more basic agricultural activity. While there was some continuing trade with the outside world, it was a more inward-looking economy and did not have the trade and market opportunities that had been afforded by the Roman Empire.

Above: Leovigild, who came to power in 568, consolidated the Visigothic kingdom in the Iberian Peninsula.

Below: Visigothic stone carving. © Catedral de Córdoba.

The Emergence of Islam

As the Visigothic kingdom was consolidating across the Iberian Peninsula in the seventh century, on another peninsula, a man of destiny emerged. The Prophet Muhammad was born in Mecca, in the Arabian Peninsula, around AD 570. Mecca was an important commercial centre at the intersection of many trade routes. Muhammad was a minor member of one of the leading families in Mecca. A thoughtful and charismatic personality, he began to ponder on religious and moral questions. It is written that, at the age of 40, he had a vision in which the Angel Gabriel revealed to him that he was God's messenger. He began to preach about the revelations and started to gain followers. Muhammad's new religion was a monotheistic one. It holds that he was the last in a line of prophets including Abraham, Moses and Jesus. People who believed in these prophets, such as Christians and Jews, were regarded as 'People of the Book'. Muhammad set down a sequence of revealed messages in the holy book of Islam, the Koran. In the following years Muhammad and his followers, under pressure in Mecca, moved to Medina in AD 622, which is the start-date of the Islamic calendar. There Muhammad took command and developed a society which was to be a model for later Islamic rule and organisation. There were ongoing attacks from the Meccans and local tribes but the Muslims retaliated successfully and expanded their control. By the time Muhammad died in Medina in 632, most of the tribes in the Arabian Peninsula had acknowledged him as their principal leader.

Under Muhammad's successor Abu Bakr and subsequent caliphs, Islamic armies continued to expand outwards and mounted numerous raids in the region. These armies ranged afar and wrested land from the Byzantine and Sassanian Empires. Most of Byzantine Syria and Sassanian Iraq was seized by 637. By 642 northern Syria and Iraq were captured, as was Egypt. Damascus became the capital of the new Islamic empire. After 647, the Islamic forces thrust further west from

Below: the rapid spread of Islam across North Africa.

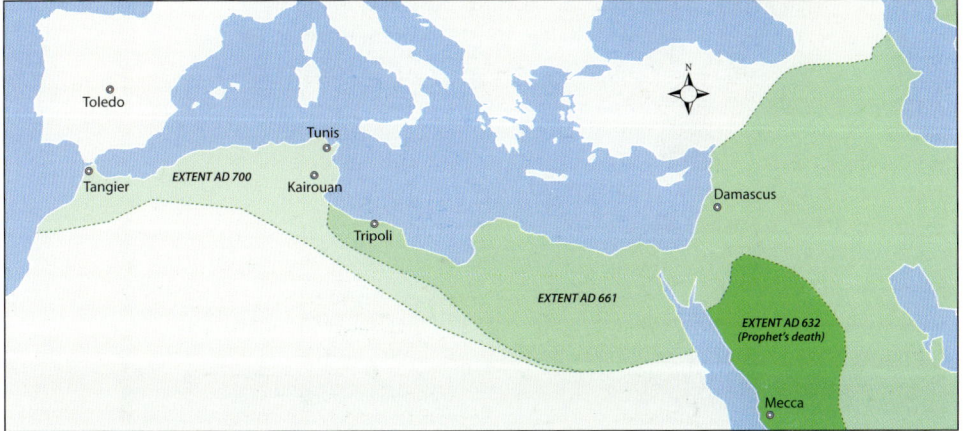

Left: in AD 711, the Muslim invaders, led by Tariq bin Ziyad, landed on this promontory known in Roman times as Calpe. He is remembered in the place name, Jebel Tariq or Gibraltar.

Egypt through North Africa. Moving through Libya, they mounted raids in (modern day) Tunisia.

Tunisia was captured by 670. Kairouan was founded and developed into the administrative centre of the region which in a few decades became the province of Ifriqiya. The Atlantic Ocean was reached in 681. All through the westward expansion the indigenous Berbers offered stiff resistance. To this day, the Berbers are located in the mountains, deserts and plains of North Africa, particularly in Morocco, Algeria, and Tunisia. The rolling form of conquest employed in the Muslim expansion involved the incorporation of the conquered peoples into the armies, thus making them available for the next phase of conquest.

As the Arab conquerors consolidated their hold on North Africa, their gaze now turned north. The death of the Visigothic king in 710 had resulted in a civil war between his two sons, Agila and Roderic. Maybe news of this weakness in the brittle Visigoth kingdom came to the Arabs, as they looked north to Iberia, with its perceived riches and fertile terrain, across the Strait. of Gibraltar, only 14 kilometres wide.

The Muslim Conquest of Iberia
And so, the momentum of conquest was channelled northwards. There were exploratory raids to the south of the Peninsula in 710. The invasion proper began in 711 when an army led by Tariq bin Ziyad, Governor of Tangier, sailed across the Strait. They landed at the point dominated by a prominent rock, which was called Calpe (now known as Gibraltar, or *Jebel Tariq*). The invading army was led by a core of Arab warriors but was predominantly made up of Berber soldiers.

Roderic returned from his civil-war campaigning in the north. He met the invaders in 712 in the south and was decisively defeated.

Right: the maximum extent of the conquest. The newly established state, al-Andalus, around AD 720.

Roderic disappeared, assumed dead. One account speculates that the battle occurred by the river Guadalete; another account gives a location adjoining Barbate (near Vejer de la Frontera). Irrespective of the actual location, the most important fact is that the Arabs triumphed over the Visigothic army and eliminated their king. The Visigothic troops fled northwards, spreading terror and despair. The Arab-led armies rapidly advanced northwards and Toledo was captured. The Visigothic Kingdom had now lost both its leader and its capital. The weak bonds of the realm disintegrated and the Arabs met with little further resistance. Military expansion continued throughout the Peninsula. The network of roads laid down by the Romans was a boon for the invaders, providing easy access through the difficult terrain. As they entered regions, the Arabs adopted a pragmatic approach. If a local leader submitted to them they would conclude a treaty on favourable terms. The people were allowed to continue to practise their religion but had to pay a special poll tax.

By 720 most of the Peninsula had been conquered, with the exception of the mountainous regions of Cantabria and the Pyrenees. The invaders began to assimilate, consolidate and organise their new territories. Córdoba became the capital a few years after the invasion. The newly conquered fertile lands attracted members of the army and its numbers were reduced as soldiers settled around the Peninsula. The new entity was called *al-Andalus*. Various theories have been presented for the origin of the name. One is that 'al-Andalus' comes from the Arabic version of the Visigothic description of how the land was divided into lots '*landa-hlauts*'. Another theory is that the name is a permutation of the Berber for 'land of the Vandals' (who had passed through the territory in the fifth century).

Meanwhile, back in Damascus, in the early part of the eighth century, the Umayyad dynasty was engaged in organising and consolidating its sprawling empire. Arabic was designated as the official language. But all was not well. The level of taxes had been raised by the Caliph, which resulted in much discontent. By the early part of the eighth century the Islamic empire extended from the Pyrenees to Persia, to Central Asia and as far as the Indian sub-continent. It was an empire of extreme distances. From Galicia in the west to the Indus in the east is around 7,000 kilometres. This enormous territory was to prove too big for any polity of that time to hold together, even one with the benefit of the unifying bond of Islam. In addition to the difficulty of ruling from such a distance, weaknesses also arose from social stratification and were exacerbated by the human frailties of the caliphs and their supporters.

Al-Andalus had a mix of new settlers, from various parts of the Arab lands, as well as Berbers. There was tension among the Arabs as well as with the Berbers. Thus was laid the seed of factionalism which contributed to the turmoil of later years. Soon the Berbers revolted as they had been treated as second-class citizens by the Arab elite. The Governor of al-Andalus stamped out the revolt using troops from Syria. Once this was accomplished he settled the troops across the south of Spain, mainly in districts of present-day Andalucía. These soldiers, organised in sections called *Junds*, from denominated regions of Syria, were given advantageous conditions. These warriors, unlikely farmers, were allowed to collect taxes from the local people. In turn they were required to make a fixed payment to the central government.

In 750 the Umayyad Caliph in Damascus was overthrown by the Abbasid clan, who began a new dynasty (they later moved to their new city of Baghdad – the Abbasid Caliphate survived until the thirteenth century.) The overthrow was a bloody affair, with members of the Umayyad family and their supporters being rounded up and massacred.

The Umayyad Dynasty in al-Andalus

Some Umayyads escaped the slaughter. Among them was a grandson of the Caliph Hisham who had ruled from 724 to 743. This young man, Abd al-Rahman, spent five years making his way through North Africa. Contacts were made with elements loyal to the Umayyads in al-Andalus. In August 755 he landed at Almuñécar on the coast (south of Iliberris, now named *Elvira*). Abd al-Rahman immediately moved north to the *Cora* or district of Elvira, where the Jund of Damascus had chosen to settle. One account says that these 500 warriors had been attracted there by the countryside that looked like the irrigated farmlands around Damascus. The junds in nearby coras were also from other parts of Syria. By the spring of 756, Abd al-Rahman had

Below: from the time of al-Andalus. A four-flame ceramic oil lamp from Pechina, near Almería. © Museo de Almería.

Above: statue of Abd al-Rahman I at Almuñécar. In 756 he established the Iberian branch of the Umayyad dynasty.

Below: delicate design. A pair of gold earrings, from the era of the Córdoba Caliphate, found near Lucena. © Museo Arqueológico de Córdoba.

assembled an army amounting to around 2,000. It was comprised of the loyalist junds, along with disaffected factions. He advanced on Córdoba, defeated the forces of the Governor and entered the city in May 756. Shortly afterwards, this young man, only 25 years old, declared himself Amir (or commander, with civil, but not religious, power). In the re-establishment of their power in Iberia, the Umayyads did not at first directly challenge the religious authority of the Abbasid caliph in the east. This only changed when the Caliphate in Córdoba was established nearly two centuries later. Al-Andalus at that time was made up of a myriad of individual fiefdoms. Abd al-Rahman I commenced the task of binding it together and establishing order. He gained control of the Guadalquivir valley and continued to expand his authority.

Far away to the north, the Asturians, successors to the Christian Visigoths, expanded their domain from a strip of land on the Cantabrian coast to become a kingdom. The expansionary Franks had also taken advantage of weaknesses on the northern border with the Muslims. The Frankish King Charlemagne mounted an unsuccessful expedition against Barcelona and Zaragoza. In the light of these threats the Amir changed the military organisation and set up a standing army composed of slaves. The border territories were divided up into what was termed a March or frontier region. The Upper March had its capital at Zaragoza. The Middle March was based in Toledo and the Lower March was governed from Mérida. The central area around Córdoba was divided into districts, with administrators appointed by the Amir. In 784 Abd al-Rahman I gave instructions to start construction of the Great Mosque of Córdoba. The building of the Great Mosque reflected the increase in population of Muslims in Córdoba, as the Amir consolidated his rule and developed his capital.

The young fugitive Abd al-Rahman I had the tenacity and courage to arrive in a land many thousands of kilometres from his homeland, seize power and subdue a mass of factions. By the time he died in 788 in Cordoba he had set up a centralised administrative and military system which formed the basis of a dynasty that reigned for around 250 years and represented the crowning glory of al-Andalus. However, in the unstable north, the seeds of the Christian legacy had been laid with the successors of the Visigoths, now well ensconced in their mountain fastnesses. The number of Visigoth inhabitants had always been small, being an estimated one-tenth of the indigenous population of Roman and Iberian origin. At the time of the Muslim conquest, the population of the Peninsula as a whole has been estimated to be around 4 million. The initial Muslim settlers, being mainly of military origin, were small in number and constituted a tiny minority of around 40,000.

15

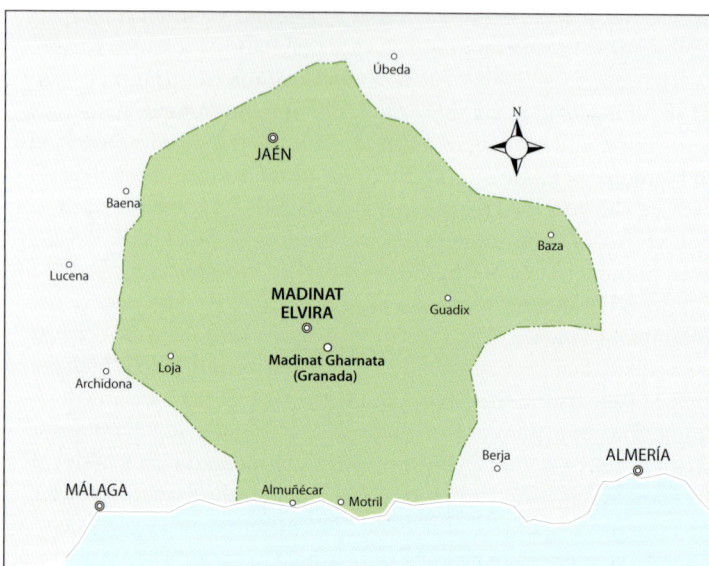

Above: Madinat Elvira was located on the side of the Sierra Elvira (near Atarfe). Roman Iliberris had possibly been in the vicinity. As al-Andalus developed, Elvira became the centre of the prosperous Cora (region) of the same name. © Fundación El Legado Andalusí. Photograph Miguel Rodríguez.

Left: map of the Cora of Elvira during the Umayyad Caliphate (929 to 1031).

Above: lamp with a bronze plate of four concentric circles, from the mosque at Madinat Elvira, dating from the period 726-850. © Museo Arqueológico de Granada.

Below: waterwheels (norias) over the river Orontes at Hama, Syria. The Muslims brought new plants and advanced techniques (particularly in irrigation) to al-Andalus. Agricultural output greatly increased.

And what of the Cora of Elvira, under the new Umayyad era of al-Andalus? During the centuries of Visigoth rule, this agricultural area, sheltered by the mountains, had become, like the rest of the Peninsula, a backwater. The productive ways of the Roman era had declined. No longer linked to the international trade of the Roman Empire, crops were produced to satisfy the local market. Roads, bridges and other infrastructure had been neglected. The arrival of the Arab settlers was a boost to the local economy. New sophisticated techniques of irrigation were introduced to the plain or *Vega*, around Elvira, as well as expansion into previously uncultivated areas. Water was channelled from the nearby mountains and from the river Genil in *acequias* (water channels) with sophisticated arrangements for distribution among the various settled tribes. *Aljibes* (reservoirs) and *norias* (waterwheels) were installed as part of this complex hydraulic system – sophisticated techniques, well developed in Syria. In addition to those previously introduced by the Romans, such as wheat and vegetable crops, the Arabs brought to al-Andalus a large variety of plants found in the east of their Islamic Empire. These included oranges, lemons, aubergines, peaches, figs, melons, cotton, rice and sugar cane. As the decades passed, the Vega benefitted from all of this and became garlanded with vast seas of wheat and other cereals. Orchards produced abundant fruit. Vines, figs, pomegranates (later to become the symbol of Granada) flourished in the fertile soil. Mulberry trees were planted and a great silk industry developed, producing a silk regarded as the best in al-Andalus. Flax was also produced, allowing the production of linen, another luxury textile. Sugar was produced in the southern areas near the coast at Almuñécar. Amidst this developement, a new Muslim settlement grew up in the area between Atarfe and Pinos Puente towards the end of the tenth century. This expanded into a city located on the side of the Sierra Elvira. In a different location from the original Roman settlement of Iliberris, Madinat Elvira grew as the administrative centre of the Cora (in turn subordinate to the central administration in Córdoba). This new urban centre handled the collection of tax, as well the management of the irrigation system of the Vega, and was also a centre for agricultural trade. As the city grew an *alcazaba* (fortress) was built as well as a mosque.

Al-Andalus continued under the Umayyad Amirs. Given the tribal composition of the Arab settlers, the Berber settlements and the new converts from Christianity to Islam, the *Muwallads*, the polity was not cohesive and there were continuous uprisings. This instability was coupled with the friction with the nascent Christian kingdoms to the north, which gradually expanded their territory southwards. Despite this, the successors of Abd al-Rahman I in the decades that followed, to a greater or lesser degree, battled with the internal and external threats and managed to maintain their hold.

The most persistent, colourful and potentially dangerous challenge to Umayyad rule was the rebellion of Umar Ibn Hafsun. He came from a well-to-do Muwallad family in the Ronda region. Towards the end of the ninth century, with a small band of outlaws, he set up in the rugged mountainous district around the Guadalhorce valley, 35 kilometres north-west of Málaga. From his base there at Bobastro he made attacks around the region and his rebellion spread. By 891 he was threatening the capital itself, Córdoba. The story runs that in 899, Ibn Hafsun made a strategic mistake: he converted to Christianity. There was an almost universally negative reaction to this by his Muwallad supporters, who took their Islamic religion seriously.

With the advent of a new Amir, Abd al-Rahman III in 912, things changed. As he took office, the state he inherited was in a ramshackle condition, near to collapse. It took 20 years of inspired and methodical exertion to restore equilibrium. Immediately he took power he began to deal with the threat from Ibn Hafsun. Promptly in January 913 an army was dispatched to capture Ecija (the nearest centre of resistance to Córdoba) – whose inhabitants promptly professed loyalty to the Umayyad Amir. The momentum continued as another expedition was sent out in March 913. It soon joined forces with a senior leader

Above: the remains of the Mozarab church at Bobastro (north of Málaga). Towards the end of the ninth century, Ibn Hafsun launched a rebellion which severely tested the Umayyad rulers in Córdoba. He converted to Christianity and set up his headquarters at this location.

Right: the arched portico of the palace-city of Madinat al-Zahra, near Córdoba. This was developed on the orders of Abd al-Rahman III after he took the title of Caliph in 929.

Below: restored part of the Salón Rico. Madinat al-Zahra is one of the great monuments of Islamic Spain.

from Úbeda, who had been deposed by Ibn Hafsun. Once the army entered the Cora of Elvira, the prominent men of the district soon professed loyalty to Abd al-Rahman III. After swinging by Fiñana and Juviles, they relieved the garrison of Elvira, which had been kept under pressure by Ibn Hafsun's forces. The Amir's army then ranged through the west, along the Serranía de Ronda and Málaga. Thus, by his diligent efforts Abd al-Rahman III snuffed out the Ibn Hafsun rebellion. However, the old rebel remained in his Bobastro lair, praying piously in the Mozarab church he had built there. He died there in 917 and was given a Christian burial.

After he had comprehensively dealt with the Ibn Hafsun rebellion, Abd al-Rahman III decided to take the title of Caliph. This is the supreme position in Islam, claiming both temporal and spiritual leadership of believers. There were several reasons for this. His rule was now well established throughout al-Andalus. The Christian threat on the frontier had been significantly reduced. The growing peace across the state was in tandem with a new era of prosperity and the administration of the state had reached a new level of sophistication. In Umayyad eyes, the Abbasids in the east had usurped the Caliphate and, in addition, they had now grown weak and decadent. The concept of a single 'Caliph' had been damaged, by virtue of the disunity in the Islamic world. Another was that the nearby proclamation of a Caliphate by the 'heretical' Fatimids in North Africa presented an affront as well as a direct threat. For Abd al-Rahman III, well-consolidated and firmly in control, it was time to restore the Umayyad caliphal line. Thus, in a solemn ceremony in the Great Mosque in Córdoba, Abd al-Rahman took the title in early 929. His name as Caliph, the Commander of

Left: detail in the Mosque in Córdoba. Mosaic cubes, sent as a gift by the Byzantine Emperor, were used in al-Hakam II's extension.

the Faithful, was proclaimed from the minarets of mosques all over al-Andalus.

In the Islamic society of the time great importance was attached to learning and knowledge and this was manifest throughout the history of al-Andalus. The level of education on offer was sophisticated, where students spent lengthy periods under the tutelage of scholars. Many travelled to gain further knowledge to study with learned men in the east and North Africa. The rulers were well educated and were patrons of literature and science. Many were poets. The whole environment was one of encouragement of learning and knowledge, with a rich cultural and intellectual tradition. In the time of the Córdoba Caliphate, coinciding with the rise in economic prosperity, there was a corresponding surge in culture and science. Poets, scholars and scientists flocked to the court of Madinat al-Zahra, the palace-city built by Abd al-Rahman III. During his reign great works were carried out all over al-Andalus. As its port grew in importance Abd al-Rahman III made Almería (to the east of the Cora of Elvira) the capital of its province and expanded and developed the city.

Al-Hakam II was into middle age, at 46 years old, when he assumed the reins of power on his father's death in 961. Despite being in the shadow of his illustrious father, he was to bring the Caliphate to a new level of achievement and sophistication, a time of great learning and development. His lasting legacy is the outstanding and exquisite extension that he made to the Córdoba Great Mosque.

However the new Caliph had no children. Thus, there was joy when, in 965, a son was born, the future Hisham II. In the meantime,

Below: the state of the Iberian Peninsula during the middle of the tenth century – al-Andalus and the expanding Christian kingdoms.

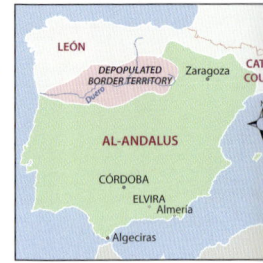

a clever and astute man, Ibn Abi Amir, had deviously insinuated his way to the top of the bureaucracy in Córdoba. When al-Hakam II died in 976, this resolute and cunning Vizier seized power, arranging that the young son of al-Hakam II, now Caliph, stayed within the confines of the Alcázar, in Cordoba, remote from the reality of state business. Having achieved supreme control, in 981 Ibn Abi Amir decided to award himself the honorific title of *Al-Mansur bi-Allah* or 'made victorious for God' – popularly known as Almanzor.

Under Almanzor's rule al-Andalus continued as a prosperous land with its interior generally at peace. A reorganised army, reinforced by troops from the Maghreb and a strong and ruthless ruler: these were the ingredients that were to spell trouble for the Christian states on the northern frontiers of al-Andalus. Over the last 20 years of the eleventh century, Almanzor instigated around 50 offensives against the lands and peoples of León, Castile, Navarra and the Spanish March. There was a resulting flow of booty and captives to Córdoba.

Almanzor was very interested in North Africa as a source of military manpower and over the course of his reign, he recruited Berber tribesmen from there into his army. Large numbers of Berbers (allies, or very frequently, former enemies), in cohesive tribal units, were inducted into the armies of al-Andalus. On the way back from a raid on the north in 1002, Almanzor, now in his sixties, fell gravely ill. He was brought to the frontier fortress of Medinaceli. A few days later, in August 1002, he died.

Back in Córdoba Almanzor's sons took power. They were politically clumsy and had only a brief period of rule. The Caliphate started to fall apart and civil war ensued. Since 756, the Umayyad dynasty was the glue that had held al-Andalus together. In the eyes of the populace, Almanzor's usurpation of power was acceptable in that he maintained what was in effect, a fiction – the legitimacy of the reigning Umayyad Caliph.

There now followed over two decades a time of extreme instability and a descent into chaos. The Caliphate became a revolving door. New claimants to this office, who reigned for short periods, were supported variously by different factions like the Cordoban mob, Berber soldiers, the slaves and the Arab aristocracy. The end of the Caliphate was in sight. With turmoil all around, leaders in Córdoba decided, in 1031, to abolish it.

Below: Ibn Abi Amir (Almanzor) intrigued to become the de facto ruler of the Córdoba Caliphate, on the death of al-Hakam II in 976.

The Taifa Era

So who stepped into the vacuum caused by the fall away of central power? Step forward the Taifas. Over 30 *taifas* (or 'party') statelets were formed all across the territory of al-Andalus. Some were large, others small. The smallest were scarcely more than a fortress and its immediate surroundings. These were set up by local notables or strong leaders who were invited in. These stepped, with agility, into the vacuum left by the rapid fall away of central power and control. They comprised three main categories: the Andalusis (those with established roots in al-Andalus) and two types of outsiders; the Slaves, who had risen to leading posts in the palace and upper levels of administration, and the 'new' (recently arrived) Berbers. Andalusis set up taifas in such places as Córdoba, Zaragoza and Seville (which turned out to be the most predatory – it expanded and swallowed up the nearby small taifas). Slaves formed taifas across the Levante, including Valencia, Dénia (which ruled the Balearic Islands), Játiva, Tortosa, Almería and Murcia.

The Berber heritage ran deep in al-Andalus. They had formed a major part of the Muslim army during the conquest of 711. Throughout the years of the Amirate and the Caliphate, there had always been a flow of Berbers from the Maghreb to the Peninsula and they eventually melded into the Andalusi population. However, it was during the reign of al-Hakam II (to 976) that a new and large influx of Berber mercenaries arrived. This reflected the fact that, as al-Andalus grew more prosperous, the citizens of the State lost their appetite for military service, forcing more dependency on the buying-in of those who were willing to do military service. During Almanzor's rule there was an acceleration in the recruitment of Berbers from the principal tribes in the al-Andalus zone of influence in the Maghreb. These were dispersed across the State and dislike of them built up amongst the 'old' Andalusis. The Berbers played a leading role during the civil war that led to the break-up of the Caliphate, with their faction laying siege to and capturing Córdoba. As the Caliphate began to disintegrate, several of these 'new' Berbers took power in various districts of southern al-Andalus and formed taifas. Amongst these were the small taifas of Carmona, Ronda, Arcos and Morón. The taifas of Algeciras

Left: as the Caliphate disintegrated over 30 taifas ('party') statelets were formed. The map shows the situation after the capture of Toledo by the Christians in 1085. The taifa frontiers were ever-changing. The Taifa of Granada had taken over that of Málaga in 1058. However, time was running out for Granada. In 1090 it was the first taifa to be taken over by the Almoravids.

and Málaga may be classified as part of the 'new' Berber category. They were led by the Hammudids from North Africa. Each of these taifas had a turbulent history, riven by inter-family feuds. In general, the rationale for 'new' Berber taifas rested on the military power of the Berbers rather than having any great roots in the community: the local people paid the Berbers in return for protection and defence. Most were small taifas and did not have great lasting power and, with the exception of the powerful and dynamic Taifa of Granada, were absorbed by expansive Seville by 1069.

Taifa of Granada
The significant Taifa of Granada was established by 'new' Berbers. Its emergence can be traced to the arrival of Zawi bin Ziri and his Sanhaja Berber tribesmen in the Peninsula at the beginning of the eleventh century. Their Zirid branch of the tribe had originated from Ziri ibn Manad (935-971), who had risen to prominence as governor of the central Maghreb in the territory of what is now Algeria. Zawi had previously played a prominent part in the conflicts in the al-Andalus zone of influence in North Africa. He had been a principal leader of the Berber faction during the civil war. In 1010-13 he led the siege of Córdoba. In the period following the defeat and sack of Córdoba by the Berbers, Zawi is reported to have been assigned the province and city of Elvira by the Caliph Sulayman (who had been installed by the Berber faction). The residents of Elvira, fearful of disorder, petitioned Zawi to rule them, promising money and land in return, Zawi and his Sanhaja made it their base while they continued to make further interventions in the civil war. In due course they set up their rule centred in Elvira over a territory which extended north to Jaén and south to the Mediterranean coast.

Seeing a need to move to a better, more defensive location, they abandoned Elvira, which was located adjacent to the wide plain irrigated by the river Genil. They made the short move east to Madinat Gharnata, a settlement situated in the foothills of the Sierra Nevada (one possibility is that this had been the site of the original Roman Iliberis) and developed a new city there. In his memoirs, the last Zirid Amir of Granada, Abd Allah, gave a succinct account of why that location was chosen: *'They gazed astonished on that lovely plain, interlaced by streams and clothed with trees…and by the mountain. They recognised its central position set amongst the rest of the territory. In front of it extended the vega and either side were the natural areas of al-Sawuja and al-Sath, behind the mountain…They also noted that if the position were attacked by enemies, it would be difficult to mount a siege on it, and also it would be hard to cut it off from the necessary provisions. So they decided to found a city there, and everyone, Andalusi or Berber, set about building a house, and soon Elvira fell in ruins'.*

It is not known why Zawi decided to return to North Africa around 1020. He was succeeded by his nephew, Habus. Habus and his descendants proved to be able governors and administrators. They established good organisation, security and order in the taifa. Granada grew to be a powerful state and expanded its borders. The Zirid dynasty proved its ability in manoeuvring through the snake-pit that was the taifa politics of al-Andalus. Neighbouring taifas were predatory, particularly that of Seville, which expanded its borders many times, swallowing up and extinguishing the neighbouring minnows. The Zirids were not as predatory but expanded their territory as a defensive stratagem. They took Málaga in 1058, in a pre-emptive move arising from Seville's takeover of Algeciras.

Reflecting the shortage of experienced administrators among the Berbers, Habus appointed as close advisor the Jewish Samuel Ibn Naghrela. From early days Granada had a particularly high Jewish population. When Habus died in 1039, he was succeeded by his son Badis, who appointed Ibn Naghrela as his Vizier. Ibn Naghrela had risen from humble origins, but proved to be a skilled administrator. He was also a poet and a rabbinical scholar. Such was his influence, that when he died, his son Joseph was appointed to replace him as Vizier. Accounts tell of the younger man's wealth and mansions. In 1066 Joseph made contact with the ruler of the nearby taifa of Almería with the intention of mounting a takeover of Granada. This treasonous initiative did not succeed, but the episode resulted in a major pogrom against the Jews of Granada (in which thousands were killed, including Joseph), reflecting the resentment of the Muslim population that too much power was in Jewish hands.

Immediately after the move to Granada, the Zirids improved and expanded the existing urbanisation of Madinat Gharnata, located on the right bank of the river Darro. It was set on a sloping height, above the fertile Vega that extends to the west. This town was probably an

Above: with the snow-capped Sierra Nevada mountains as background and the Vega (plain) all around, this was a perfect location for the Zirids to move to and set up the headquarters of their taifa in Madinat Gharnata. In his memoirs, Abd Allah, the last of the Zirid rulers, recounted: 'They gazed astonished on that lovely plain, interlaced by streams and clothed with trees…and by the mountain.'

Right: tiles in Plaza de España in Seville show an illustration from the thirteenth-century book Cantigas de Santa Maria. A Muslim king holds court before his subjects.

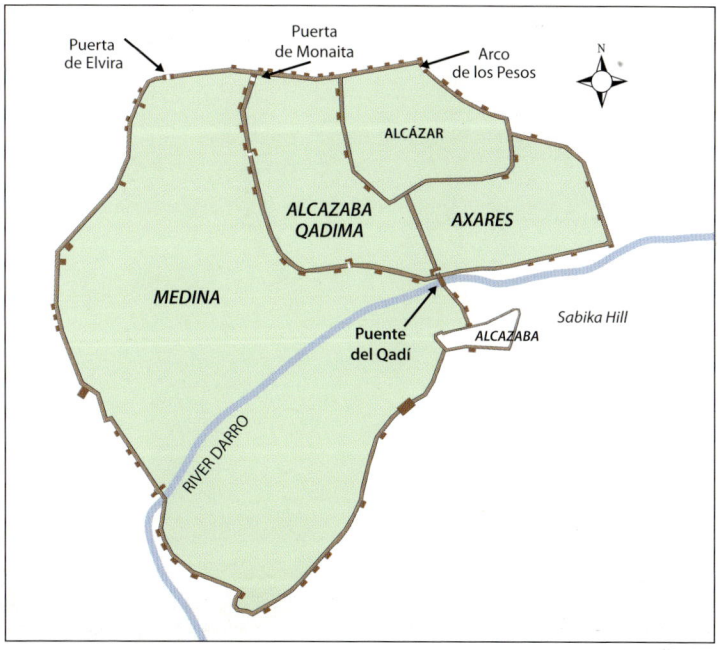

Above: in Granada, the eleventh-century Puerta de Elvira. This principal gate allowed access to the Elvira road.

Left: a tower and arch of the Puente del Qadí, by the river Darro. Dating from the reign of the Zirid ruler Badis, it connected, over the river, the defensive walls of the Alcazaba Qadima with new walls leading to a fortification on the Sabika Hill.

Right: Zirid Granada in the mid-eleventh century.

Above: the Puerta de Monaita dates from Zirid times.
Left: Arco de los Pesos. The first Zirid king upgraded an existing fortress. This arch allowed access to it through the walls. The name pesos (weights) comes from the Christian era. Inspectors confiscated the rigged weights of the traders in the nearby market and hung them by the arch.
Gold dinar from Granada, issued by the Zirid king Badis. © Museo de Jaén.

Above: tapial (rammed earth) walls, their solidity reinforced by semi-circular towers. These formed part of a second northern defensive line around the Alcazaba Qadima. Some sources say these were built during the Almoravid or Almohad eras, later than the Zirids. This is part of a 350-metre long section between the Arco de los Pesos and the Puerta de Monaita. There are three semi-circular towers and 11 of rectangular section.

outlier settlement of Madinat Elvira. Defences, as always, were the priority. The fortifications around the existing medina were strengthened. High walls of rammed-earth construction were erected, interspersed with watchtowers, and four new gates were built. Within this was the *Alcazaba Qadima*, (the 'old' fortress), located on the flank of the Albaicín hill and bounded by the Darro. Defensive walls extended up and around the hill (now known as the Albaicín district), then down to the river Darro. A bridge, the Puente del Qadí (one abutment still survives) was built across the Darro. This allowed access to guards to continue across on to the defensive walls on the other side which ran to a small fortress located high on the Sabika Hill. In the heart of the city was the Great Mosque, much of which demolished to make way for the Cathedral of Granada in the sixteenth century. Baths, now known as the 'Bañuelo', were situated on the right bank of the Darro,

Right: Zirid walls near the Puerta de Elvira.

29

Above: the well-preserved Zirid hammam, or baths, located near the river Darro.
Left: the Church of San José in the Albaicín, with nearby aljibe. The tower was a minaret of a Zirid-era mosque.
Below: carved capital of a column in the baths.

near the Puente del Qadí. These baths, one of the oldest still in existence in the Peninsula, were built during the eleventh century, and had a capacity for around 50 people. The city's growing suburbs and estates with orchards were fed by water from the Darro and the Genil using a network of acequias (water channels). In addition the plentiful water of Fuente Grande in the mountains by Alfacar was brought to the heights of the city and the Alcazaba along the 13-kilometre distance by the Aynadamar irrigation channel. This was commenced during the reign of Badis and completed by Abd Allah.

In 1073 Abd Allah, who was to be the last in the Zirid dynasty, came to power in Granada. The grandson of Badis, he was a well-educated man. He left behind his memoirs which, as we have previously seen, give an illuminating description of the history of the time. Abd Allah was the last ruler of the taifa of Granada. He was to fall foul of the Almoravid Amir and, as we shall see, end up as an exile in North Africa.

In the Peninsula as a whole, the balance of power had been inverted. Over the period from the end of Abd al-Rahman III's reign all the way through to the rule of Almanzor, the Christian kingdoms had

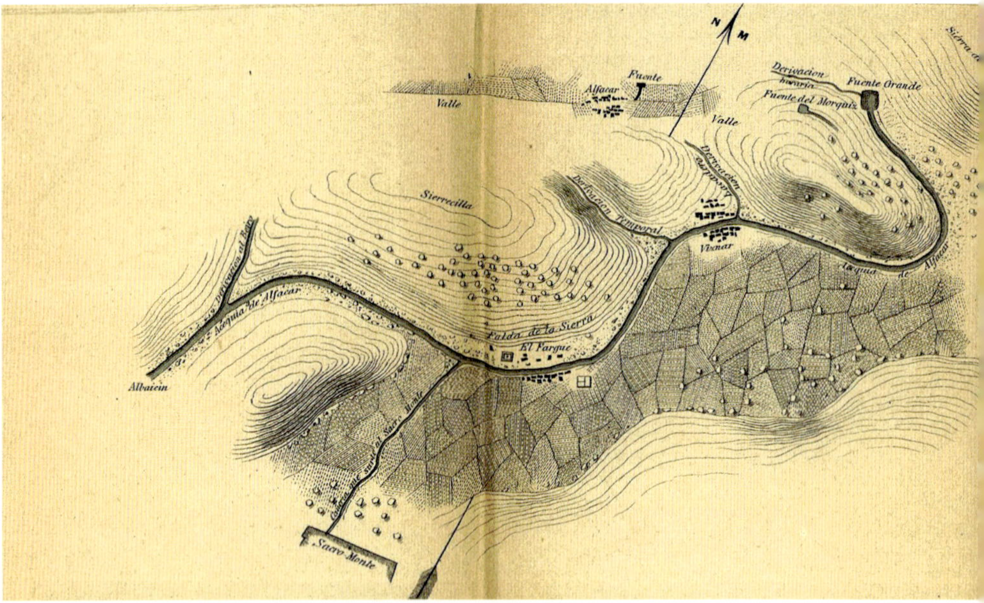

Above: a plan of the water supply system to the Albaicín. It starts at the Fuente Grande, located in Alfacar, eight kilometres north of Granada). The channel or acequia of Aynadamar contours 13 kilometres along the undulating countryside, cutting through hills, to end at the Aljibe del Rey. The acequia project was commenced during the reign of the Zirid ruler, Badis and finished under Abd Allah (r. 1073-1090).

Left: between Alfacar and Viznar, the acequia of Aynadamar crosses an aqueduct before entering a tunnel through the hill.

Above: clear water from the mountains. The Fuente Grande is at an altitude of 1,100 metres at Alfacar on the edge of the Sierra de Alfaguera. The Zirid monarchs are reputed to have come here to rest and celebrate the autumn harvest.

Right: Zirid masters of hydraulic technology. The acequia of Aynadamar supplied several aljibes (cisterns) in the Albaicín, before culminating in the Aljibe del Rey, near the Alcazaba Qadima. The principal aljibe of the locality, this has four chambers with barrel vault roofs and a capacity of 300 cubic metres.

been reduced by the powerful al-Andalus state to mere vassalage and had to undergo payment of tribute, interspersed with regular raids through their territory. With the fragmentation of the Umayyad state into small quarrelling statelets, the Christian kings were now able to flex their muscles and make expansive moves. Thus they raided deep into Muslim territory. They soon established the practice of offering protection through non-aggression pacts to the taifas on the basis of the payment of parias or annual tribute. The populace of the taifas were in high outrage at the level of these parias they had to pay, which in turn weakened the authority of the taifa rulers.

Almoravids and Almohads
Significant events were occurring far away in the south of the Maghreb in the middle of the eleventh century – events which were, in time, to greatly affect al-Andalus. A scholar emerged among the Berber tribes (a branch of the Sanhajas) in the far south of present-day Morocco. These tribes disliked the rigorous regime he promulgated and the scholar and his followers had to seek refuge in a fortified monastery or ribat. The name 'Almoravid' that emerged is possibly derived from *al-murabitun* (or people of the ribat). The number of Almoravid adherents grew rapidly and they began to spread their orthodoxy by military force on the neighbouring tribes. The Almoravids expanded and founded their new capital, Marrakech, in 1071. The development of Marrakech marked a transformation for the Almoravids from their nomadic origin to a more sedentary, urbanised way of life. Under their Amir, Ibn Tashufin, they continued their northwards expansion across Morocco and reached Ceuta in 1083.

Back in the Iberian Peninsula, the taifas were in trouble. As we have seen, the Christian kingdoms were harassing them and extorting large parias. The beleaguered Muslims began to look southwards at the powerful new Islamic movement that had become established. A defining blow occurred when Alfonso VI took the strategic heart of al-Andalus, the taifa and city of Toledo, in 1085. This was a huge and central swathe of territory. No longer able to rely on the frontier defences of the Upper and Middle Marches, al-Andalus was now wide open to attack at its very centre. The shock of the fall of Toledo resulted in a rare example of unity: the disparate taifas agreed to assemble a delegation of senior representatives, which travelled to see the Almoravid Amir and ask for help.

Ibn Tashufin agreed to assist, making a condition that the port of Algeciras be handed to him. The Almoravid army commenced landing there in July 1086 and Ibn Tashufin followed in September. The massed Almoravids defeated the forces of Alfonso VI at Sagrajas, near Badajoz, in October 1086. Ibn Tashufin returned to the Maghreb

Right: the taking of Toledo in 1085 was a seminal event. The Christians seized a huge swathe of al-Andalus and now reached deep into its heart. This event spurred the takeover by the Almoravids.

shortly afterwards. At this stage he did not seem to harbour much interest in extending his power in al-Andalus. However, he left behind 3,000 horsemen. Despite the heavy defeat of Sagrajas, the Christians soon reverted to their old and profitable ways of harassing the taifas and extracting parias. Their activity became particularly intense in the Levante (the eastern region of the Peninsula). In a daring move, Christian forces moved south and set up in the castle of Aledo, located between Murcia and Lorca. This strategic location was soon used by the Christians as a springboard to penetrate deep into the surrounding region.

The Almoravid Amir set out with his troops for the second time. His army, with forces from the taifas, laid siege to Aledo. The siege was not successful. Ibn Tashufin, much displeased, returned to the Maghreb. He was to return within two years and achieve a more decisive outcome. By now, Ibn Tashufin had lost patience with his wayward co-religionists in al-Andalus. In the summer of 1090, he set out for al-Andalus for a third time, determined to secure al-Andalus for Islam and to put an end to the decadent taifas. He had previously written to Abd Allah, ruler of Granada, reproaching him for what he perceived to be his scheming ways and false declarations. Alfonso VI's troops had made a raid through the territories of Granada and Almería. Abd Allah resorted to making a huge payment to Alfonso, a *paria* – effectively the payment of protection money. This most definitely constituted a grave offence in Almoravid eyes. Abd Allah harboured the mistaken hope that his Sanhaja lineage would win him favour with the Almoravid leader of similar but distant tribal origin. It was not to be. Granada proved to be the first in Ibn Tashufin's sight. The taifa there was in a troubled state: Abd Allah's treasury was depleted; the populace was much disaffected. Ibn Tashufin, now actively planning

Left: the Ermita de San Sebastián in Granada. This oratory originally was a ribat, a small mosque where a holy man would live. It was constructed in the Almohad era, in 1219, close to the river Genil at the same time as a nearby Alcázar or fortress.

a campaign against Granada, sent a message to Abd Allah, advising him that if he surrendered, he would receive protection. The Zirid king set out to meet the Almoravid leader and capitulated. Such was low morale and the feeling against the Zirid dynasty that the various strands of the population of Granada (Berbers, merchants and general populace) welcomed the Almoravids when they arrived in September 1090. Abd Allah was sent into exile to Aghmat, a Berber town, just to the east of Marrakech. As we have seen, once there, he wrote his enlightening memoirs. Granada now became the premier city of al-Andalus within the Almoravid Empire. Ibn Tashufin set up in the Zirid palace in the city.

The Almoravid campaign against the rest of the taifas continued and they were soon taken. By autumn 1092, the advance had continued to within a day's ride of Valencia (taken by the Almoravids much later in 1102). Completing their conquest of al-Andalus, the Almoravids took Zaragoza in 1110 and the Balearics in 1116.

In al-Andalus, the Almoravid presence constituted a thin (mainly military) layer. The Governors were part of the Almoravid select few. However, most of the administration was left to the existing Andalusi leaders and officials. The Maghreb, by contrast, began to benefit from the more advanced culture of al-Andalus. A steady stream of Andalusi administrators, craftsmen, engineers and architects went south and gave of their expertise in North Africa. Granada, being the foremost city of the Almoravids on the Peninsula, experienced strong growth.

The population soared and the Medina became full to capacity. The Almoravids improved the fortifications of the city, expanding the towers and walls erected by the Zirids.

On the Iberian Peninsula the Christian kingdoms were, understandably, vexed by the Almoravid invasion. The energetic King of Aragón, Alfonso I, the *Batallador* (Battler), took the northern bastion of Zaragoza in December 1118 and moved on to take the region around the Ebro. Alfonso I continued south and pushed the frontier south of such places as Calatuyud and Daroca. Over the rest of the decade, Alfonso continued the offensive and made a triumphal pass deep through southern al-Andalus. As the Christian pressure built up, a change occurred in the relationship between the Andalusis and the Almoravids. Originally, the North Africans were seen as upright, powerful saviours of the faith. When it turned out that the Almoravids couldn't actually hold back the Christians, the halo slipped and Andalusi opinion swung against the Almoravids.

To exacerbate the problems of the Almoravids, a rebellion by new fundamentalists, the Almohads, broke out in the High Atlas Mountains near Marrakech. These rebels then moved out from their mountain strongholds and captured the plains of Morocco. The end was swift for the Almoravids – the Almohads captured their capital of Marrakech in March 1147. Over on the Iberian Peninsula, as Almoravid power faded, Andalusi leaders and notables in the various regions emerged to seize power. Thus, for a second time, taifas began to emerge, albeit for a brief time. One of the groups, the Banu Ghaniya took over Seville and Córdoba, but were eventually displaced from there. They went to rule in Granada and remained in power there until the Almohads took it in 1154.

Right: the foothills of the High Atlas Mountains in Morocco, heartland of the Almohads.

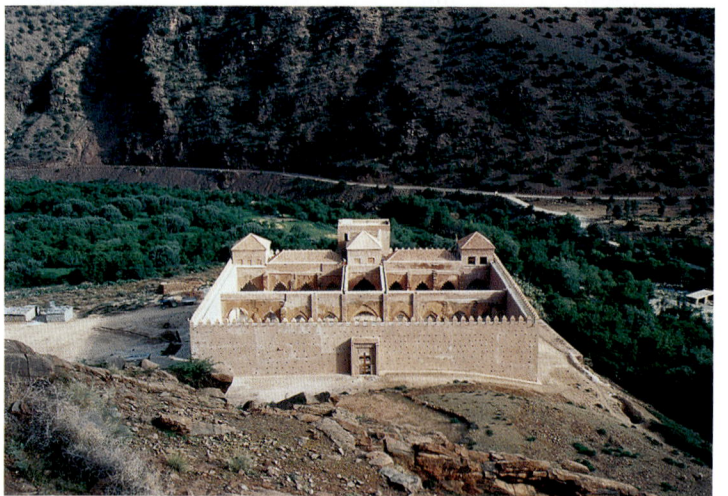

Left: the Tin Mal Mosque in the High Atlas Mountains. It was built in 1156 to commemorate the founder of the Almohad dynasty, Muhammad bin Tumart. © Museum With No Frontiers/Discover Islamic Art.

Al-Andalus had not been the principal priority for the Almohads in their first years, as they expanded across North Africa. Eventually they turned their attention northwards and in 1147 detachments of Almohad troops landed and seized the western half of al-Andalus, taking Seville early the following year. The Almohads expanded progressively until, by around 1160, most of the west and centre of al-Andalus had declared allegiance to them. Amid all this expansion, enemies remained on many fronts. The Christians, sensing weakness during the interregnum following the collapse of the Almoravids, had increased their attacks. The Count (later King) of Portugal emerged as a strong new Christian leader, attacking Muslim strongholds to the west of the Peninsula. However, it was not all bad news for the Almohads. There was a respite from Castilian pressure when Alfonso VII died in 1157 and Castile and León reverted to two separate and disputatious kingdoms.

The Almohads ruled al-Andalus from Seville, now their capital on the Peninsula, thus dislodging Granada from the leading status that it held during the Almoravid era. Conflict with the Christians continued. Alfonso VIII of Castile kept up the pressure. The Portuguese also persisted with their attacks, on occasion coming within sight of Seville. There were many battles between the Christians and Almohad armies. In 1195 the Almohad army marched from Seville and met with the forces of Alfonso VIII in July 1195 near the Castle of Alarcos, (south-west of Ciudad Real). The Almohads prevailed in this battle.

This era proved to be the apogee of the Almohad Empire. They controlled roughly the lower half of the Iberian Peninsula, and in the Maghreb from Morocco all the way to Tripoli. The Almohads were prodigious builders, and constructed a large number of buildings, both in the Maghreb and in al-Andalus. They constructed exceptional

Right: Granada lost its place as a principal location when the Almohads set up their capital in al-Andalus at Seville. Prodigious builders, they began construction in 1172 of a great mosque there. Its minaret is now the Giralda tower of the cathedral and was influenced by the Koutoubia in Marrakech.

Below: the Koutoubia Mosque was constructed in Almohad Marrakech in 1158.

39

Left: the tower of San Juan de los Reyes in the Albaicín in Granada, once a mosque. The lozenge-style decoration is Almohad. The simplicity of the plain geometric decoration reflects the ascetic tendencies of the Almohads.

Below: decorated ceramic jar dating from the Almohad era. © Museo de Almería.

buildings in their capital of Seville and throughout the south-west. There is an account that around 1210 an Almohad governor of Granada added many new buildings to the city, including a splendid residence for himself along the Darro. They built canals, gardens and a large number of new *almunias*, or country villas, in the Vega. Almohad designs can still be seen on the minaret of a mosque in Granada, now part of the church of San Juan de los Reyes.

There followed a period of relative peace in al-Andalus arising from truces made with the Christians but storm clouds were gathering. Alfonso VIII had not forgotten the bitter defeat of Alarcos and

Above: an Almohad brass incense burner. © Museo Arqueológico de Córdoba.

secured, from Pope Innocent III, a declaration of a crusade against the infidels of al-Andalus. Detailed preparations were put in train in early 1212. Christian knights from northern Europe came to Toledo for the crusade. The armies of Castile and Aragón assembled there. The combined Christian forces headed out in mid-summer 1212 and moved towards the Muslim frontier. The Almohad army left Seville and headed to las Navas de Tolosa (around 64 kilometres north-east of Jaén). The Christians attacked here on July 16 1212. The Muslim army was decisively defeated and it scattered in disarray. This battle was to prove a pivotal event. While the Almohad presence continued in the Peninsula for two more decades, their military capability was severely damaged and this defeat sounded the death knell for their rule.

In the years that followed, the Almohad ruling family descended into feuding – in turn three separate rebellions broke out in the Maghreb. To the east, the Hafsids had set up in Ifriqiya. The Zayyanids took over Tlemcen in 1236. The Marinids took Fez in 1248, making it their capital. In 1269 they eventually captured the Almohad capital of Marrakech. We will see these North African dynasties, particularly the Marinids, influencing events in the Peninsula during the later Nasrid era.

The Christians took advantage of the vacuum in Muslim power and launched vigorous offensives. Amidst the strife, a new Muslim leader Ibn Hud (descended from the family that had ruled the taifa of Zaragoza) set up in Murcia. All the main cities (including Seville, Córdoba, Granada and Almería), with the exception of Valencia, recognised him. However, Ibn Hud failed the litmus test of being able to defend Muslim lands against Christian attacks: in 1230 he suffered a serious defeat in a battle with the King of León, Alfonso

Right: the Battle of las Navas de Tolosa. Francisco de Paula Van Halen. In July 1212, the Christian armies conclusively defeated the Almohads at this location, north of Jaén. The battle was a seminal event as the Almohads never recovered militarily from this decisive defeat. © Patrimonio Histórico-Artistico del Senado, Madrid. Photograph: Oronoz.

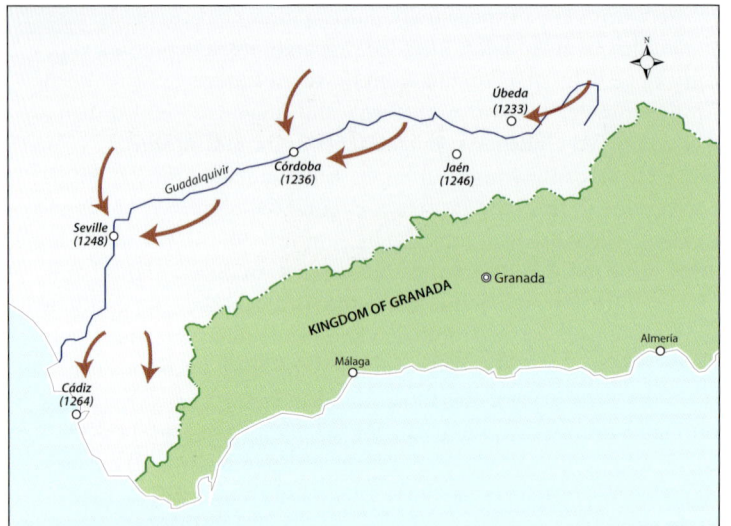

Left: as the Almohad dynasty disintegrated during the early thirteenth century, the Christians were able to take advantage of the power vacuum. The Kings of Castile and León made sweeps down the Guadalquivir valley, capturing great swathes of territory. All that remained of al-Andalus was the newly-established Kingdom of Granada.

IX, at Alange, near Mérida. The Christians continued their advances and took Mérida and Badajoz in 1232. The way was now open to the south and the Guadalquivir valley. On the death of Alfonso IX in September 1230, Castile and León were reunited and thus the Christian advance proceeded with even more energy. The new King of Castile and León, Fernando III, put Córdoba under siege and it surrendered in 1236. Córdoba had been the capital of the Umayyad Caliphate and its loss was deeply demoralising for the Andalusis. The inhabitants were ordered to leave the city and the Great Mosque of Córdoba was consecrated as a Christian cathedral. The Christian army continued its traverse along the Guadalquivir valley, seizing territory and strongholds. Ibn Hud moved to Almería where he was assassinated in January 1238.

Seville, the wealthy capital of Almohad al-Andalus, was now in Christian sights. Fernando III commenced the siege of the city in July 1247. This was an era of changing allegiances and ruthless self-interest, as witnessed by the help the Christian forces besieging Seville, received from Muslim troops dispatched by a leader from Arjona, one Ibn al-Ahmar (of whom much more later). Seville capitulated in December 1248.

Most of the rest of al-Andalus was progressively taken over by the Christians, either directly or indirectly, with submission by the rulers as vassals until the final takeover. Murcia lasted under Muslim rule until 1266, Minorca until 1287. Thus, in this turbulent thirteenth century, the Christians made enormous gains and the Reconquista was in full ascendance. They now controlled three-quarters of the former Almohad al-Andalus. Only the lands of what was to become the Kingdom of Granada remained under Muslim control.

Chapter 2
The Nasrid Kingdom of Granada

Over the course of two centuries the balance of power was totally reversed in the Peninsula. In the period around AD 1000, towards the end of the Umayyad Caliphate, the Christian realms were the weaker entities, relegated to the poorer north and kept in check by regular raids by large Muslim armies. During the time of the taifas, the Christian kingdoms had developed an assertive and expansionary approach, with the demographic and military might to roll back their Muslim foe, by now fragmented and weak. In the era of Almohad decline the Muslim world of al-Andalus was being torn apart. In the following three decades, three-quarters of the territory of al-Andalus was seized by the Christians. Under Fernando III the Kingdom of Castile acquired a new dynamism since its union with León in 1230. The Christians, coming south from the arid Meseta Central, penetrated the rich heart of what remained of al-Andalus under the Almohads, and ranged down the fertile valley of the Guadalquivir. Only one portion of territory was to remain out of their control. This was the mainly mountainous lands, comprising part of what is known today as Andalucía. This area became the Nasrid Kingdom of Granada, which was to maintain Islamic rule on the Peninsula for another 250 years.

As the conquest ground on, the Muslims were expelled from the captured cities. There was great seizure of land and booty. In the division of spoils, the Christian lords were granted vast swathes of territory. A stream of Christian settlers flowed in from the north, eager to exploit the new opportunities. As the remaining Islamic territory shrank, the local population was frantic to find a protector. As we have seen, in the vacuum that followed the demise of the Almohads, Ibn Hud had seized power as an independent ruler of al-Andalus. He had originally been seen by the Muslims as a protector, with the potential to save them from the Christian assault. However, they soon lost confidence in him: he was defeated in several battles and he raised taxes to pay parias to the Christians who were in the ascendant.

The emergence of Ibn al-Ahmar

As the Castilian raids increased along the border in the south, a frontier fighter came to prominence and gained high status as a tough and astute defender. Ibn al-Ahmar, later better known as Muhammad Ibn Yusuf Ibn Nasr, came from the town of Arjona, around 30 kilometres to the north-west of Jaén. He belonged to an established land-owning family. These were from a strand of al-Andalus society, that of Arabs with a military heritage, who had supported the Umayyad dynasty, and regarded the Berber Almoravids and Almohads with distaste.

In 1232, this local strongman rose up in Arjona against the domination of Ibn Hud and was proclaimed leader in the local mosque. Ibn al-Ahmar, then aged 37, attracted adherents from other prominent families (including the Banu Asqilula, of whom more later) around the region, and the ranks of his followers grew. He soon expanded his domain as far as Baza and Guadix. The people of the large regional capital of Jaén invited him to be ruler in 1233. He set up his headquarters there, improving and expanding the defences. Saviours were in short supply and his reputation preceded him. In the same year he was invited to rule in Córdoba and, sometime later, in Seville. In each case, his rule lasted only a few weeks. These big city dwellers did not take to the style of the man from Arjona and reverted back to Ibn Hud. Ibn al-Ahmar took the strategic decision in 1234 to recognise Ibn Hud as Amir. In return Ibn Hud conceded to him the lordship of Arjona, Porcuna (south-west of Arjona) and Jaén. This trimming of his sails to obtain the best opportunity was an early manifestation of the essential skills of Ibn al-Ahmar that allowed him to survive, expand and establish the Kingdom of Granada. All through his career, he demonstrated his capacity as a master tactician, combining pragmatism, shrewdness and a touch of deviousness. He was also reputed in his earlier years to have had an ascetic and religious nature, verging on the mystical. Later, after forming his kingdom, he subscribed to the

Above: bust of Ibn al-Ahmar at Arjona, his birthplace. Shrewd and decisive, this tough frontier fighter, a member of the Banu Nasr family, founded the Kingdom of Granada. Once he had established himself in that city, he became Muhammad I of the Nasrid dynasty. © Visita Arjona. Photograph: Antonio Salas Sola.

Below left: a view of the castle of Santa Catalina, with, in the foreground, remains of defensive walls from the Almohad period. The castle overlooks the city of Jaén and dates from the eighth century. In 1233 the people of the city invited Ibn al-Ahmar to be their leader He strengthened the castle and fortifications. Fernando III laid siege to the city in 1245. The following year, Ibn al-Ahmar, now in Granada, sued for peace and signed a treaty. Amongst the conditions was the handover of Jaén and its region.

Above: the Surrender of Córdoba. The King of Castile and León, Fernando III, put the city under siege and it surrendered in 1236. In those febrile times, survival was more important than religion. Ibn al-Ahmar, calculating for his advantage, had entered negotiations with Fernando and did not oppose the siege.

Right: Fernando III of Castile and León (r. 1217-1252), the conqueror of large tracts of al-Andalus.

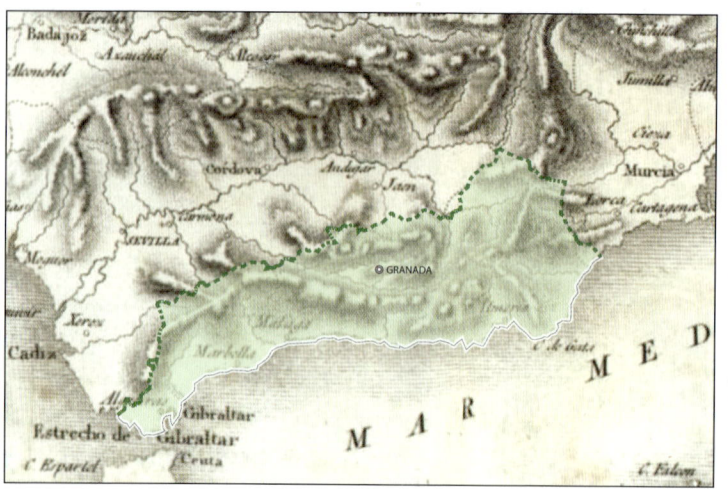

Left: the area of the Kingdom of Granada superimposed on an old relief map. The Christians had proved that they held the advantage in open warfare across the plain of the Guadalquivir. The new Granadan border was set back from this plain, The mountainous territory of the Baetic Cordillera formed a spine along the length of the kingdom, which, coupled with a new series of frontier fortresses, presented a more secure defensive barrier against attack. In addition, the ports along the southern coast allowed access to support from the Islamic kingdoms of the Maghreb.

rigid Maliki tradition (a useful attribute, as it was to garner a lot of religious support from the *alfaquis* of Granada).

It was common practice in those times to treat with the Christian enemy. Ibn al-Ahmar soon negotiated a treaty with Fernando III. One consequence was that he facilitated the Christian seizure of Muslim Córdoba in 1236. One wonders how he wrestled with his conscience, imbued with Islamic mysticism, on the issue of helping Christians defeat Muslims. However, his pragmatic side was the victor. His dilemma must be seen against the background of those dangerous times as the remaining Muslim enclaves around the Peninsula were being progressively captured by the Christians. Survival was a sensible choice and we later see Ibn al-Ahmar allying with the Christians anytime it suited. Whatever his mix of attributes, it appealed to the people of Granada who now requested him to be their ruler.

Against the background of the continuing defeats of the Amir Ibn Hud, a group of prominent Granadans had rebelled against the governor that had been appointed by Ibn Hud. After executing the governor, they declared for the new rising star, the man from Arjona. A delegation was sent to Jaén. They submitted to Ibn al Ahmar and requested his protection for Granada. He responded by sending his right-hand man, the leader of the Banu Asqilula clan, to meet with the great and the good of the city. Assured of the arrangements for handing over of the city, Ibn al-Ahmar travelled to Granada in May 1238, assumed control of the city and set up his headquarters and kingdom there.

Shortly afterwards, news came of Ibn Hud's assassination in Almería. Ibn al-Ahmar seized the moment, headed there and took over the port city in mid-1238. Málaga submitted to him in the same year. Over the space of six whirlwind years, he had moved from being the

Right: the Nasrid Kingdom of Granada in its original form around 1270.

Below: a Koran attributed to the Nasrid period, Muhammad I had the useful ability to combine his devout adherence to the Maliki version of Islam with a touch of pragmatism. © Metropolitan Museum of Art, New York.

leader in small-town Arjona to Amir of the Kingdom of Granada, in command of a significant part of the southern Peninsula.

Accord with Castile

Ibn al-Ahmar's treaty with Fernando III expired in 1242. Christian accounts claim that he made attacks on the Christian frontiers to the west of Jaén, which provoked retaliation. In any case, the Castilians advanced and devastated the countryside around Jaén. They totally encircled the city and began a siege there in August 1245. Dominated by a castle on a hill over the city, it presented a difficult target. As the siege wore on and the city's inhabitants starved, Ibn al-Ahmar made an attempt to send relief supplies to the defenders but was not successful.

Finally, in early 1246, he decided to resolve the conflict and signed a treaty with Fernando III. The conditions were hard. Jaén (including nearby Arjona, Ibn al-Ahmar's hometown) was to be handed over to Castile together with the payment of a huge sum of money (150,000 maravedis) every year. Ibn al-Ahmar was to be the King's vassal and give military support when required. However, the positive feature was that the treaty was of 20 years' duration. Thus, Ibn al-Ahmar, now Muhammad I of the Kingdom of Granada, bought himself time to consolidate his rule, set up all the necessary organisational structures for his new kingdom, and build fortifications along the frontier. As the last outposts of Muslim rule elsewhere on the Peninsula were being extinguished, this treaty also brought the new ruler of Granada protection, as a vassal of Castile, from the attacks of neighbouring Aragón on his Levante frontier. On a strategic level, the removal of the Jaén region from his domain marked a retrenchment to a more defensible line. The Christians had proved that they held the advantage in open warfare across the plains of the Guadalquivir. The mountainous territory of the Baetic Cordillera formed a spine along the length of the Kingdom of Granada, which, coupled with the new series of frontier fortresses, now presented a more secure defensive barrier against Christian attacks. In addition, the ports along the southern Mediterranean coast allowed access to support from the Islamic kingdoms of the Maghreb, which had set up as the Almohad Empire disintegrated. Apart from the ports of the Strait, which it was to lose at an early stage, the Kingdom of Granada was now in the shape it was to retain for most of its existence. It comprised, more or less, the present-day provinces of Málaga, Granada and Almería and ranged in the west from Tarifa along the Mediterranean coast to the eastern frontier with Murcia. Thus, the bargain that led to the painful surrender of his former stronghold of Jaén, as well as his birthplace of Arjona, allowed Ibn al-Ahmar to bring a new, larger and as it turned out, more durable, entity to life – the Kingdom of Granada.

The peace also made sense for the kingdom of Castile. It bought respite – Castile had recently seized enormous swathes of territory. It needed time to absorb these, divide up the spoils and introduce Christian settlers from the north. There had been an exodus of Muslims from the captured lands, either to North Africa or to the new Kingdom of Granada. These Muslim lands had been highly productive, requiring intensive farming with a large labour force. Thus with their exodus the land had become depopulated and time was needed to import new settlers and consolidate agriculture. At that time, as well as a

Above: the military quarters of the Alcazaba at the Alhambra. Once established in Granada, Muhammad I moved from the Zirid alcazaba and built a new fortification, expanding an older fortress here on the Sabika Hill.

Below: the red conglomerate earth of the Sabika Hill proved ideal for the defensive walls made of rammed earth. The name Alhambra is from the name 'Qalat Al-Hamra', or red castle.

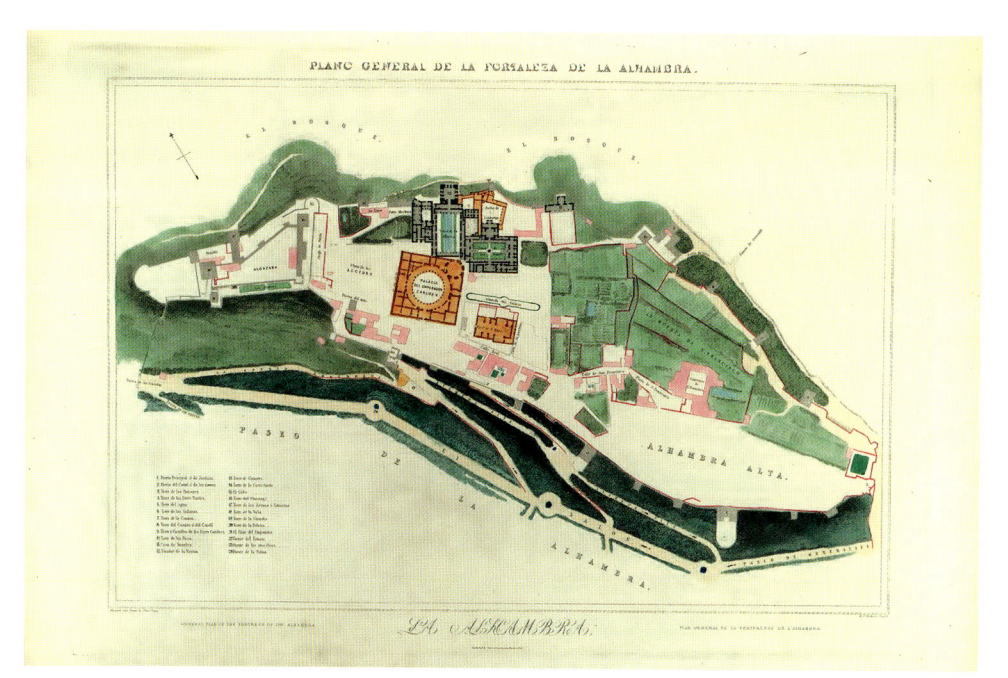

Above: a nineteenth-century plan of the Alhambra by the English-born architect Owen Jones. The Alcazaba was the start of what was to become a palace-city. In time there were to be many palaces, administrative buildings, baths and a great mosque. This was at the heart of the Nasrid dynasty: it was the residence of the Amirs over the centuries.

scarcity of Christian settlers, Castile was short of military manpower and found it difficult to garrison its new domain; to continue the expansion would have overstretched its army, far from its Castilian and Leonese domains. An additional benefit was that it was a very lucrative deal: the Christians, weaned on parias, were reaping a huge annual payment from the Nasrid kingdom, to be paid over 20 years.

Granada at the dawn of Nasrid Rule

So what was the city of Granada like at the beginning of the Nasrid era in 1238? Essentially it was in the shape that had been developed during the Zirid taifa and amplified during the rule of the Almoravids and Almohads. It was an extensive city surrounded by the prosperous farming areas on the plain along the banks of the rivers Darro and Genil. It had all the usual attributes of an Islamic city: within the extensive series of defensive walls there was an Alcazaba (the *Alcazaba Qadima* – the 'old') on the heights north of the Darro. Down in the medina was a Great Mosque, baths and a souk. Various suburbs extended north and south of the Darro.

Ibn al-Ahmar set up in Granada, initially basing himself in the Alcazaba Qadima. Muhammad decided to move from here and build one afresh on a hill above the city, the Sabika. This new Alcazaba was the start of what was to become a palace-city, similar to the great Madinat al-Zahra of the Córdoba Caliphate. In time many palaces, administrative buildings, baths and a great mosque were built. This

50

Left: a view up the valley of the river Darro, fed by the melting snows of the Sierra Nevada. Using their mastery of hydraulic technology the Nasrid builders constructed a major water channel to supply the Alhambra. This channel commenced at a dam on the north of the river Darro some six kilometres upstream of the Alhambra. It is known as the Acequia Real, or Royal Channel.

Left: the water entered over an aqueduct to the the Alhambra complex, by the Torre del Agua, seen to the right. It continued onwards via the Acequia Real (the channel to the left).

Below: just visible in the foreground is an albercón, a hydraulic system with reservoir, located above the Generalife gardens. To the front is a tower, which formed a platform for an animal-powered water wheel. The water was pumped up from the Acequia Real to the reservoir, for onward distribution.

was to be the heartland of the Nasrid dynasty: the residence of the Amirs, who over the centuries continued to expand the palatine complex, known as the Alhambra.

Construction of the new fortress, the Alcazaba, began on the narrow plateau that sits on a spur of the Sierra Nevada, the hill of the Sabika which dominates the city. To the north is the valley of the river Darro, and the Albaicín hill. On its southern side lies the broad valley of the river Genil. An eminent Spanish archaeologist has referred to the Sabika Hill as an *'enormous boat anchored between the mountain and the plain'*. The name Alhambra derives from *Qalat al-Hamra*, the red castle, particularly due to the colour of the ferric oxide in the clay (known as 'Alhambra conglomerate', which proved an excellent material for construction of the rammed-earth defensive walls).

Ibn al-Ahmar, (now Muhammad I of his newly-established Nasrid dynasty) first took steps to ensure that a secure water supply be put in place for his new fortress enclave. The Muslims of al-Andalus had been masters of hydraulic technology and this expertise was demonstrated in the construction of a major water channel which intercepted the river Darro (fed by the melting snows of the Sierra Nevada) by means of a dam on its north side some six kilometres upstream of the Alhambra. A channel, known as the *Acequia Real*, crosses the river via an aqueduct and runs parallel to it on its southern side for several kilometres, contouring the hillside along the valley. Nearing Granada, it changes direction to the east and crosses a gully via another aqueduct to the Alhambra area. The water channel ran directly along the Sabika plateau to the new citadel. As the building work began, one account relates that Muhammad had a tax collector from Almería (and later others of the same profession) put to death on the Sabika grounds, as he was dissatisfied with the flow of funds necessary to fund his building programme.

The Alcazaba was located on the site of a smaller earlier fortress, on the western end of the Sabika hill, facing the Granadan Vega. Sources are vague on this older structure – some say that, around 1056, Samuel Ibn Naghrela, the Jewish Vizier of the Zirid Amir, rebuilt and enlarged this relatively small building and that the last Zirid ruler, Abd Allah, had also upgraded it.

Within the new Alcazaba grounds was an *aljibe* (cistern) fed by the Acequia Real. There was a residential quarter and all other requirements for an encampment of elite royal guards: a bathhouse, barracks, dungeons, stables and storerooms. The older walls were reconstructed and reinforced so that the new Alcazaba, triangular in shape, was flanked by strong high defensive walls punctuated by many towers.

Under the shelter of his treaty with the Castilians, Muhammad I had ample time to consolidate his new kingdom. In contrast to the previous decades of chaos, a new public order was established. Cor-

Left: elaborately decorated ivory pyxis with a flat lid and silver fixings. It is from the Nasrid period – the late thirteenth century. On its body is a poem, referring to the object itself: 'Truth is in me like something stored in a pyxis; and they say faithfulness is my share in life; never did I betray this confidence (in me); thus my name soared so I serve only the great'. © Catedral Basilica del Pilar, Cabildo Metropolitano de Zaragoza.

ruption was discouraged. That indispensable element of any state, tax collection, was made more efficient (presumably the execution of some tax collectors, previously mentioned, had concentrated minds!) and fair.

As the Reconquista continued, a surge of Muslim refugees from the former territories of al-Andalus fled to the Kingdom of Granada. This resulted in a boost for the new kingdom. The stream of skilled and talented people from the conquered lands stimulated the economy. Refugees flooded into the main cities: Granada, Málaga and Almería and the capital. Granada grew rapidly, absorbing the new migrants. The Zirid walls of the city were strengthened and a new line of walls to the north was constructed to incorporate the Albaicín district, newly swollen with refugees from Baeza (taken by Fernando III of Castile in 1226). The name of the district is thought to have come from the Arabic *al-baezan* – people from Baeza.

Ten years after setting up in Granada, Muhammad I gave assistance to Fernando III who was besieging Muslim Seville. No more than his assistance to Fernando in extinguishing Muslim Córdoba years before, this represented the Faustian aspect of his pact with Castile. As vassal of Castile, he sent 500 horsemen to take part in the siege of Seville, which was taken towards the end of 1248. This is a less than honourable part of early Nasrid history but one could argue that, had Muhammad I been more principled, it is likely his Granada kingdom would not have survived for the two and a half centuries that it did.

Assistance from the South

There was another significant power to the south across the Strait of Gibraltar: the Marinids. They had taken over from the Almohads, across what is more or less present-day Morocco and had set up their capital in Fez. The Marinids were eager to help their co-religionists in Granada against the Christian threat. Thus began their involvement in the Peninsula, which was to last for around 80 years. This commenced around 1263 when the Marinid Amir sent a detachment of *Guza*, or 'fighters of the faith' to Granada. Muhammad I was strengthened by these new arrivals, which may lend weight to suggestions that he encouraged an uprising in 1264 of the *Mudéjars* (Muslims living under Christian rule) in Christian territory, which erupted all along the frontier. The rebellion ran from towns like Vejer de la Frontera, to Jerez and along the south of the lower Guadalquivir valley – as well as in Murcia. Significantly, the treaty with Castile was coming to an end, with only a few years to run.

Muhammad I sent troops to aid the rebels in Jerez, but the Granadan troops were repelled. He sent more troops to Murcia, but Jaime I of Aragón eventually ejected them. As the Mudéjars were expelled by the Christians, a fresh wave of refugees flowed into Granada. Castile responded by establishing military orders with their knights in positions along the border with Granada. Thus, Muhammad I's brief attempt to roll back the Reconquista turned out to be a failure.

Trouble now broke out on the internal front. The Banu Asqilula family had been close supporters of Muhammad and had been prominent in supporting his rise to power. This family was related by marriage to the Granadan Amir; also one of the Banu Asqilula was head of the army. The family had built up expectations of sharing power and were frustrated by Muhammad's naming of his sons as heirs. The Banu Asqilula were also perturbed by the presence of the Marinid Guza, who they perceived as displacing their control of the army. In 1266 the Banu Asqilula rose up against the Amir in two strategic locations to the east and west of Granada: Málaga and Guadix, both places where family members had been governors. The rebels looked for help to Alfonso X of Castile who sent to their aid a thousand-strong detachment of cavalry led by one Nuño González. Despite his best efforts, Muhammad failed to put down the rebels and Málaga remained out of his control.

He tried diplomacy and negotiated with Alfonso X, but this did not succeed. In the fast-changing fortunes of the era, Ibn al-Ahmar had a stroke of good luck: the nobles of Castile had become disaffect-

Below: Nasrid ceramic oil lamp, fourteenth century. © Museo de la Alhambra.

ed with the king. With the help of these, known as the *Ricos Hombres*, and led by the self-same Nuño González, the Nasrid forces attacked and took Antequera from the Banu Asqilula in July 1272. Despite this advance, the conflict with the Banu Asqilula was still ongoing when Ibn al-Ahmar tumbled from his horse in Granada. He died in January 1273. He was 77 years of age and had reigned for over 40 years.

He was succeeded by his son, Muhammad II. Aged 38, he was very experienced, having occupied senior positions of state. On his accession, the immediate task that faced him was that of suppressing the Banu Asqilula uprising. He first tried to treat with Alfonso X and went to meet him at his court in Seville. The Castilian king proved to be difficult – in effect he was readily accepting Muham-

Above: a view of the Strait of Gibraltar, looking northwards from the Moroccan coast, with the bare and rocky Isla de Perejil in the foreground. Control of the Strait has been a constant allure, even up to the present day, as evidenced by the enclaves of Gibraltar and Ceuta on the northern and southern coasts, respectively.

Left: over two centuries the Nasrids struggled with, variously, the Castilians and the Marinids, amongst others, for domination of the Strait and its ports. Eventually the Castilians gained control and captured territory north of the Strait.

mad's tribute money but not responding with any assistance with the Banu Asqilula problem. Muhammad II now looked further afield to the Marinids in Fez who had sent an earlier detachment of troops, the Guza. The Marinids agreed to give substantially increased help. In addition to their jihadi instinct, this reflected the hegemonic desire of the Marinids to reconstitute the old Almohad Empire, as well as to control the Strait of Gibraltar. The Marinid Amir, Abu Yusuf, made plans to lead a large army to the Peninsula. Thus a new and potent dynamic was added to the competing forces on the Peninsula and it was the beginning of a bewildering tableau of ever-changing alliances. The Nasrids were playing with fire – over the history of al-Andalus previous requests from harried Muslim rulers on the Peninsula for relief from Christian pressure had resulted in complete takeover by the Almoravids and the Almohads.

The Marinid advance troops landed in Tarifa, setting up there and in Algeciras by May 1275. Abu Yusuf followed in August, leading the main force. Once installed, he convened a meeting attended by Muhammad II and representatives of the Banu Asqilula. This was a failure, with Muhammad II storming off at what he perceived as the pro-Asqilula attitude of Abu Yusuf. The Marinid army then embarked on a series of raids on Castilian lands, sacking the regions of Córdoba, Seville and Jaén. With Algeciras and Tarifa still under Marinid control, Abu Yusuf, laden with booty, returned to the Maghreb. However, the genie was now out of the bottle: the Marinids proved to be as much a danger to the Nasrids as were the Castilians. Without prior consultation with the Nasrids, the Marinids mounted another expedition to the Peninsula. Abu Yusuf led this new campaign, making several raids against localities from Jaén to Cádiz during the second half of 1277.

Left: the castle at Tarifa, originally built in 960 during the reign of Caliph Abd al-Rahman III. Throughout the Nasrid era it was the scene of much conflict during the battles for control of the Strait of Gibraltar.

Fearful of being attacked by the Nasrids, the Banu Asqilula ceded Málaga to the Marinids. Muhammad II, now alarmed by the danger the Marinids posed to his kingdom, made an arrangement with Alfonso X to join forces and eject the Marinids from the peninsula. Bringing another ingredient into what was already an explosive mix, Muhammad II also reached an agreement with one of the other Maghrebi dynasties and rivals of the Marinids, the Zayyanids in Tlemcen, in present-day Algeria.

Sieges of the Strait Ports

Events moved swiftly: in February 1279 the Castilians besieged Algeciras (in Marinid hands) from the sea but were beaten back by a large Marinid fleet. Around the same time, Muhammad II manoeuvred, by bribery it is suggested, to achieve the take-over of Málaga. The Marinids then made peace with the Castilians and the swirling dance continued, with the protagonists rapidly changing partners. In 1280, the Castilians, the Banu Asqilula and Marinids embarked on attacks on the Nasrids who succeeded in fending them off. Fortunately for the Nasrids, there was dissension within Castile: in 1282 Alfonso X fell into dispute with his son Sancho who entered the fray on Granada's side.

Alfonso X died in April 1284 and was succeeded by the Granadan's erstwhile ally, now Sancho IV. In 1285 the Marinids mounted another military campaign in the Peninsula, this time against Sancho. The Marinid Amir Abu Yusuf died in Algeciras in March 1286. At this time his kingdom was still in control of Algeciras and Tarifa. However, priorities had changed for the Marinids. They now wanted merely to maintain the status quo on the Peninsula: new challenges such as that from the neighbouring Zayyanids now loomed large in the Maghreb and they wanted to concentrate their efforts there. In any case, the vicissitudes of dealing with the wily Nasrids and the quicksands of the

Below: with a regal lion at his side, Sancho IV, King of Castile and León, presides at Tarifa. In alliance with the Nasrids, he seized this port from the Marinids of North Africa, in 1292.

ever-changing peninsular power alliances did not present an attractive prospect. Abu Ya'qub, the new Marinid Amir, signed a peace agreement with the Nasrids (although the ever-present lure of control of the Strait was to persuade the Marinids to return to the fray over later centuries). In 1288, the Banu Asqilula faded out of the history of the Peninsula, as they emigrated to the Maghreb, where they were granted lands by the Marinid Amir. They set up a small dynasty in Ksar el-Kabir, inland from the Atlantic coast, around 85 kilometres south of Tangier.

Muhammad II, who still wanted control over the Strait, signed an accord with Sancho IV in May 1291. The understanding was that the Castilians would take Tarifa from the Marinids, which they would then hand over to Granada in return for some frontier fortresses. In this tale of intrigue, the Christian kingdoms in turn had designs on North Africa. Castile and Aragón had signed a treaty which agreed spheres of influence for themselves in North Africa. Thus Sancho IV began the siege of Tarifa with the help of the Aragonese navy, which blockaded the city from the sea. Muhammad's troops came from Málaga and joined the siege. Tarifa fell in October 1292. However,

Right: silk textile from Nasrid Granada, with cursive script. The silk industry was an important part of the economy and magnificent textiles, as evidenced by this splendid example, were produced. © Museo Lázaro Galdiano, Madrid.

Muhammad may have been too clever by far in his manoeuvring, as the deal ended up with a loss for him. Sancho reneged on the agreement, refused to hand over Tarifa and at the same time seized the promised frontier fortresses.

For Muhammad II, understandably angered, it was time to switch partners. He reverted back to the Marinids. The agreement that he now reached was that he would get Algeciras and Ronda, with the Marinids having possession of Tarifa. In the opposing corner were the Castilians, along with the Aragonese but now in an alliance with the Zayyanids in Tlemcen, enemies of the Marinids. So, in April 1294, the Marinids started the siege of Tarifa. Although the Granadans were their allies, they gave only nominal support. Then the famous event happened, when the leader of the Castilian defenders Alfonso Pérez de Guzmán or 'Guzmán the Good' was confronted by the demand of the besiegers: surrender or they would kill his son whom they had captured. He defied them and legend has it that he threw his dagger down at them to do it, whereupon the son was killed. This event had poignant later resonances for an event in the twentieth-century Spanish Civil War when Colonel Moscardó, Nationalist commander of the besieged Alcázar in Toledo, was confronted with a similar proposal by the Republican forces. They had captured his son and threatened to shoot him unless the Alcázar was surrendered. It is recounted that he told his son, over the telephone, to die bravely.

Above: dagger in hand, Guzmán 'the Good'. He defended Tarifa against the attempt by the Marinids to retake it in 1294.

The siege of Tarifa lasted just four months – it was lifted when Aragonese ships came to the rescue. After the failure of the siege, the Marinids decided to leave the peninsular stage. The two Amirs met to discuss this in Tangier in 1295 and, as a result, Granada was able to finally incorporate Algeciras and Ronda. Sancho IV died in April 1295. Castile was weakened by internal dissension, as the new successor to the throne was only nine years of age. Granada was now in a position of strength. As the Aragonese wished to avoid a pact between the Castilians and Nasrids, they signed a treaty with the latter.

When Muhammad II died in April 1302 he was succeeded by his son Muhammad III (one source suggests that the Amir was poisoned by his son). He was not a very attractive personality: the great Arab chronicler Ibn al-Khatib depicts him as brutish and cruel. He also turned out to be inept: the Kingdom of Granada created by his grandfather and father was now to enter into a whirl of instability. The new amir started off sensibly enough: he signed a pact with the Castilians (it included three years of vassalage), which gave him confidence to begin his new adventure. Desirous of total control of the Strait, he cast his sights on Ceuta in the Maghreb, just across from Gibraltar. For more than two centuries, the dynamic of invasion had come from the Maghreb, north to the Peninsula. This marked a reversal of that pattern. The Granadans fomented a revolt in Ceuta and subsequently

Right: in Ceuta, a tile depicting the city. This strategic port is now a Spanish enclave surrounded by Morocco. The Umayyads had gained control of the port and the surrounding region. Following attacks on al-Andalus fleet by the Fatimids in 955, Caliph Abd al-Rahman III ordered the fortifications here to be strengthened. Ceuta featured in the struggles for control of the Strait during the Nasrid era.

took it over in 1307. This Nasrid venture, establishing a bridgehead on the North African coast, proved to be a step too far: it propelled the Marinids to re-emerge on the scene. Conveniently, the Marinids had just ended their war with the Zayyanids in Tlemcen. They, together with the Castilians and Aragonese, now formed a triple alliance against Granada.

As this grave external threat rose up on the horizon, there was understandable popular unease in Granada at the parlous state of affairs. It resulted in Muhammad III being forced to abdicate in March 1309. He was replaced by his brother Nasr. (Muhammad was assassinated in January 1314 – assassination of amirs was to become a speciality over the remaining Nasrid era). The situation facing the new amir was bleak: Granada stood alone against three kingdoms. The Marinids attacked Ceuta with the assistance of an Aragonese fleet and ejected the Nasrids. In July 1309 the Castilians began the siege of Algeciras and eventually seized nearby Gibraltar in September 1309. In August 1309 the Aragonese attacked Almería by land and sea.

The members of the Nasrid dynasty seemed to inherit the ability to skilfully negotiate their way out of dangerous situations (an ability that had evaded Muhammad III). Nasr, only 21 years of age, behaved adroitly: he took the difficult decision to negotiate with the Marinids and hand over to them Algeciras and Ronda, enclaves that had been in Marinid hands in the past. He also offered his sister in marriage to the Marinid Amir. In exchange, the Marinids sent an army to his aid. On the Castilian side, internal dissent broke out among the nobles. Against all this the Castilian Fernando IV decided to raise the siege of Algeciras in January 1310 and sign a treaty with Nasr. It involved the usual vassalage and the handing over to Castile of two border towns and tribute. The siege of Almería by the Aragonese had been long. There were many assaults using siege engines including catapults. However, storms meant the Aragonese were running out of food, while the defenders (who had planned ahead) were well supplied. The Granadans sent a relieving force and the siege was lifted in 1310.

Fernando IV of Castile died in 1312 in Jaén. His heir Alfonso was a child of only one year of age, which led to dissension in the kingdom. In the same year an uprising broke out against Nasr with the Amir's nephew, Isma'il, at the head of the rebels. Eventually, in 1314, Nasr was forced to abdicate and Isma'il I took power in the Alhambra. Nasr headed for Guadix and set up in opposition there. The Castilians supported Nasr and various encounters took place between these and Isma'il's forces. Eventually Isma'il's army decisively defeated the Castilians in what was termed the Battle of the Vega in June 1319.

Isma'il spent some time recapturing lost fortresses and consolidating his kingdom, including signing treaties with the Aragonese. In a frontier skirmish with the Castilians, we hear of what sounds like the first use of gunpowder on the Peninsula. It was the vigorous mastery of artillery by the Christians that was to later destroy the Kingdom of Granada, although ironically, it seems the first use was by Muslims. The historian Ibn al-Khatib tells how, in a Nasrid attack on Huéscar in 1324, a device made a thunderous roar, and an iron ball was projected with great velocity at the enemy.

Above: the Alcazaba in Almería (constructed by Abd al-Rahman III in 955). It was one of the important ports of the Nasrid Kingdom of Granada. In August 1309 the Aragonese attacked Almería by land and sea. The siege was long and hard. Eventually due to storms the Aragonese ran out of food. A relieving force was sent from Granada and the siege was lifted in 1310.

Left: engraving by the Irish architect James Cavanagh Murphy in his 1816 book 'The Arabian Antiquities of Spain'. Based on one of the painted scenes on a ceiling in the Sala de los Reyes in the Alhambra, it depicts a joust between Muslim and Christian horsemen.

Continuing dynastic intrigue

In time, the Nasrid tendency for dynastic intrigue manifested itself: Isma'il was assassinated in July 1325, following a dispute with his cousin, who was governor of Algeciras. Isma'il's son, only ten years of age, succeeded him and became the new ruler, Muhammad IV. Initially, he was under his Vizier's tutelage but eventually grasped the reins of power. Over in Castile another young sovereign, Alfonso XI, reached his majority. The Castilian now planned to take the initiative and avenge the great defeat of the Vega of less than a decade before. Imbued with a crusading spirit, Alfonso XI tried to organise a coalition of the Iberian Christian states, together with support from the northern European kingdoms, against Granada. It did not work as he had planned and it was only the Castilians, with some European knights, that eventually set out on the offensive. They began their

Right: a Nasrid dignitary, probably a ruler, with his highly decorated jineta (a light cavalry sword), symbol of power. This is part of a scene on the painted ceiling of the middle vault in the Sala de los Reyes. © Archivo y Biblioteca del Patronato de la Alhambra y Generalife.

Left: the Madrasa al-Sahrij in Fez, constructed in 1321. Fez was the capital of the Marinids, who became involved in the struggle for control of the Strait. At times they supported the Nasrids rulers, at other times they posed a direct challenge to Granadan power.

assault and took several frontier fortresses, including that of Teba, around 30 kilometres north-east of Ronda, which fell after a long siege in 1330.

Muhammad IV asked for help from the Marinids and together they attacked Gibraltar, which they took in June 1333, after several months of siege. With the Marinid troops once more in the Peninsula, Alfonso XI decided to sign a truce in August 1333. Shortly afterwards, Muhammad IV, only 18 years old, was assassinated nesr the river Guadiaro, near Algeciras, on his way home from Gibraltar, by sons of the leader of the Guza (the Berber fighters for the faith stationed in Granadan territory). This group were superb fighters and an essential element of Granada's army. However, ever since the first group had been established on the Peninsula in the reign of Muhammad I in 1264, they were expensive to maintain, and were resented by the Granadan populace (echoing how the Berber mercenaries had generated huge resentment during the last days of the Córdoba Caliphate). They were light horsemen, able to out-manoeuvre the more heavily armoured Castilians. The Spanish word *jinete* (horseman) comes from

Right: the Corral de Carbón in Granada, built at the beginning of fourteenth century. This was a funduq (or inn) where visiting silk merchants could lodge as well as store their wares. Silkworms were cultivated on the mulberry trees of various areas such as the Alpujarras and Almería. Granadan silk was renowned for its quality. Silk textiles were exported across the Mediterranean and to Christian Spain. The export trade was controlled by Genoese merchants. Trading families from Genoa settled in the capital and also in Almería and Málaga.

the Zanata Berber tribe. In Granada the Zenete quarter near the old Alcazaba is named after the Guza who settled there. As we have seen from the events by the banks of the Guadiaro, the Guza had gained power and influence. They were habitually involved in palace intrigue and in the assassination of Granadan leaders.

Yusuf I and his son, Muhammad V

Muhammad's brother, another young man (only 15 years old), Yusuf I, succeeded to the throne. He immediately accomplished the first essential task: that of expelling the family of his brother's assassins to the Maghreb. He then signed peace treaties with the Christian kingdoms. However, the ongoing rivalry over control of the Strait led to an arms race between the Marinids and the Castilians, with both sides building up their navies. This came to a head when the Marinid and Granadan navies struck at the Castilian fleet near Algeciras in April 1340 and soundly defeated it. Emboldened by this, the Marinid Amir crossed the Strait with a large force and laid siege to Tarifa in August 1340 – using at least 20 siege engines according to one account. The Christian forces (led by Alfonso XI of Castile and supported by his brother-in-law, the King of Portugal) set out to attack the numerically more powerful Muslim army, predominantly Marinid, but with some Nasrid troops. The armies met at the Rio Salado (near Tarifa) and this time the heavily armed Christian cavalry overcame the opposing light horsemen, unable to manoeuvre in the confined space of the battlefield. The Muslims suffered huge losses and fled, leaving behind arms, precious metal and, according to one account, slaves and concubines. A huge amount of treasure was seized by the Christians. As L. P. Hartley relates in his book *Islamic Spain 1250 to 1500*, such was the quantity that prices crashed in the bullion markets of Paris, Barcelona and other cities. The Marinids hurried back across the Strait and the Nasrids to Granada. Capitalising on this great victory, Alfonso seized Granadan frontier fortresses. He mustered a substantial force of northern European soldiers and began the siege of Algeciras in August 1342. This was an important strategic objective for the Castilians: to seize the main port through which reinforcements had flowed northwards from Morocco. Despite a strong defence by the Muslims, including their use of cannon, the port surrendered in 1344. The tech-

Above: the cupola of the Madrasa in central Granada. This university was built in 1349 during the reign of Yusuf I. It was much altered following the Christian conquest, when it was used as the Casa del Cabildo (city hall).

Above: engraving by James Cavanagh Murphy of the Patio de los Arrayanes, part of the Palacio de Comares. The palace was commissioned by Yusuf I, and was completed by his son Muhammad V who commenced his reign (one of several) in 1354.

nology of gunpowder and cannon was absorbed by the Christians and it is reported that English knights who had been at the siege brought this knowledge back to England. Later we shall see how the Castilians achieved a sophisticated mastery of artillery, which hastened the end of the Kingdom of Granada.

As part of the handover of Algeciras, Yusuf I concluded a ten-year truce with the Castilians. This peace and the resulting external stability led to a period of prosperity which fostered a flourishing of architectural, cultural and literary development in Granada. However, Granada did not escape the Black Plague, which had spread to Europe at this time. This pestilence was generally more virulent in urban centres than in the countryside. From 1348 onwards it passed through the kingdom and killed thousands.

This did not stop Yusuf I from embarking on major construction works in Granada and throughout his kingdom. In the Alhambra, he built three imposing gateways as well as many towers including those of Machuca and Comares. The latter includes the main reception area, the Hall of the Ambassadors, which was his throne room. The Patio de los Arrayanes (of the myrtles) was also commenced. In 1349 Yusuf I built in the city itself the *Madrasa*, a theological seminary and law school. In the kingdom's second city, Málaga, he built the great

Left: decorated stucco at the Madrasa.

fortress, the Gibralfaro castle on the hill which dominates the city and its port. As well as architecture, the arts flourished in the kingdom. He attracted many famous writers to his court. Yusuf's reign marked the beginning of Granada's golden age and this continued during the reign of his son Muhammad V.

Alfonso XI of Castile had no scruples about breaking the truce he had made with Granada. He began a siege of Gibraltar, but the Black Plague struck and he died there in March 1350. He was succeeded by his young son Pedro I, who later gained the soubriquet of 'Pedro the Cruel'. He maintained good relations with the Nasrids and soon signed a peace treaty with them. However, the energetic Yusuf I was not to enjoy peace for long. He was cut down in his prime at only 36 years of age by a demented slave, while he prayed at the mosque in the Alhambra, in October 1354.

He was succeeded by his son, Muhammad V. The new ruler was nearly 16 years old but had the support of a talented and powerful group of court advisors, including the vizier Ibn al-Khatib whom we have previously encountered. Muhammad V was a polymath, a poet and historian and regarded as one of the greatest writers of the Nasrid era. When personal energy and ability are combined with a long reign, external peace and a certain amount of luck, extraordinary things can be achieved. This was the case with Muhammad V, whose rule spanned 37 years, albeit including an unplanned interruption of three years. This enlightened amir presided over a period of stability and prosperity, which included the construction of some of the finest buildings in the Alhambra. In short, it was to represent the apogee of the kingdom's splendour. At the beginning of his reign, Muhammad V and his phalanx of advisors set about to copper-fasten the peace that he desired with the main powers which surrounded Granada.

Right: a tangled web – the reigns of the Nasrid dynasty, 1238-1492. It commenced in a stable fashion: there were only two reigns over the first 64 years. As the years progressed the throne was occupied by a rapid succession of amirs: each Nasrid ruler was either deposed or assassinated. Some rulers reigned several times. Over the last 65 years to the downfall in 1492 there were 16 separate reigns.

Left: the parapets of the Gibralfaro castle, on a hill 130 metres above Málaga, which was the most important port of the Kingdom of Granada. The fortification was built on the orders of Yusuf I. This energetic ruler constructed many magnificent buildings across his kingdom.

1238-1427

- MUHAMMAD I — *1238-1273*
- MUHAMMAD II — *1273-1302*
- MUHAMMAD III — *1302-1309*
- NASR — *1309-1314*
- ISMA'IL I — *1314-1325*
- MUHAMMAD IV — *1325-1333*
- YUSUF I — *1333-1354*
- MUHAMMAD V — *1354-1359*
- ISMA'IL II — *1359-1360*
- MUHAMMAD VI — *1360-1362*
- MUHAMMAD V — *1362-1391*
- YUSUF II — *1391-1392*
- MUHAMMAD VII — *1392-1408*
- YUSUF III — *1408-1417*
- MUHAMMAD VIII — *1417-1419*
- MUHAMMAD IX — *1419-1427*

1427-1492

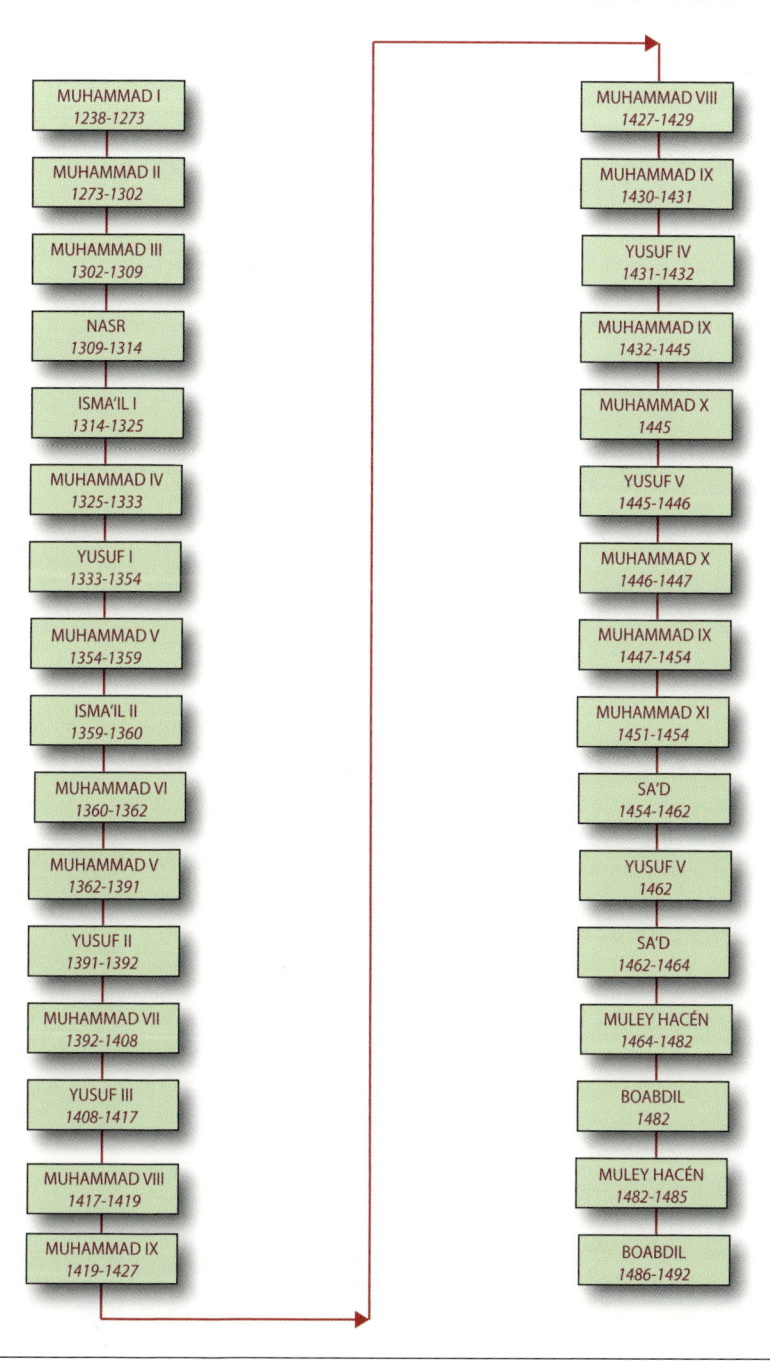

- MUHAMMAD VIII — *1427-1429*
- MUHAMMAD IX — *1430-1431*
- YUSUF IV — *1431-1432*
- MUHAMMAD IX — *1432-1445*
- MUHAMMAD X — *1445*
- YUSUF V — *1445-1446*
- MUHAMMAD X — *1446-1447*
- MUHAMMAD IX — *1447-1454*
- MUHAMMAD XI — *1451-1454*
- SA'D — *1454-1462*
- YUSUF V — *1462*
- SA'D — *1462-1464*
- MULEY HACÉN — *1464-1482*
- BOABDIL — *1482*
- MULEY HACÉN — *1482-1485*
- BOABDIL — *1486-1492*

He signed new peace treaties, initially with Castile and later with Aragón. Not forgetting his co-religionists in the Maghreb, he sent Ibn al-Khatib to Fez in 1354, with the aim of establishing good relations with the Marinids. However, the peace was broken when, in 1358, Pedro I of Castile went to war with Aragón. Granada was sucked into the fray by virtue of its vassalage and had to send ships and land forces to support the Castilians. Domestic issues suddenly intervened when there was a takeover of the Alhambra in August 1359 by discontented palace plotters. Muhammad's stepbrother was proclaimed the Amir Isma'il II. Muhammad, who happened to be outside of the Alhambra complex, fled first to Guadix and eventually headed to the Maghreb and found refuge with the Marinids in Fez. Back in Granada, the new ruler was reputed to be weak, slothful and dominated by his ambitious mother. He ruled for less than a year, his rule ending as suddenly as it had commenced. In July 1360 he was assassinated and replaced by his ambitious second cousin, Muhammad VI. This new ruler decided to establish close relations with Aragón. This proved to be a bad tactic, as, in consequence, Pedro I of Castile, engaged in conflict with Aragón, gave assistance to Muhammad V to reclaim his throne. Muhammad V returned in 1361, met Pedro in Seville and established himself in Ronda, supported by Pedro. With Castilian assistance, Muhammad V began a campaign to reclaim his kingdom. After a slow start he eventually managed to take the important city of Málaga in 1362. This proved to be the tipping point and the other cities of the kingdom declared for him. Muhammad VI, unwisely as it turns out, fled (taking his finest jewels) with his supporters to Castile seeking refuge. Pedro received them as guests in Seville and gave them a meal. Then, displaying his appellation of 'the Cruel', they were seized, stripped of their valuables and executed in a field. Their heads were sent to Muhammad V, now reinstalled in Granada.

Following this episode of inter-family intrigue, Muhammad V now enjoyed an uninterrupted reign of nearly 30 years. After an initial period of conflict, this was to prove the longest and most peaceful period in the history of the Kingdom of Granada. Muhammad continued his skilful diplomacy, with the objective of achieving peace. While maintaining good relations with the Marinids, he kept a wary eye on any possibility that they might re-establish themselves in the Iberian Peninsula. He also maintained connections throughout the Maghreb and beyond, from the Zayyanids in Tlemcen and the Hafsids in Tunis to the Mamelukes in Egypt.

As we have seen, Pedro I of Castile had assisted Muhammad V in regaining his throne. Pedro I was fascinated by the brilliance of Muslim architecture. This appreciation was demonstrated by Pedro's construction of the extraordinarily graceful Real Alcázar in Seville, which he began in 1364. This was built on an earlier Almohad build-

Below: statue of Pedro I of Castile (who ruled 1350-1369, who was given the name of 'the Cruel'. He established close relations with the Nasrid ruler, Muhammad V.

Right: the exquisite Real Alcázar in Seville, begun in 1364. Pedro I appreciated Muslim architecture. He employed craftsmen from Granada during the construction of this palace.

ing in the Islamic style, using master craftsmen from Granada. It was constructed during the same era as the Alhambra buildings – many of the styles and techniques are similar. However, Pedro had to concentrate on arms, not architecture. A war of succession flared up when Pedro was challenged by his half-brother, Enrique II of Trastámara, who now stepped up his attempts to seize the throne. One of the accusations made against Pedro was that he was too pro-Muslim. In the midst of this civil war, Muhammad V backed Pedro and sent a detachment of troops to fight on his behalf. However, with the aid of French mercenaries and the support of Aragón, Enrique managed to seize the Castilian throne in 1366. Muhammad V, mindful of the danger of attack and with the Nasrid facility for survival, switched sides and recognised Enrique.

Skilful diplomat that he was, Muhammad V negotiated a tripartite peace treaty involving Granada, Aragón and the Marinids in Fez. However, in 1367 Pedro returned to regain his throne, this time with the aid of the English royal adventurer, Edward, the Black Prince. Muhammad V once again reverted to allying with Pedro. He used the dissension in Castile to attack anti-Pedro enclaves like Priego, Jaén, Úbeda and Baeza. However, in March 1369 Pedro was defeated and murdered by his half-brother. As Enrique II was still preoccupied with consolidating his kingdom, Muhammad V took advantage of this situation and ranged along the border with Castile: he conquered Cambil and Rute in April. He gained a major advantage when he seized Algeciras in July – the lure of control of the Strait hadn't gone away. Muhammad, by now in a strong position, signed an eight-year truce with Enrique II in 1370. This brought peace to Granada, which continued when Enrique died in 1379, as his successor Juan I was preoccupied with conflict with Portugal and England. Muhammad also further improved his command over the Strait when he retrieved Gibraltar from the Marinids in 1374. On taking Algeciras earlier, he had demolished its strong defences in order to deny it to the other powers that coveted the Strait.

Right: the Patio de los Leones in the Alhambra, constructed by Muhammad V, whose reign marked an acceleration in the development of architecture, art and literature.

The fruit of the peace was prosperity. It allowed a flourishing of art and literature as well as the construction of great buildings. Muhammad V continued work on the Alhambra, enhancing its unequalled splendour. His chief vizier was the poet Ibn Zamrak. However, this poet was also a great intriguer who had his illustrious predecessor (who had also been his tutor), the poet Ibn al-Khatib, put to death on a charge of heresy. Nevertheless Ibn Zamrak was able to elegantly eulogise the palace-city thus:

'The Sabika hill sits like a garland on Granada's brow,
In which the stars would be entwined
And the Alhambra (Allah preserve it)
Is the ruby set above that garland.
Granada is a bride whose headdress is the Sabika
And whose jewels and adornments are its flowers.'

Muhammad V added to his father's work in the Comares Palace. One of his outstanding buildings is the Patio de los Leones, a complete palace which includes royal pavilions. It is arranged around an oblong court with colonnades, which surround a central fountain with 12 stylised stone lions. In the city of Granada, he built civic structures such as the *Maristan* or hospital for the poor.

The effect achieved in the decoration of the buildings of the Alhambra is enthralling. The use of delicate and beautifully carved, moulded

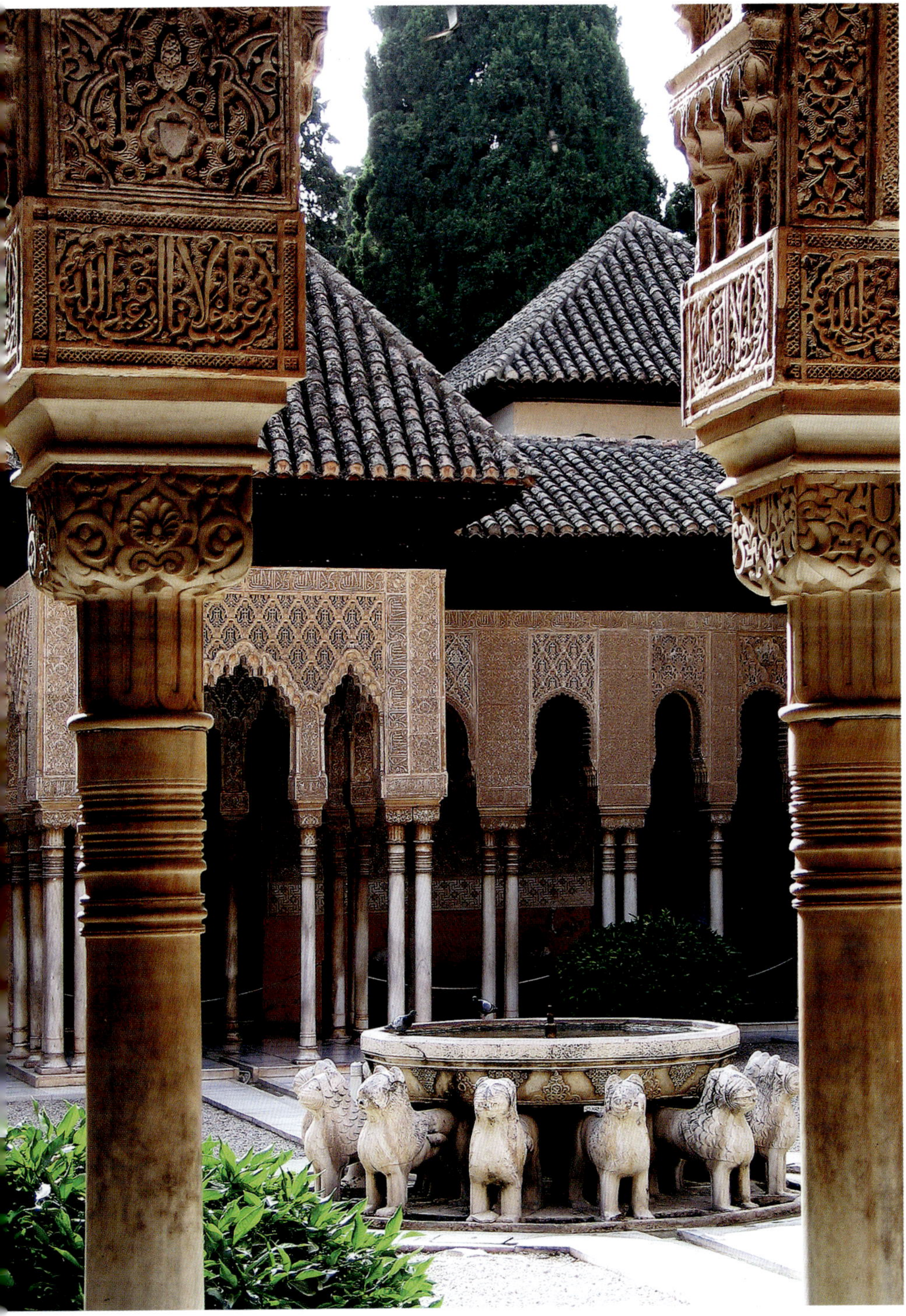

Left: one of a set of two, a large carved limestone lion from the Maristan. The Maristan was built as a hospital in the Albaicín district in the period 1365-1367 by Muhammad V. The lions, with water spouts in their mouths, were at either side of a courtyard pool. The Maristan was demolished during the nineteenth century. Afterwards the lions were moved to the Partal in the Alhambra. Now restored, they can be seen in the museum at the Alhambra. © Museo de la Alhambra.

and painted surfaces of wood and plaster achieves a stupendous result. This breath-taking accomplishment in human art was achieved at a relatively low cost. The materials used were not expensive. The necessary inputs were imagination, inspiration and many skilled hands, which were obviously available in abundance during the Nasrid era. The Kingdom of Granada, while it achieved wealth and prosperity, was relatively small. There was not an enormous expanse of fertile land (even though it was hugely productive), when one discounted the mountains. The Córdoba Caliphate was many times its area and population, thus Granada's economy was much smaller. The unprecedented wealth flowing from what encompassed most of the Iberian

Peninsula, during the tenth century, allowed Abd al-Rahman III to spend vast amounts of money on importing luxury materials (such as marble from Ifriqiya) from far and wide for the construction of his palace-city Madinat al-Zahra. Thus, the Alhambra had to be built with cheaper materials, but it still achieves the sublime.

Intrigue and Upheavals

And so the peace continued, to come to an abrupt end when the Amir Muhammad V died in January 1391 at the age of 52. He was immediately succeeded by his son, Yusuf II. His reign marked the beginning of a turbulent era which lasted for a century and ended with the demise of the Nasrid dynasty and the final remnant of Muslim rule in the Peninsula. Yusuf harshly stamped out the conspiracies which emerged. This included putting to death three of his brothers and consigning his vizier, the poet Ibn Zamrak, to imprisonment in Almería. He reigned for little more than a year and a half and died of mysterious causes in October 1392. The art of assassination had reached high levels in those times: there is an allegation that he died after donning a poisoned gold tunic received as a gift from the Marinid ruler.

Yusuf II's younger son Muhammad VII seized the throne, in contravention of the rule of primogeniture. This 16-year-old promptly had his elder brother locked up in the fortress of Salobreña. This location proved very useful as a royal prison during the next century of Nasrid dynastic intrigue. The poet Ibn Zamrak made a brief reappear-

Above: fourteenth-century Nasrid textile made of silk. Kufic inscriptions read 'beatitude' while other insriptions repeat the words 'happiness' and 'prosperity'. © Metropolitan Museum of Art, New York.

Right: the castle at Salobreña. This coastal location, south of Granada, served as a royal prison during the dynastic intrigues of the Nasrids.

Above: the neighbourhoods around the city grew rapidly during the Nasrid period. The most heavily populated area was the Albaicín. During the reign of Yusuf I (r. 1333-1354) a wall was built around the district. It was adapted to the contours of the terrain, reaching an altitude of 850 metres at the top of the hill near the Christian-era Ermita de San Miguel Alto.

Left: the walls, near the Sacromonte, as they descend down the hill, eventually reaching the river Darro

Above: Nasrid walls are still intact on the western side of the old city. The tapial or earth walls were made by compacting the local conglomerate soil behind wooden shuttering. The holes left by the tranverse timbers used to secure the shuttering can still be seen.

Right: the Puerta de Fajalauza, on the northern end of the Nasrid walls. The Aynadamar irrigation channel entered the city here via an underground passage.

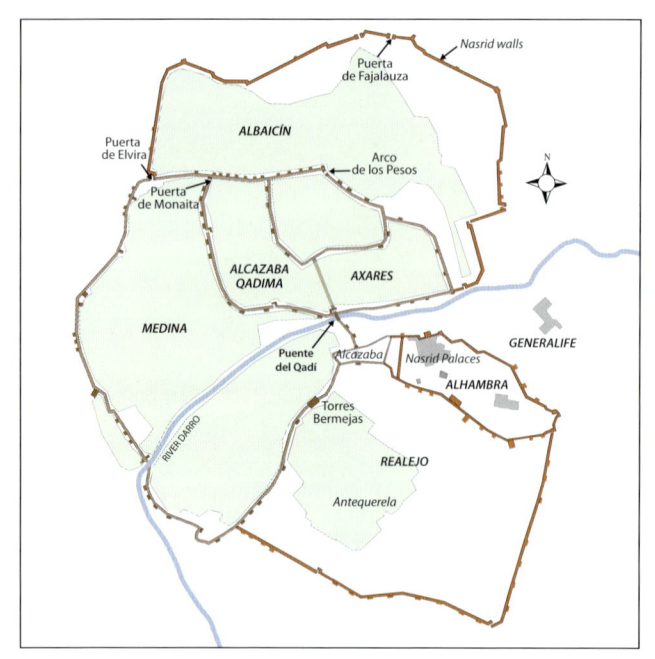

Left: map of Nasrid Granada. From the very beginning of the dynasty in 1238, Granada had grown, its population swollen by the refugees fleeing from the Christian conquest. As the districts grew and expanded outside of the old Zirid walls, an outer ring of new defensive walls was constructed.

ance, freed from his captivity. Brought back into the amir's retinue, he was assassinated a year later. It was in this era that the Abencerraje family (or Banu Sarraj) emerged as a highly influential group at the top levels of Nasrid power and exerted a dark influence in upheavals and intrigues up to the end of the Granadan kingdom. Muhammad VII, forgetting the skilful husbandry of peace by his grandfather Muhammad V, rashly provoked the Castilians. Taking advantage of internal squabbles in the court of Enrique III of Castile, he launched attacks across the frontier. A series of frontier raids by both sides followed and continued for well over a decade. One significant Granadan reverse was the loss of the stronghold of Zahara (to the north-west of Ronda), where the Castilians used their artillery to batter the defences. The Granadans came under pressure, not least because of the growing Castilian mastery of artillery, and requested a truce with the Castilians. This was agreed at the beginning of 1408.

Muhammad VII was not to savour the peace, as he died in May 1408. His brother was freed by supporters from his royal incarceration in Salobreña and seized power, becoming Yusuf III. The new ruler sought peace and a new truce was achieved with the Castilians, which lasted until April 1410. Shortly after the truce expired, the Granadans retook Zahara by stealth and sacked it. This tweaked the tail of the mightier Castile. The Castilians responded by besieging the strategically important centre of Antequera, taking it towards the end of 1410. The victory reflected the fact that the Castilians had grown

Below: art meets the Nasrid walls in the Alto Albaicín. In 2006, a missing section of wall near the Ermita de San Miguel Alto was reconstructed. An interesting architectural statement, it consists of two layers of stacked stone slabs.

Above: a much disputed frontier fortress – Zahara and its Castle. The Castilians used artillery to capture this stronghold at the beginning of the fifteenth century. In 1410 the Nasrids retook and sacked it. The Castilians seized Antequera in revenge. History repeated itself when in 1481 the Nasrids again took Zahara. The Castilians responded in force and struck at Alhama de Granada, deep in the heart of the Granadan kingdom.

Right: a view from the Alcazaba at Antequera. At the end of 1410, the Castilians responded to the attack on Zahara by capturing Antequera. The loss of this city and its fertile region was a blow to the Granadan economy and morale.

rapidly in strength over the years. In comparison to Granada, Castile comprised a much larger territory with vastly greater resources and a larger population. The siege revealed how the Castilians had pushed forward the frontiers of military technology. They had developed two super-crossbows, which they mounted on high platforms. They were able to fire down on the defenders with bolts which could penetrate armour. Undoubtedly one of the more important factors in the demise of Granada during the fifteenth century was the significant Castilian superiority in artillery. To properly deploy artillery, great numbers of skilled artillerymen and support personnel were needed, together with the logistics of smooth delivery of large quantities of gunpowder and projectiles. The Castilians had mastered these skills. Some large cannons required up to 200 men to service each one. They had also set up

Left: statue depicting refugees from Antequera. After the fall of the city in 1410, refugees fled to Granada and settled there, in a district that became known as Antequerela.

the necessary support organisation, such as the makers of charcoal and cannonballs.

Granada was also bereft of the assistance of their co-religionists in the Maghreb. It was in a weak situation in comparison to its Christian neighbours on the Iberian Peninsula and this was to tell in the coming decades. The loss of Antequera and its fertile region was a blow to the Granadan economy and morale. In the face of this loss, Yusuf III negotiated a peace and Granada enjoyed a period of general external peace up to 1428. Yusuf himself died in 1417.

The period from now until the final decades of Granada is a bewildering one of internal conflict. One should pause here and wonder why the Nasrids in this, the latter part of their dynasty, had such a penchant for deceit, disruption and instability; it was in total contrast to the sublimity of their creation – the Alhambra. Thus, within walls of this magnificent and awe-inspiring palace city, the stage was set for a revolving door of rulers, with usurpations, abdications, murders and incarcerations. There were eight rulers between 1417 and the beginning of 1464 (the advent of Muley Hacén), with 15 separate reigns. Usurpation was the order of the day: one ruler, Muhammad IX, possessing a certain persistence, enjoyed four separate reigns. All of these

Above: a detail from the fresco painting of the Battle of Higuerela, in the Monastery of the Escorial.
The battle was fought in 1431 between the armies of Castile and the Nasrids. In reality it was little more than a cavalry skirmish in the Vega. However the Christians came close to the heart of the Granadan kingdom: in the event they were driven from the walls of Granada by crossbow fire.

Right: a view of Gibraltar from the Moroccan coast. The struggle for control of the Strait continued. Muhammad V retrieved Gibraltar from the Marinids in 1374. The struggle finally ended when it was taken by the Christians in 1462.

Left: parade helmet in steel, gold, silver and enamel, dating from the late Nasrid era. © Metropolitan Museum of Art, New York.

rulers had Nasrid blood, a few tending to the periphery of the family tree. In the heart of this turmoil, we see the sway of one family, the Abencerrajes (or Banu Sarraj), who insinuated themselves into positions of influence in the corridors of the Alhambra. They had an acute eye, ready to spot and enlist pretenders to power, and promote these, to their own gain.

In mid-1431 the Castilians decided to mount a large onslaught on the ruler of Granada (Muhammad IX) who had refused to become their vassal, having secured the assent of a pretender to the Granadan throne. The resulting battle of Higuerela took place in the Granadan Vega, by the river Genil. Although celebrated as a huge battle in a magnificent mural in the Escorial, it was, in reality little more than a cavalry skirmish. The significant thing is how close the Christians came to the heart of the Granadan kingdom: in the event they were driven from the walls of Granada by crossbow fire. At the beginning of 1432 the pretender favoured by the Castilians (Yusuf IV) ascended the throne and made a treaty, suitably onerous and with a large tribute, with his sponsors. The treaty was deeply unpopular and Yusuf was deposed, put to death and replaced by Muhammad IX.

Castile took full advantage of the internal dissent. At various stages, the Castilians took sides, trying to impose their favoured candidate as Amir. They were in the ascent and gradually pushed back the border, seizing Muslim fortresses and towns. The incursions proved to be particularly wounding as the Castilians now took to burning down the groves of olive and mulberry trees, which took decades to regrow. The Kingdom of Granada was in a weakened economic state. Any benefits there might have been to Castile of a neighbouring vassal state were receding. There was little tribute to be extracted. The Amir in Granada did not have the authority to impose his will on local warlords who mounted opportunistic raids on the Castilian frontier. Some of the frontier enclaves to the east, like Galera and the two towns called Velez (Blanco and Rubio) sensing that they were not going to be saved by any Granadan central power, decided to treat with the Castilians and secure a more favourable outcome. As the historian L. P. Hartley has written: *'By the mid-fifteenth century, Granada was living on borrowed time'*. Its time was to run out by the end of that century.

Muley Hacén
Within Granada, the Abencerraje family continued to play a sinister role in affairs of state, achieving high positions, manipulating the throne and intriguing to place their favoured candidate, Sa'd (of Nasrid lineage) as Amir, in opposition to the appointed heir of the previous ruler. Both claimants occupied parts of the kingdom, with the heir, Muhammad XI (dubbed *el Chiquito*, or the 'small one'), reigning over Granada and Málaga. After a period of turmoil Muhammad XI was lured back to Granada (from where he had fled in 1455) from his refuge in the Alpujarras. He was waylaid by Sa'd's son Ali bin Sa'd, later to be known by the Castilians as Muley Hacén. The captive was brought to the Alhambra and had his throat cut in a hall leading to the patio of the Court of the Lions. To seal the deed, Muhammad XI's two small sons were suffocated. Sa'd had initially been supported by the Abencerraje family. Although the specific reason for his displeasure is not known, Sa'd now turned on them and their excessive control and influence. The story runs that in July 1462 he invited leading family members to a banquet in the Alhambra, where two principal members (including the grand vizier) had their throats cut. (As we have seen, Sa'd and his son had form in throat-cutting and murder in the Alhambra.) However, several Abencerrajes managed to escape and fled to Málaga, a family stronghold, where they promptly proclaimed a new pretender to the throne. Two other shocks to the kingdom occurred soon afterwards, with the loss of the important strongholds of Gibraltar and Archidona, to the Castilians. In 1464 Sa'd was overthrown in turn by his son Ali bin Sa'd, the previously mentioned Muley Hacén, now supported by the Abencerraje clan, who now operated with vigour from Málaga. Accounts say that Sa'd was exiled to Salobreña, the castle there having functioned as a royal prison for the Nasrids over the previous century.

Muley Hacén proceeded to strengthen his army and the economy. He consolidated his rule and, amongst other initiatives, began a campaign to suppress the Abencerrajes, who, master survivalists, fled to take shelter with the Christian lords along the borders. Despite some upsets, Muley Hacén, who had knowledge of Christian ways, having spent time in the Castilian court in his youth, broadly achieved an external peace up to 1481. Mention must be made of a feud in the harem which has grown into the stuff of legend. Muley Hacén had married the widow of Muhammad XI, Ayesha, herself of Nasrid lineage. He then fell for the charms of an alluring Christian captive, Isobel de Solís, who had converted to Islam, taking the name of Zoraya. A feud ensued between these wives, which was to have implications in the later overthrow of his father by Boabdil, son of Ayesha.

The Catholic Monarchs

An important event for the future of Granada occurred in 1474 when Isabel of Castile proclaimed herself Queen on the death of her brother Enrique IV. In 1469, aged 23, she had married Prince Fernando (a year younger than her), the heir to the throne of Aragón, under a veil of secrecy. The marriage took place despite the opposition of Louis XI of France, as well as of the powerful lords of Castile, who, for different reasons, foresaw a threat from the increased power due to the union of two of the kingdoms of Iberia. Castile was the greater power on the Peninsula and had a population of around six million. The Crown of Aragón was smaller, with around a million people (the same as Portugal, the other significant Christian kingdom in Iberia). Despite being the largest kingdom, Castile's central power was weak, with a multitude of powerful lords, enjoying huge estates. Originally it was a pastoral, inward-looking economy that had been shaped by the continual conflict of the Reconquista. However, a dynamic element was the boom in the wool industry. From the introduction of Merino sheep over a century previously, sheep farming flourished on the Meseta Central. An insatiable demand for Spanish wool had grown in Northern Europe, and this opened up Castile to international trade and the outside world. In the Kingdom of Aragón, by contrast with Castile, the distribution of power was better defined, with an established system of rights and obligations. It was outward-looking, reflecting its mercantile tradition. Its focus on the Mediterranean, led by Catalonia, resulted in the acquisition of overseas domains such as Sardinia and Sicily. However, in the years before the accession of Fernando, a debilitating civil war had sapped the dynamism of Aragón.

Isabel's marriage had precipitated conflict over her rights to the Castilian throne. A claimant, Juana (with the nickname of la Beltraneja), asserted that she was the daughter of Isabel's brother, King Enrique IV and her claim was actively supported by Portugal. A civil war

Above: the patio of the Nasrid Palacio de Dar al-Horra, located in the Albaicín district. It is reputed to have been the residence of Ayesha, mother of Boabdil, the last Amir.

Below: even against the background of disintegration of the Nasrid state, science continued at a high level. Bronze astrolabe dating from 1481, found in the Albaicín. © Museo Arqueológico de Granada. Photograph: Javier Algarra.

Right: statues of the Catholic Monarchs, on high at either side of the altar in the Cathedral in Granada.

Above right: King Fernando II of Aragón (1452-1516). His marriage to Isabel of Castile led to the dynastic union of the kingdoms which, together, covered most of the Iberian Peninsula. It represented the birth of Spain, as we know it today.

Below right: Isabel I of Castile (1451-1504). Highly religious, she had great character and a steely determination. Together the Catholic Monarchs, planned, financed and implemented the downfall of the Kingdom of Granada.

ensued and it was to take until 1479 for Isabel to prevail and gain full control of Castile. One factor in her success was that Fernando imported Aragonese military experts who instructed the Castilian troops, loyal to Isabel, in improved military techniques. Juan II of Aragón died in that same year and the two powerful states became finally entwined when Fernando succeeded his father. From many perspectives, this union of Castile and Aragón, whose territories encompassed most of the Iberian Peninsula, represented the birth of Spain, as we know it today – up to then there had been only the limited concept of Hispania, as a geographical entity. The result of the union added up to more than the sum of the parts. To Castile's power, growing wealth and energy, Fernando brought Aragón's better organisation and Mediterranean territories. The internal dynastic problems had been resolved and the two monarchs were now able to pay full attention to a prime pressing objective: the elimination of the last vestige of Islamic rule from the Peninsula, in final achievement of the Reconquista.

The Catholic Monarchs (the appellation of *Reyes Catolicos* or Catholic Monarchs was latterly conferred on the couple in 1494 by Pope Alexander in recognition of their capture of Granada) were an extraordinary couple. Isabel has been described as a woman of great character and determination. Fernando in turn was astute and brought energy and resourcefulness. Both had overcome many challenges and dangers to achieve their present elevated status. Imbued with religious fervour, they were now determined to wage a holy war to eliminate what they

Above: a crossbow from Nasrid times. The art of war had moved from the arrow to the cannonball. The Nasrids also had artillery but this was not at the level of sophistication or organisation of the Castilian forces. © Museo Arqueológico de Granada. Photograph: Vicente del Amo.

Below: stone cannonballs at the Alcazaba in Alcalá la Real.

Right: a fifteenth-century cannon at Edinburgh Castle. This type of large-calibre cannon was heavy and difficult to transport over the poor medieval roads. Yet the Castilians, with superior organisation managed to move these cannon around the Kingdom of Granada where they efficiently demolished the Nasrid fortifications.

Right: illustration of heavy cannons of the Holy Roman Emperor dating from the second half of the fifteenth century. The Catholic Monarchs acquired the most modern artillery of the era, which proved to be a game-changer in their offensive against the Kingdom of Granada.

Below: a model of a bombard, or mortar, on display near Lanjarón in the Alpujarras. Bombards, with a steep vertical trajectory, could rain heavy fire down on defenders within fortified city walls.

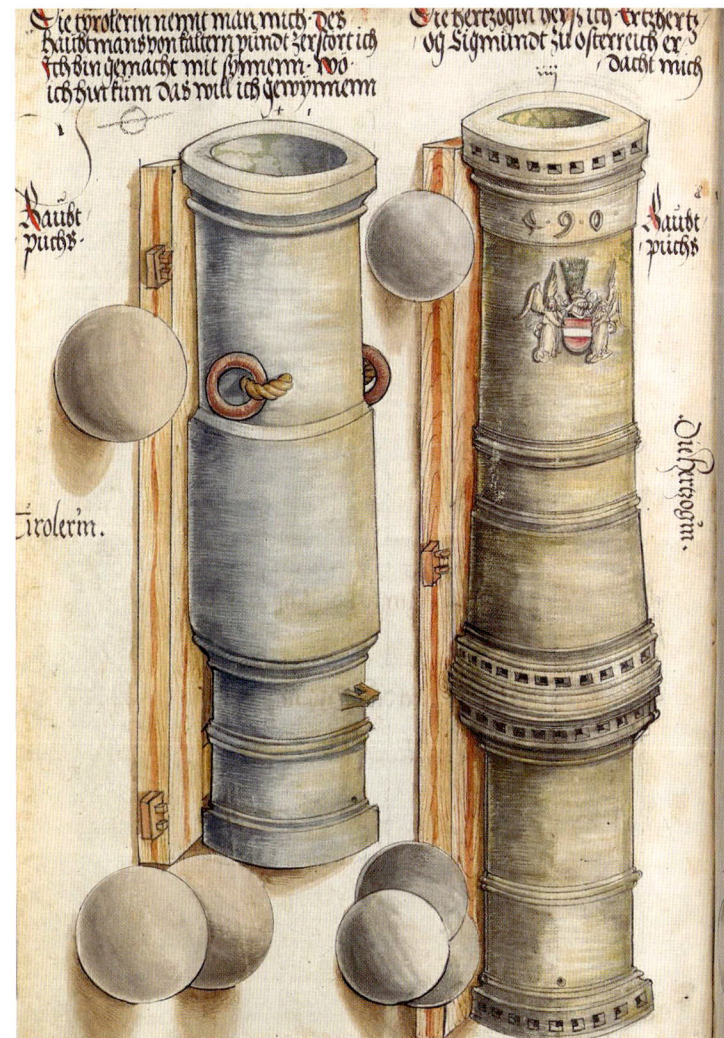

85

regarded as the infidel religion of Islam from the Iberian Peninsula. As in all wars of conquest from time immemorial, there were other benefits: booty and land to be won. The Catholic Monarchs proved to be highly effective in achieving their aims. Once their internal dynastic turmoil had been overcome, they were free to meticulously plan a campaign against Granada, and allocate the large sums that were necessary. The royal couple had the will, the steely determination and now the means, to overcome the Kingdom of Granada. This now faced a resolute foe with vastly greater resources and population, infinitely more powerful than before. Granada now entered the last chapter of its history.

Continuous attrition, due to Christian attacks over the decades, meant that Granada's borders had shrunk. By the end of 1481, it comprised less than three-quarters of the area of the early years of the Nasrid dynasty. The frontier now ran from just west of Estepona, looping inland to the north of Ronda, then south of Antequera, north of Granada, onwards to the east around Huéscar and to the coast north-east of Mojácar. The Kingdom of Granada still contained within its territory its mountainous spine and its main ports of Málaga and Almería. However, it had lost the ports near the Strait, thus denying it more direct access to the co-religionists in the Maghreb. Another factor was that the kingdoms in the Maghreb were in a state of decline, so Granada now had to stand alone. In addition, some of Granada's most fertile plains had been lost to the Castilians. Coupled with the

Above: the Kingdom of Granada in 1482. It had lost around a quarter of its original territory of 1270. Over the last decade up to the fall in 1492, the rate of loss of Granadan territory accelerated greatly.

Below: the Crown of Isabel I of Castile in the Capilla Real, where she is buried. © Capilla Real, Granada

Above: Alhama de Granada. After the capture of Zahara by the Granadans, the Castilians responded in force. In February 1481, using stealth, they sent a large force to reach the important town of Alhama, a mere 50 kilometres from Granada. After a bloody struggle, the Castilian army captured the town. It became a forward base for the imminent dismemberment of the Kingdom of Granada.

Christian razed-earth policy of cutting down crops and fruit trees when raiding, this put severe strain on the Granadan economy.

Initially Isabel, beset by the struggle for the Castilian throne, had taken the pragmatic step of signing treaties with the Kingdom of Granada. Once she had achieved internal peace the way was clear for the assault on Granada. A key date was December 1481, when the Granadans, with a large force, seized the castle of Zahara (even though a treaty was in place). This was against the background that, over the decades, both sides had made border raids. However, the taking of Zahara proved to be a step too far. The Castilians responded in force and this time, not just with a classic border raid on a town. They struck deep into the heart of the kingdom. In February 1482 they sent along mountain tracks a large force which, undetected, managed to reach Alhama de Granada. The expedition surprised the inhabitants and the town was captured after a hard struggle, with much loss of life. Muley Hacén responded quickly. He brought an army from Granada and put the captured town under siege. After hard fighting, the siege was lifted when a large Castilian relieving force arrived, forcing Muley Hacén to retreat. Alhama was a severe loss. At only 50 kilometres' distance, it was uncomfortably close to Granada and could interdict the main route from Málaga to Granada. It was to become a forward base which would support the future dismemberment of the Kingdom of Granada. In July 1482, the Christians besieged Loja, an important town at the western end of the Granadan Vega. The inhabitants mounted a stiff resistance. When a relief force appeared the Christians withdrew in disarray, leaving behind artillery, supplies and siege equipment. The Granadan army had proven that it still was a formidable force and difficult to overcome. However, the Kingdom of Granada was about to be fatally weakened by internal feuding.

Above: the mountainous Axarquía region, to the east of Málaga. In 1483 the Castilian army made a disastrous incursion through here.

Boabdil's erratic rise to power

At the same time as the Loja engagement, a significant event was taking place in Granada itself, 50 kilometres away to the east. Muley Hacén was overthrown by his son Abu Abd Allah bin Ali, Muhammad XII, (popularly known as Boabdil) who was supported by those perpetual intriguers, the Abencerraje. Opposition to the high taxes raised to fund the war was one reason for the coup. An Arab chronicler claimed that the discord was due to the conflict between Ayesha, Boabdil's mother and his father's slave Zoraya. According to this account, Ayesha was fearful of Muley Hacén's wrath and moved to protect her son. After fleeing to Guadix, Boabdil returned to establish himself in the Alhambra and Muley Hacén (accompanied by his brother, Muhammad bin Sa'd, known as 'al-Zagal', the brave) left and set up in Málaga and Ronda, which remained loyal to him.

The assault by the Christians continued. In 1483 they made a major incursion into the Axarquía, a region to the east of Málaga bounded by inland mountains and the Mediterranean coast. The aim was to split the Kingdom of Granada into two – but it turned out to be a disaster. In this area under Muley Hacén's control, the Muslims fought back and soundly defeated the Castilian forces, who floundered through the steep, mountainous terrain. Thousands of Christian prisoners were taken.

Wishing to boost his prestige, Boabdil resolved to emulate this success. In April 1483 he mounted a raid northwest towards Lucena, north of Antequera, deep into the heart of Christian territory. The Christian army reacted strongly and the Granadan forces were badly defeated – thousands were killed or captured. Boabdil was taken prisoner. Back in Granada Boabdil's star had fallen; a delegation went to Málaga and requested Muley Hacén to return to the capital, which he did. Meanwhile, after some consideration, Fernando had decided that backing Boabdil provided his best chance to take Granada in the longer term. By releasing him the civil war would continue; Granada would be in a weaker state. Following negotiations, a truce was signed. Boabdil was freed, with the payment by his supporters of a large sum of money, the return of Christian prisoners and the handover of hostages (including Boabdil's sons) to the Castilians. Boabdil set up in Guadix in October 1483.

Below: bronze coin from Granada, minted during the reign of Boabdil. © Museo Arqueológico Nacional. Photograph: Lorenzo Planas Torres (N.I. 2004/123/639).

Right: statue of Abu Abd Allah bin Ali, or Muhammad XII, (popularly known as Boabdil) at Granada. He was the last of the Nasrid Amirs. In 1482 he rose aginst his father Muley Hacén. The civil war that followed made it easier for the Christians to finally overcome the Kingdom of Granada and seize the city. Boabdil at times allied with the Catholic Monarchs and then resisted them. As the last ruler, he negotiated capitulations and surrendered Granada to Fernando and Isabel at the beginning of January 1492.

Right: Torre del Moral in Lucena. Boabdil was imprisoned here following his unsuccessful raid through the region in 1483.

89

Above: jineta sword and scabbard. Boabdil had been captured at Lucena by the Castilians led by Diego de Fernández de Córdoba. This sword, surrendered by Boabdil, remained in the Fernández family over the centuries. In 1906 it was bequeathed to the army museum. The hilt of the sword has a spherical pommel with a carved ivory grip and highly decorated curved quillons (crossguard). The scabbard is made up of sections of wood covered by leather, decorated with silver-gilt embroidery. © Museo del Ejército, Toledo.

The Castilians' attacks continued during 1484 and, with the skilful use of artillery, they began to steadily capture Granadan towns. The campaign was directed by Isabel, as Fernando had urgent business to attend to elsewhere. The Castilian army was immense: thousands of infantry and light horsemen; enormous quantities of pack animals to carry supplies, and the sophisticated and well-provisioned artillery division. The artillery train had to be preceded by men who repaired and widened roads and mountain passes. In the midst of this conflict, Muley Hacén was increasingly incapacitated by a serious illness, similar to epilepsy, and his brother, al-Zagal, came to the fore. Al-Zagal led an expedition to Almería, a stronghold of Boabdil, and captured it at the beginning of 1485. In the meantime, the Castilian advance continued. To the west of Málaga, Coín and Cártama fell in early 1485. In May the strategic town of Ronda was attacked. The Castilian artillery demonstrated its power and accuracy – as well as an abundance of cannonballs and gunpowder. The large walls were systematically destroyed by a continuous stream of cannonballs and the people within were terrified. With the water supply cut off, the town surrendered within a few weeks. The population was ignominiously expelled. Back in the Nasrid capital, al-Zagal consolidated his grip on power and Muley Hacén, a sick old man, was forced to leave the city and died a few months later. Al-Zagal repelled a Castilian attack on Moclín. However, the Christians managed to capture Cambil and other enclaves to the north of Granada.

Boabdil, in the meantime, capitalising on the hunger for peace among the population and on the premise that he could secure peace with the Castilians, gathered support in the east of the kingdom. Within Granada itself, his supporters spread this message in the Albaicín and an uprising broke out there in March 1486. The rebels were attacked by al-Zagal's forces, which didn't shirk from using artillery, pouring fire on the Albaicín from the Alcazaba of the Alhambra. After several months of struggle, reconciliation between uncle and nephew came about in May 1486, with Boabdil recognising al-Zagal. Boabdil

Above: Loja, with its alcazaba, seen on a height to the left of the Cathedral bell-tower. Fought over several times, the city was finally taken by the Christians in May 1486. The Granadan Vega was now vulnerable to attack.

was assigned Loja. The city came under siege by the Castilians and Boabdil headed there. Despite a strong resistance, the Christian artillery prevailed and Loja was captured at the end of May. Montefrío, Moclín and Illora were then taken. The Vega of Granada was now vulnerable. Boabdil once again submitted and made another arrangement with Fernando, who recognised him as ruler in the eastern Granadan territories, with vassalage and support for him in his endeavour to capture more territory. An additional inducement was the offer of a three-year truce with the Christians for those towns and districts that rose up to support Boabdil. With this secured, Boabdil made a pass through the east, gathering followers. Once more he headed for Granada, secretly moving into the Albaicín in October 1486. There he rallied his supporters. In January 1487 al-Zagal assembled his forces, entered the Albaicín and made a great effort to stamp out the rebellion. In the meantime, news came that the Castilians were marching on Vélez-Málaga to the east of Málaga. It was most likely that they were complicit with Boabdil, to relieve pressure on his uprising. Al-Zagal took the difficult choice to split his forces and, at the end of April, led a contingent across the mountains through the Axarquía towards Vélez-Málaga. He made a vain attempt to destroy the Castilian artillery train, slow and

Right: in the choir stalls of Toledo Cathedral, made of mahogany, there is a series of elaborate carvings denoting the conquest of the principal towns and cities of the Kingdom of Granada. This shows the taking of Montefrío (north-east of Loja) in 1486, which occurred just after the capture of Loja.

Left: another of the carvings on the choir stalls at Toledo. It depicts the siege of a large fortification, with an adjacent walled hill surmounted by a castle. It possibly shows the siege of Málaga. There are tents shown to the left, which may be where the following took place: in a fracas during the siege a Muslim holy man, planning the assassination of the royal couple, was taken captive. He requested to see the Christian Monarchs, saying he had important information. He was brought to a tent adjacent to the royal one. Observing the fine clothing of the people within, he mistakenly thought he was in the royal presence and struck out with a dagger, severely wounding a courtier. The assailant was promptly cut to pieces.

spread out. However, the town capitulated at the beginning of May 1487 and al-Zagal led his failed expedition back towards Granada. On the way, he received the news that, in his absence, Boabdil had prevailed and was now in control of the city. Al-Zagal had no choice but to divert to Guadix.

The final reduction of the Kingdom of Granada

Having gained control to the east and west of Málaga, the Castilians began the siege of the city in May 1487. This was the second city of the Nasrid kingdom and it was a key step in the campaign of the Catholic Monarchs. A major advantage of capturing this port city would be to further deny the possibility of passage of reinforcements and supplies from North Africa to Granada. Initially, the Castilians tried to negotiate a surrender. The Malagans refused, no doubt comforted that they had a resilient detachment of Berber soldiers (from the Gomara region in the Rif Mountains) on hand. The Castilians opted for direct assault rather than a long-drawn out siege. However, the inhabitants, ably led and well organised, put up heroic resistance. The city was well fortified with natural defences. It was dominated by the Gibralfaro fortress on top of a steep hill, linked by a curtain wall to the Alcazaba, further down. As it happened, the defenders received no assistance from Boabdil, in compliance with his compact with the Castilians – he even went to the extent of intercepting reinforcements sent from Granada by al-Zagal. However, it turned out to be one of the bloodiest encounters of the Castilian campaign. In Málaga, the initial Christian assault was held up, meeting a hail of arrows and artillery fire. Changing tactics, the Christians now carried out an extensive

Right: Málaga was well fortified. This is the defensive curtain wall snaking down from the Gibralfaro castle to the Alcazaba.

exercise, building a ring of trenches and temporary towers around the city walls and fortifications. The Castilians brought more cannon on shore from the royal fleet moored in the harbour. The battle changed to a static form, with both sides exchanging artillery salvoes. The combat was so intense that the royal tent had to be moved back out of the line of fire. Castilian spirits fell to a low ebb at this stage, and the supply train failed on occasion resulting in food shortages. There was an outbreak of plague nearby, which alarmed the soldiers. At this stage Isabel urged Fernando to abandon the siege. However, he arranged for Isabel to join him at the siege with the intention of raising morale. Eventually, the defenders were reduced by starvation and the city fell after three and a half months of attack. Such was the stench that the city had to be cleaned of dead bodies before the Catholic Monarchs could set foot within. The inhabitants now had to endure the ordeal of being reduced to slavery, as punishment for their strong defence of the city. As a gift, the Pope received 100 Berber soldiers as slaves. Batches of Muslim girls were sent as presents to the Queens of Naples and Portugal.

During 1488 the Castilians received the submission of strongholds to the east, from Galera to Mojácar, perhaps encouraged by the harsh consequences of resistance to the Castilian steamroller, just as happened at Málaga. These were places promised to Boabdil and it broke the understanding the Christians had made with him. The seizure of these towns is likely to be one of the causes of Boabdil's subsequent strong resistance to the takeover of Granada. When 1489 dawned, all that remained in Muslim hands were a few cities and their immediate hinterland. There was Boabdil in Granada and al-Zagal who held Almería, Baza and Guadix. The Castilians now turned their sights on that beacon of resistance, al-Zagal – it would be necessary to eliminate this tenacious foe before the final assault on the Granadan capital. The Castilians advanced towards Baza and put this formidable stronghold

Left: the surrender at Málaga. The siege on this, the second city of the Kingdom of Granada, began in May 1487. After three months of heavy bloodshed the defenders were afflicted by starvation and the city fell. The inhabitants now had to endure the ordeal of being reduced to slavery, as punishment for their strong defence of the city.

under siege in June 1489. The Castilians assembled what were by now the usual ingredients: a large body of troops and heavy artillery, with the necessary logistical support. Al-Zagal sent reinforcements to the defenders from Guadix. As the siege dragged on, once again like at Málaga, Queen Isabel travelled to the front to boost Christian morale. The defenders ran out of supplies, negotiations were entered into and the enclave fell at the beginning of December 1489, with the Muslim commander receiving a substantial bribe (in those fluid times, he, Sidi Yahya al-Najjar, eventually transformed himself into a Castilian noblemen, as Don Pedro de Granada Venegas).

Events moved swiftly: al-Zagal had had enough and was convinced that resistance was now futile. By the end of December 1489, he reached an agreement with the Castilians – agreeing, in effect to their (in modern parlance) hostile takeover. He surrendered his territories of Guadix and Almería. In return, he received a lordship in territory which encompassed parts of the Alpujarras and the valley of Lecrín, as well as a large sum of money.

All that now remained for Castilian attention was the city of Granada and its surrounding district. Christian envoys were sent to meet Boabdil's representatives at the beginning of 1490, with the intention of negotiating the takeover of the city. However, it was clear to Boabdil that his previous agreements with the Castilians had been torn up and this mercurial monarch reverted to fighting back on behalf of his Muslim people. He launched an expedition, which fought its way through the Alpujarras and headed south to Salobreña on the coast. Most likely, this had the objective of establishing a supply line to the coast and possibly to reinforcements from North Africa. This expedition had a consequence for his estranged uncle. With Boabdil on the horizon, al-Zagal had become disheartened. He decided not to occupy

Right: the monumental gate, Puerta de Granada, at Santa Fe. In 1491, in preparation for the siege of Granada, the Catholic Monarchs set up a great fortified encampment at this location around ten kilometres to the west of the city. A hamlet was demolished, a great enclosure erected and buildings were cosntructed for the royal couple and their army.

his assigned territory in the Alpujarras. He arranged for his lands to be sold and then transferred with his family to Oran in the Maghreb, which he did in mid-1490.

The Fall

Receiving the news that the Castilians were marching on Granada, Boabdil headed back to the city in August 1490. There was skirmishing in the countryside. The Castilians captured many towns and hamlets surrounding the city. In addition they ravaged the crops throughout the Granadan Vega. This proved an effective tactic and disrupted supplies to the city. At the beginning of 1491 the last piece of the Castilian plan was put in place: the siege of Granada. In April the massed armies set out for the city, attacking districts on the way. The Catholic Monarchs set up their great fortified encampment in a location around ten kilometres to the west of Granada. A hamlet was demolished, a great enclosure erected and buildings were constructed for the royal couple and their army. It was given the appropriately inspirational name of Santa Fe. Skirmishes and attacks continued into the winter, with all the remaining fortifications in the outlying countryside eventually being overrun. One of the last villages to be attacked was Alfacar where there was a fierce encounter – one reason for the attacks being possibly that it was the location of the Fuente Grande, an important source of water supply for the Albaicín. As the cold weather set in, the strategic route that brought supplies to the city on mountain tracks from the Alpujarras was cut off by snow. Food became scarcer and hunger intensified. The inhabitants made representations to Boabdil that he should begin negotiations with the Christians. Unbeknownst to the Granadans negotiations began in secret between the representatives of Boabdil and the Catholic Monarchs. By the end

Left: 'The Surrender of Granada' by Francisco Pradilla. On 2 January 1492 Boabdil met the Catholic Monarchs at the gates of the city and rendered homage to them. This event marked the end of 780 years of Muslim rule in the Iberian Peninsula. © Patrimonio Historico-Artistico del Senado, Madrid. Photograph: Oronoz.

of November terms for the surrender of Granada were worked out in detail.

These terms, or capitulations, incorporated many detailed conditions including: the entitlement for the Muslims to remain in the city under Christian rule, with freedom to practise their religion, customs and laws and to keep their property and belongings. They were also entitled, for a period of three years, to emigrate with their possessions, with free passage to the Maghreb ports. There have been suggestions that Boabdil was acting as a puppet of the Castilians and according to a predetermined script. This may have been the case. However, in the context of the times, the capitulations that he signed were fair. As we shall see, the fatal flaw was that there was no safeguard if these were broken, as they were by the Castilians later on. Boabdil, of course, did not neglect his own interests. He was to be allowed to set up in the Alpujarras and establish a statelet there under Castilian vassalage.

The deal being agreed, the end was orchestrated rapidly and clandestinely, so as not to inflame the passions of the citizenry. The Alhambra was vacated on the night of 1 January 1492 and, in secrecy, a detachment of Christian troops, led by Gutierre de Cárdenas, arrived at the city-palace. The next morning, in the Salón del Trono (also known as the Hall of the Ambassadors) in the Comares Tower, Boabdil handed over the keys of the Alhambra to de Cárdenas. The Christian troops secured the palace. The Castilian flag was hoisted on the Torre de la Vela of the Alcazaba, and now flew high over the conquered city. Later in the afternoon, Boabdil met the Catholic Monarchs at the gates of the city and rendered homage to them – receiving back his son who had been a hostage. Curiously, one account tells that the Catholic Monarchs had dressed in Muslim attire for this occasion. If true, it would have added a certain theatrical touch to the pathos of the fall of Nasrid Granada, the last vestige of al-Andalus and it marked the end of 780 years of Muslim rule in the Iberian Peninsula.

Chapter 3
Conquest and Decline

By the beginning of 1492 the Iberian Peninsula was under full Christian control, with the Peninsula's kingdoms in a state of ascendance. To the west, Portugal, (the smaller kingdom comprising a mere 15% of the Peninsula), with its Atlanticist outlook, was in a phase of great exploration and conquest across the oceans. In the greater part of the Peninsula, the new and powerful land of Spain had arisen from the matrimonial union of Aragón and Castile. With lands across the Mediterranean and with a powerful army battle-hardened in the Granadan conquest, the combined kingdoms of Aragón and Castile now had the critical mass to be a major player on the European stage. The momentum and energy created in the final Reconquista was to continue and be channelled into new expansion. In the same year as the capture of Granada, Christopher Columbus, who had received his orders from the Catholic Monarchs in the city, set off and discovered the New World. It is significant that 1492 was also when the first Castilian grammar book was published. Not as epoch-making as the discovery of America perhaps, but it was a key step in establishing Castilian as the underpinning language of the new Spanish Empire.

With strength came intolerance. The Catholic Monarchs were believers in a unified Christian State and had little tolerance for religious dissent. This had been manifested by the earlier establishment of the Inquisition in 1478, with the intention of maintaining the religious purity of Spain. The triumphant Catholic Monarchs or *Reyes Catolicos*, having conquered the infidel Muslims of Granada, issued an edict regarding the Jews of Spain in March 1492: the choice offered to these was either conversion or exile. Around 150,000 chose exile and, in one stroke, Spain lost a dynamic and talented group of its subjects, many of them administrators and merchants who would have been invaluable in supporting the future growth of the Empire and its economy. A few months earlier, the Muslim Granadans had surrendered on the basis that they had the right to practise Islam. The expulsion of the

Left: statue in Plaza de Isabel la Católica in Granada – Christopher Columbus presents the proposal for his voyage to the Indies to Queen Isabel.

Jews was not a good omen for the application of this agreement and so it turned out to be: there was to be no religious freedom.

Immediately on the surrender of Granada, the hapless Boabdil headed for the Alpujarras, bringing with him his riches, and set up there in his allocated fiefdom at Láujar de Andarax, in accordance with the terms of the surrender. Luis de Mármol Carvajal, in his book written in the sixteenth century (dealing with the subsequent rebellion in Granada), recounts the legend of how, on passing through the foothills on his way to the mountains (at a point now known as Suspiro del Moro), Boabdil is supposed to have looked back at Granada and wept, whereby his mother, Ayesha, brusquely said: *'You weep like a woman over what you could not defend like a man'*. Boabdil spent some time in the Alpujarras. However, at the end of 1493, tiring of his vassalage, he travelled to the Maghreb and settled in Fez. He was never to return to the Iberian Peninsula and died in North Africa around 1533.

The Muslims of Granada, just like their co-religionists centuries earlier in Castile, Aragón and other parts of Spain, had become *Mudéjars*, or Muslims who lived under Christian rule in the Iberian Peninsula. For a few years, life in Granada continued more or less as before. The new Christian administrators, nobles, soldiers and prelates had flooded into the city. They operated at one level, beneath which the Granadan Muslims were able to continue their daily life. The latter now enjoyed a respite from the recent strife of the Reconquista. Some

Right: 'The Moor's last Sigh', a painting by Marcelino de Unceta y López. Legend has it that Boabdil looked back at Granada on the way to his exile in the Alpujarras and wept. This is a nineteenth-century painting which reflects that century's perception of the Andalusis as dark, exotic and alien. © Museo de Zaragoza.

Below: Francisco Jiménez de Cisneros, Archbishop of Toledo, a former confessor of Isabel. This austere and energetic prelate applied pressure on Muslims in Granada to convert to what he saw as the true faith.

of the Muslim leaders and alfaquis participated in the administration of the city. Just before its fall the population of the city had been swollen by refugees, fleeing from the Christian onslaught across the Kingdom of Granada – one estimate is that there had been a population of around 50,000. The Muslim population declined after the defeat of 1492. Many, particularly the upper classes, had taken the opportunity to emigrate to North Africa. As Christian immigrants arrived in the city the demographics began to slowly change. The Christians settled in the area around the Alhambra – roughly 1,000 initially. In the first few years Granada was still predominantly Muslim, with the Albaicín totally so.

However, storm clouds were gathering on the Granadan horizon. Little by little, intrusive new laws, such as that denying Muslims in the Vega the right to buy land, came into force to facilitate the settlement of Christians. The pressure was to increase sharply when, in 1499, the influential Francisco Jiménez de Cisneros, Archbishop of Toledo and former confessor of Isabel, was invited to visit the city by the Catholic Monarchs to assist with conversions. This visit was to have grave consequences for the Granadan Mudéjars. Up to now the Archbishop of Granada, Fernando de Talavera, had adopted a benign attitude towards the Muslims, attempting to convert them by preaching, even converting Christian religious material into Arabic – but with little success. Archbishop Cisneros took a different attitude to de Talavera's gradualism with the Mudéjars. Austere and energetic, he targeted those Muslims who had converted from Christianity in the recent past and who thus had consciously rejected what he saw as the true faith – these were now termed renegades. Despite a specific protection for these converts in the capitulations of Granada, Cisneros began to force them to re-convert to Christianity. He also ordered that Islamic books be gathered and destroyed. One account tells of 5,000 books of all types (including Korans) being burnt in the central Plaza de Bibrambla in 1499. However, Cisneros separated some medical works from the cull – 40 volumes were sent off to the library of the University of Alcalá de Henares, near Madrid (which he had just founded). He continued the pressure, attempting to force Christianity on prominent members of the Mudéjar community.

Uprising and forced conversions

In December 1499 the people of the Albaicín rose up in protest, outraged at the breaking of the capitulations. They seized the gates of the district and fortified them. The uproar was dampened down by the skilful negotiation of Archbishop de Talavera and the Captain-General of Granada. The rebels dispersed. However, Cisneros advised the Monarchs that the conversions should not stop; since the Muslims had rebelled, they merited death but their pardon should be conditional:

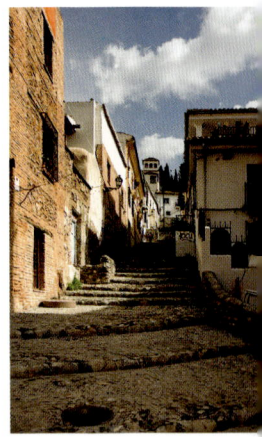

Above: the Albaicín in Granada. In the first years after the conquest this district was overwhelmingly Muslim. In December 1499 the people of the Albaicín rose up in protest, outraged at the breaking of the capitulations. This resulted in the forced conversion of the Muslim population.

Left: baptism of the Muslim men. An engraving of a relief from the Altar of the Capilla Real in Granada.

Right: Lanjarón Castle. After the Mudéjars of the Alpujarras rose up, King Fernando led the assault on the castle, which he took at the beginning of March 1500.

convert or be expelled. The Monarchs duly consented. The forced baptism of all Muslims in Granada was carried out speedily, en masse, with no time for any instruction in the faith. These now became *Moriscos* (Muslims converted to Christianity).

News of these forced conversions spread to the Alpujarras. Alarmed, but trusting in the impregnability of their mountainous region, the Mudéjars there rose up in January 1500. In reality, these Muslim farmers and townspeople had no chance against the large numbers of experienced Castilian troops, who were sent rapidly to quell the uprising. The Castilians attacked the rebels, who had set up in various strongholds across the Alpujarras, and put down the uprising with brutal force. To the east, the Count of Lerín led a force which attacked the Castle of Láujar. In the course of these hostilities, he ordered the nearby mosque of Andarax to be blown up, although full of women and children who were sheltering there. A large force of royal troops headed towards the west of the Alpujarras. King Fernando himself led the assault on the Castle of Lanjarón, which he took at the beginning of March 1500. Against these onslaughts and with no prospect of any help from their co-religionists abroad, the rebels had to give up. Conversion (or the alternative of expulsion) was now imposed on them and the rest of the Mudéjars of the Kingdom of Granada. The conversions were effected in the period from August to October of 1500. Further rebellion flared up in the west, in the Serranía de Ronda and nearby Sierra Bermeja in 1501. After an initial reverse, the Castilian forces soon put this rebellion down.

Changes in Granada
After the capture by the Catholic Monarchs, the changes to the city of Granada were initially slow, but then the pace quickened. There was an influx of Christian soldiers, part of the siege army which gradually became a garrison. The sixteenth-century writer Luis de Mármol Carvajal recounted that the proven diplomatic skills of Archbishop de Talavera were needed as *'the majority of those who came to populate (Granada) were men of war or upstarts and among them were many who were so unruly in the evils that the military life brings with it'.*

A vigorous building programme began in Granada. With a new flock of forced converts, the city was divided into 23 parishes in 1501. New churches were built on the sites of demolished mosques, or the mosques were reconstructed as churches. A host of priests, monks and other religious arrived in the city, to begin the task of putting a Christian stamp on what had been the last centre of Islam in the Peninsula. These men faced a daunting task: they had a flock of forcibly convert-

Left: the sepulchre of the Catholic Monarchs in the Capilla Real. The construction of this, the Royal Chapel, was ordered by royal warrant in September 1504. © Capilla Real Granada.

Right: the Convento de San Francisco (now a parador), in the Alhambra.

Below: the commemorative slab in the Convento de San Francisco (now a parador) denoting where the Catholic Monarchs were temporarily interred.

ed men and women – they now had to convince these 'converts' of the glories and truth of Christianity.

In the heart of the Granadan Medina the construction of the Royal Chapel, the *Capilla Real,* was ordered by royal warrant in September 1504. This was intended as the final resting place for the Catholic Monarchs – they had a choice of many prime locations across the country for this but Granada was where the most glorious event of their reign had occurred. As it happened, Isabel died shortly after in November 1504. Work began on the chapel in 1506. To make way for this, sections of the Grand Mosque and nearby buildings like baths were demolished. The gothic-style funerary building was finished 11 years later. Isabel's will had included a request for a simple resting place. As it turned out, the Royal Chapel is a sumptuous building, far removed from her wish for simplicity. Ferdinand managed the project until he himself died in 1516. Both monarchs were initially interred in the monastery, the Convento de San Francisco, in the Alhambra (built over the remains of a Nasrid palace and now a parador) until their remains were transferred to the Royal Chapel in 1521.

Some buildings were adapted for civil use. The *Madrasa*, or university, in the central area, just across from the Royal Chapel, had been erected on the orders of Yusuf I in 1349. It was decreed to become the *Casa de Cabildo* (City Hall) for the city. The nobles, who had been the principal commanders of the Castilian army during the assault on the kingdom of Granada, were awarded property in the city and great estates in the countryside. The Marqueses and the Dukes established their noble residences in prime locations in Granada. Some highly placed personages like Hernando de Zafra simply took over Nasrid palaces (his palace is now known as Casa de Zafra); others built afresh, using a mix of classical and Islamic (most available tradesmen were Morisco) styles.

Above: the decorated ceiling, from the Christian era, in the Madrasa, in central Granada. The Madrasa had been erected on the orders of Yusuf I in 1349. After the conquest it became the Casa de Cabildo (City Hall).

The headquarters of the Captain-General, the military governor of the Kingdom of Granada was established in the Alhambra. Immediately after the conquest the Catholic Monarchs moved into the Alhambra and stayed there for a while. They ordered the strengthening of its defences – adding bastions to the defensive walls. They also made renovations to stop some of the deterioration that had occurred. Alterations were also made to rooms of the Alhambra to serve the needs of their royal court. Two years after the conquest, a Nasrid palace in the upper part of the Medina was demolished to make way for the Convento de San Francisco (now part of the network of Spanish paradors). Parts of the walls of the Nasrid palace and their fine stucco work can be seen within the parador.

Left: Fernando and Isabel are commemorated in this inscription in the ceiling at the Madrasa.

Above: the Carlos V Fountain, by the walls of the Alhambra. As well as providing water for the cavalry, it declares the splendour and greatness of Carlos V.

Below: Carlos V inherited many kingdoms, including that of Holy Roman Emperor. His new palace at the Alhambra was in the classical style, acknowledging his exalted imperial status.

Carlos V and his impact on Granada

After Isabel's death in 1504, the Spanish monarchy entered into an unstable period of successional change, complicated by the extensive range of existing dynastic unions. Juana, the daughter of the Catholic Monarchs, now inherited Castile. Juana's husband, Philip (known as the '*Hermoso*', or 'handsome', son of the Hapsburg Emperor) died in 1506. Juana was mentally unstable and Philip's death propelled her into madness. She (dubbed '*la Loca*' or 'mad') travelled through Spain with his coffin. King Fernando took over the regency. On Fernando's death in 1516, Juana inherited the crown of Aragón. Enter her eldest son Carlos, living in the Netherlands. After Fernando's funeral, this sixteen-year-old was made King of Castile and Aragón to rule jointly with his mother.

Carlos was lucky in his birthright – he inherited many of Europe's kingdoms. Through his father he had already inherited the Low Countries and Franche-Comté. In 1520 he succeeded his (paternal) grandfather as Holy Roman Emperor. He was known as Carlos I of Spain and Carlos V of the Holy Roman Empire. This youth now had become ruler of a new entity, a superpower, with enormous territories across the north, south and west of Europe. This was in addition to the Spanish domains of the New World, thousands of kilometres across the Atlantic. Initially unable to speak Spanish, Carlos V transferred to Spain in 1517. It was to be 1526 before Carlos visited Granada. He came to the city just after marrying Isabel of Portugal in Seville. Mindful of his huge empire, he planned that Granada would be the magnificent centre. He duly commissioned a palace – this was to serve as his imperial residence. Symbolism, as always, was an essential element. This was where his grandparents, the Catholic Monarchs, had conquered the last redoubt of Islam in this part of Europe. It was a time when his domains were challenged by the Islamic Ottoman

105

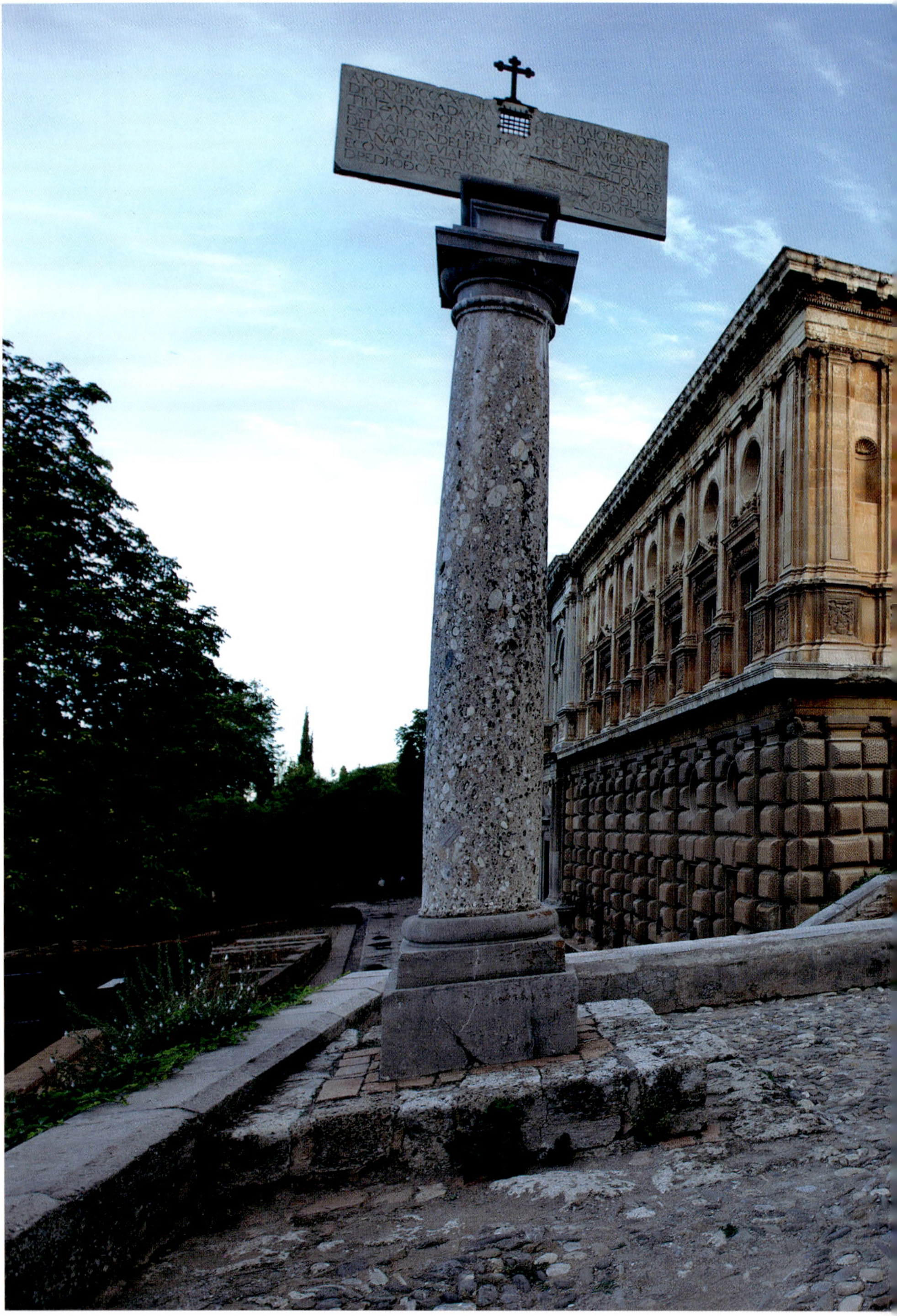

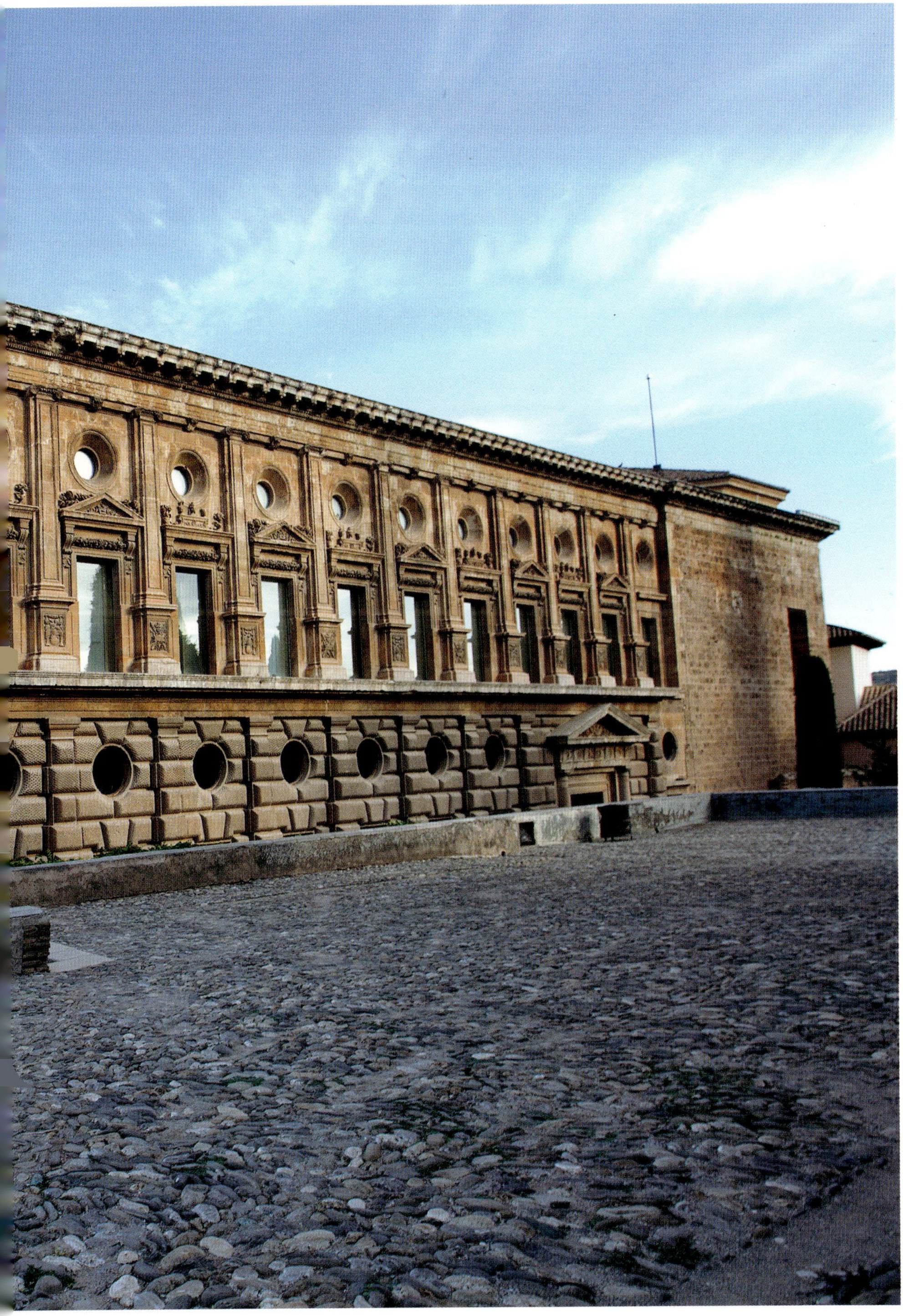

Empire. For the location of his royal palace, he chose the Alhambra, site of the Nasrid palaces, on a dominating height above the city. The designer of the palace was Pedro Machuca, polymath and architect, who had studied under Michelangelo in Italy. The Renaissance style he adopted displaced the previous orthodoxy of the Gothic style. The new style acknowledged that of classical Rome, more in line with Carlos' new imperial status – he saw himself as part of the line of succession of the Roman emperors. Construction commenced in 1527. As always, funds were in short supply. The long war of conquest of the Nasrid kingdom had sapped the coffers of Spain; new wars in Italy

Previous page: the Palacio de Carlos V in the Alhambra. The designer was Pedro Machuca, who had studied under Michelangelo in Italy. The Renaissance style he adopted displaced the previous orthodoxy of the Gothic style, popular in Christian Europe. Construction commenced in 1527.

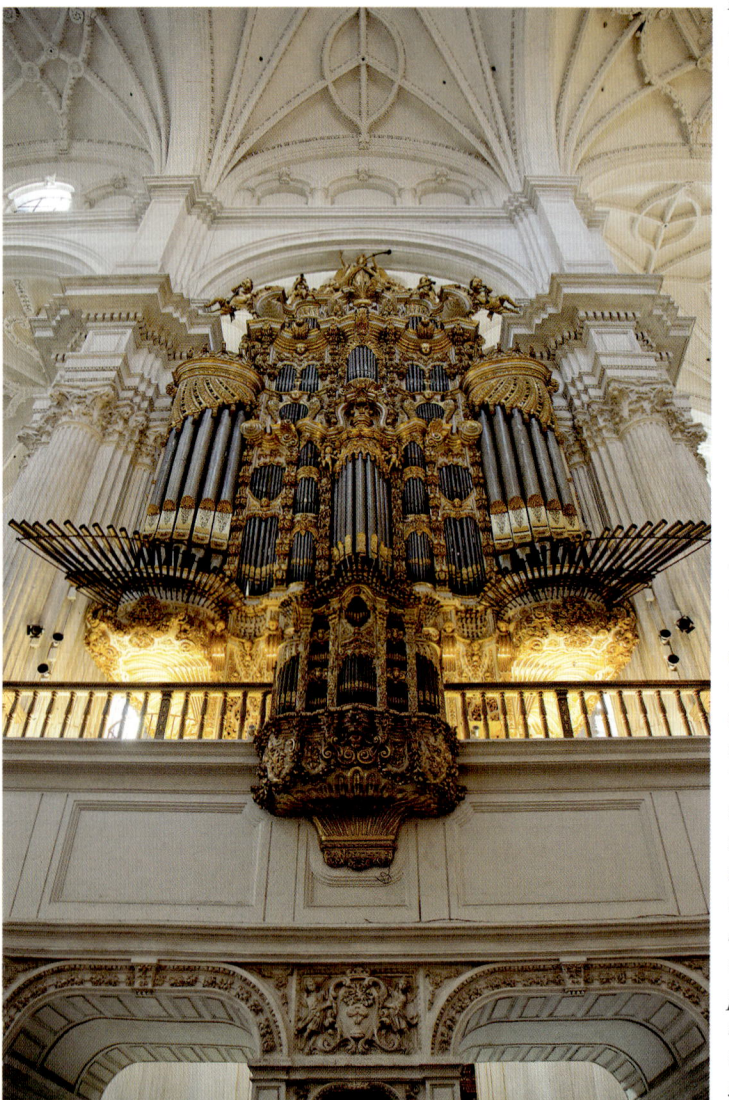

Left: organ in the Cathedral in Granada. Carlos ordered the construction of a new Cathedral on the site of the Grand Mosque in the central Medina. Work started in 1523 on a site adjacent to the Capilla Real where the Grand Mosque had recently stood. When the architect Diego de Siloé was appointed to the project five years later he changed the design to Carlos' preferred Renaissance style.

Above: the 'Door of Forgiveness', which leads into the north transept of the Cathedral. This elaborate and highly carved entrance was executed by de Siloé. An eagle with the royal shield of the Catholic Monarchs can be seen on the left-hand pier. The carved tablet located directly over the door runs: 'After 700 years of Muslim supremacy, the Catholic Monarchs gave these peoples both Justice and Faith".

and elsewhere in the Holy Roman Empire further depleted Carlos' treasury. It was a cruel irony that the building of Carlos' new palace was financed by the *farda*, a special tax that had been levied on the Moriscos from 1510. The new building was constructed immediately adjacent to the southern side of the Patio de los Arrayanes, requiring demolition of a small part of it. Work proceeded slowly, under Machuca, who died in 1550. The revolt by the Moriscos in the Kingdom of Granada in 1569 cut off the source of finance and construction stopped for 15 years. The palace, with an imposing square shaped exterior and a circular inner court, was largely finished in 1637, although the roof was still unfinished. Carlos V never got to stay in his palace – in any case, he was frequently absent from Spain, engaged in the affairs of his vast empire. Seen in its own right, it is an excellent Renaissance building. However, it is a bulky imposition in its present location. It brings a foreign, essentially Italian style, to the precinct of the Alhambra. It offers a jarring note to the magnificent, fluid and sublime courts and gardens of the Nasrid palaces. These have a unique and unequalled architectural style, which had been developed over the preceding centuries and was homegrown in the Iberian Peninsula.

Carlos ordered the construction of a new Cathedral on the site of the Grand Mosque in the central Medina of Granada. Finance, as ever, was a consideration. Funds had been diverted towards the construction of the Royal Chapel. It was only when this had been completed that a new cathedral could be constructed. Work started in 1523 on a site adjacent to the Capilla Real where the Grand Mosque had recently stood. Foundations had been initially constructed to cater for a Gothic-style building. When the architect Diego de Siloé was appointed to the project five years later he changed the design to Carlos' preferred Renaissance style. De Siloé, with some difficulty, adjusted the Renaissance-style upper elevation to fit on the Gothic-designed ground plan. Construction continued over the years until 1704, under the direction of many architects (incidentally, a record not beaten by Gaudi's long-running Sagrada Família church in Barcelona). Just in case the message on the new reality was lost, this Christian structure was built over the Grand Mosque; the cartouche over one of the principal entrances (the Door of Forgiveness) runs: '*After 700 years of Muslim supremacy, the Catholic Monarchs gave these peoples both Justice and Faith".*

Granada experienced an extraordinary amount of new construction in the sixteenth and seventeenth centuries. The urban fabric of this Islamic city was completely remodelled. Civil and religious buildings were inserted across the city, reflecting the aspirations and characteristics of the new Castilian rule. Granada underwent an abrupt change of character, from the previous Islamic city; it became a showcase of Renaissance architecture. The Royal Hospital, commissioned by the

Left: the main entrance to the Royal Hospital. Building commenced in 1511. This large and impressive hospital, intended to cater for the sick and poor, is a prime example of the extraordinary amount of new construction in Granada during the sixteenth and seventeenth centuries. The urban fabric of the Islamic city was being extensively remodelled.

Catholic Monarchs, was commenced in 1511. The Renaissance Royal Chancellery, constructed during the reign of Carlos' son, Felipe II, was built to house the courts of justice. The adage that Spain (with the flow of gold and silver from the New World) was the country that could transform silver into stone was well demonstrated in Granada: a vast amount of religious institutions, over 40 convents and monasteries, as well as churches of great splendour were constructed. Designed by talented architects, these were filled with religious paintings by eminent artists. Examples of this heritage include the Monasteries of San Jerónimo and the Cartuja. Gradually Granada was transformed. From parochial churches built over mosques, through the setting up of major religious institutions and the insertion of new squares, to the remodelling of the Plaza de Bibrambla, the city was losing the urban configuration of Nasrid times.

The Remainder of the Sixteenth Century
The uprising in the Kingdom of Granada of 1499 and the consequent forced baptisms had now freed the conversion genie from the Castilian bottle. Given the desire for religious uniformity of the Catholic Monarchs, the focus now fell on the settled Mudéjars in the rest of the Kingdom of Castile. These, many of them were speakers of Castilian, had been living peacefully and modestly under Christian rule for several centuries. A royal decree was proclaimed in February 1502, ordering that they convert.

Above: 'Moriscos in Granada'. A Morisco man leads his veiled wife, mounted on a horse with baby in the basket. This depiction is by the sixteenth-century German artist Christoph Weiditz, who brilliantly captured Morisco customs and dress during his visit to Granada. Moriscos were Iberian Muslims who became baptised Christians by decree after the conquest. In reality, in reaction to the forced conversion, most were crypto-Muslims.

The Mudéjars of all Castile (including Granada) had now been transformed into Moriscos. In reality, in reaction to their forced conversion to Christianity, most were crypto-Muslims. They had converted as they had no real alternative and to gain relief from the unbearable pressure. While they were nominally Christian, they continued to dress in Muslim attire, persisted with their cultural practices such as baths, maintained their diet, and practised their religion in private. The Granadans continued to speak Arabic. The Church made efforts to dispatch priests to instruct their new flock in the newly acquired religion, with the corollary that the converts would give up their Muslim dress and customs. However, very few priests could speak Arabic or had the desire to. Scarcely any headway was made with these reluctant converts. It was patently obvious that the conversion was not genuine and this became a source of irritation at the royal court.

The Muslims of North Africa looked on with sympathy at the travails of their co-religionists. In 1504 a *fatwa* was issued by a *mufti* (an expert on religious law) in Oran. This gave an interpretation of Islamic law in an effort to deal with the peculiar situation in which the Moriscos found themselves. In effect, it said that they could physically carry out Christian rituals and remain Muslims, so long as in their

Left: Weiditz depicts Morisco musicians and a dancer in his 'Das Trachtenbuch des Christoph Weiditz von seinen Reisen nach Spanien' (1529).

hearts they rejected these rituals and believed in Allah. As it became evident to the authorities that the Moriscos had not changed their ways, various restrictive proclamations were issued in 1511 to try to get them to change. These required the wearing of Christian dress. They inluded bans on tailoring Muslim attire; on the halal method of slaughtering animals; and on the use of Muslim-style baths. These and other measures were applied in a disorganised and half-hearted way and had very little impact.

Fernando's domain, the Crown of Aragón, comprised Aragón, Catalonia and Valencia. The Kingdom of Valencia was home to the largest population of Mudéjars in the Peninsula. They had been living in relative peace there under Christian rule for nearly three centuries. Carlos V issued an edict in November 1525 that mandated the expulsion from the state of all the Mudéjars of Aragón, Catalonia and Valencia, the alternative being conversion. Most chose to convert. Thus, in theory, the population was now uniformly Christian and no Muslims remained on the soil of Spain.

For the next decades, the pace and intensity of pressure on the Moriscos reduced somewhat. But Spain was changing, both at home and abroad. In 1556 Felipe II succeeded his father Carlos V and inherited his vast empire. The rising power of the Ottoman Empire to the east was a particular threat. To use a present-day Russian phrase, Spain's 'near abroad', the Mediterranean, was in danger of becoming an Islamic lake. During the first half of the sixteenth century, the Spanish had established a series of *presidios* or fortified enclaves along the North African coast – and the Turks had also set up enclaves along here.

Uneasy indeed lay the Crown of Spain and it was in this atmosphere that the Moriscos of Spain came to be increasingly mistrusted.

In the Crown's eyes they were seen as an Islamic fifth column, ready to support an enemy attack. The Moriscos had continued over the years to maintain their distinctive customs and dress – thus they were a very visible minority, obviously not adhering to orthodox Christianity. The general populace disliked the Moriscos and this hatred continued to mount. In Granada, at the end of the 1550s, punitive measures were enacted, which meant that Moriscos without land title were fined or had their land confiscated. Adding to the woes in Granada was the crisis in the silk industry. This had been a lucrative activity for the Moriscos in the Alpujarras and was depressed by a state ban on silk exports in the 1550s and sharply increased taxes after 1561.

In 1565 representations were made to the King by a synod of Granadan Bishops, requesting the enactment of the measures banning Muslim customs that were made in 1511. This gained consideration and finally, in January 1567, a document was published which laid down restrictions on dress, baths, religious observation, language and social gatherings. The Moriscos of Granada thought that they could buy off the enactment of these edicts by the payment of a large sum, a tactic that had worked in the past. Envoys were sent to negotiate but, by 1568, it was evident that there was going to be no change. With the economic losses due to the decline of the silk industry, coupled with years of ill-treatment, this tough new attitude of the authorities proved to be the last straw. Rebellion was in the air and secret meetings were held in the Albaicín and the Alpujarras.

On Christmas Eve 1568, in Granada, one Farax Aben Farax (said to be of the lineage of the Abencerrajes, plotters par excellence from Nasrid times) lit the flame of rebellion. He led a small group that tried to galvanise the residents of the Albaicín to rise up. This attempt failed and the rebels withdrew. However, in the Alpujarras, the real revolt began on the same day. Moriscos took over the towns and hamlets of the western Alpujarras. In the village of Béznar (less than 30 kilome-

Right: villages in the Alpujarras. Nestling below the highest mountains of the Peninsula, the Alpujarra region was the scene of the uprising by the Moriscos in January 1569. This was in response to intolerable pressure. The rebellion, known as the Second War of the Alpujarras, was put down with much bloodshed.

tres south of the city, in the Valle de Lecrín), a king was named by the Moriscos of the Alpujarras: one Aben Humeya, formerly known by his Hispanicised name of Fernando de Válor. As his Muslim name implied, he claimed to be descended from the Umayyad dynasty. The uprising in the Alpujarras released the pent-up anger of this persecuted people. The anger was focused on the unfortunate Christian clergy who had been posted throughout the region and atrocities were widespread. Priests were tortured and slaughtered. Churches were destroyed. Christians in the districts took refuge in church towers and fortifications, many of which were burnt, with great loss of life. The rebellion spread rapidly across the Alpujarras and adjacent territories. This rising was to prove difficult to put down and developed into a hard-fought conflict, known as the Second War of the Alpujarras. Full of strategic danger for Spain, it turned out to be a major preoccupation for Felipe II.

Left: the bridge over the steep ravine at Tablate, entry point to the western Alpujarras. In January 1569 the Christian forces attacked the entrenched Moriscos here, who had demolished the bridge. A Christian friar heroically leapt across the defile, inspiring the royal army to follow and decisively defeat the Morisco defenders.

Right: map of uprisings in the Kingdom of Granada in 1569. The main revolt was in the east of the kingdom, but there were also uprisings in the west, around the Sierra Bermeja, near Ronda.

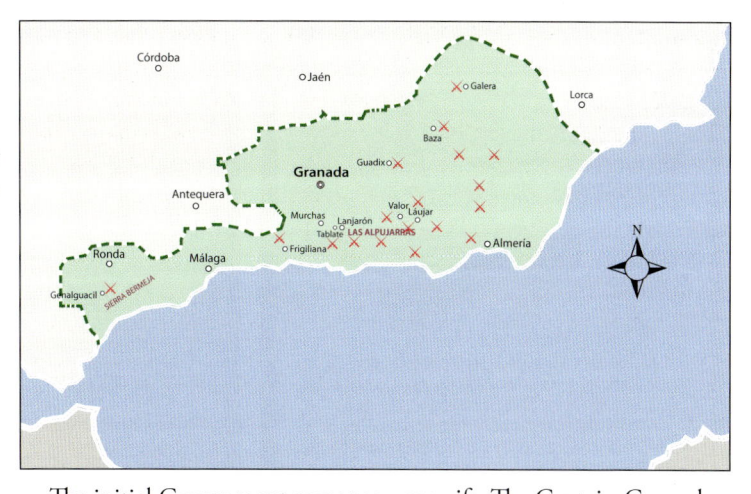

The initial Government response was swift. The Captain-General of Granada, the Marques de Mondéjar, assembled his forces and set out from the city on 3 January 1569. He headed south to the strategic hamlet of Tablate, which was the entry point to the western Alpujarras. Here, entry would be gained across a bridge that spanned a deep ravine. The rebels, anticipating the arrival of royal forces, had destroyed the bridge, save for some ancient planks which spanned the void. Both sides began an exchange of projectiles. A Franciscan friar, Cristóbal de Molino, accompanying the royal troops, now undertook one of the few heroic acts of the war. It is said that, with his habit hitched up in his belt, a crucifix in his left hand and a sword in his right, he invoked the name of Christ and leapt across the rubble and planks and scrambled his way up the other side. He was followed by soldiers, emboldened by his example. They put the Moriscos, entrenched on a height above the bridge, to flight. The bridge was quickly repaired and the Marques de Mondéjar advanced to Lanjarón and onwards to Orgiva where he set up his headquarters. Over the following months, his forces ranged over the west and central Alpujarras, harrying the rebels, capturing towns and releasing Christian captives. By March the Christian forces had pushed back the rebels. Aben Humeya and other leaders had to flee, narrowly avoiding capture. Soon, negotiations on surrender terms began. The Marques de los Vélez had also set out with troops from Murcia at the beginning of January, blundering into the more peaceful eastern Alpujarras, causing commotion among the those Moriscos who had yet to rise up. At this point, the Christians managed to snatch failure from the jaws of victory. The two Marqueses were long-time rivals and did not cooperate. Many of their troops were undisciplined and behaved in a brutal manner towards the local populace. This fanned the flames of revolt,

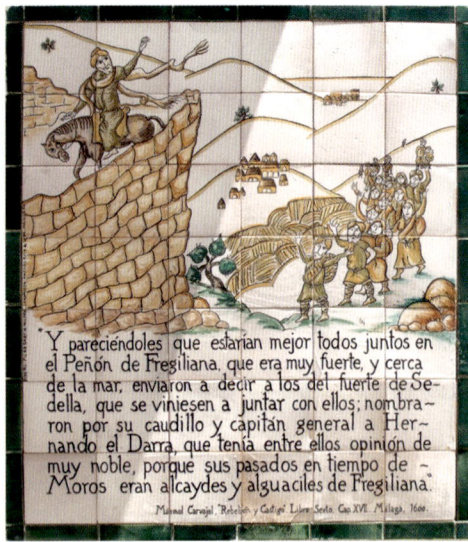

En la empresa tomaron parte fuerzas de mar a las órdenes de don Luis de Requesens, de don Álvaro de Bazán y de don Sancho de Leiva. Esa Armada contribuyó eficazmente al buen éxito de la expedición, cooperando a operaciones tan brillantes como la del Peñón de Frigiliana, posición tenida por inexpugnable, y los acometió Requesens al frente de 6.000 hombres, entre los cuales se contaban 800 marinos.

Carlos Ibáñez de Ibero, Marqués de Mulhacén "Almirantes y hombres de mar" Madrid, 1960.

Y pareciéndoles que estarían mejor todos juntos en el Peñón de Fregiliana, que era muy fuerte, y cerca de la mar, enviaron a decir a los del fuerte de Sedella, que se viniesen a juntar con ellos; nombraron por su caudillo y capitán general a Hernando el Darra, que tenía entre ellos opinión de muy noble, porque sus pasados en tiempo de Moros eran alcaydes y alguaciles de Fregiliana.

Manuel Carvajal "Rebelión y Castigo" Libro Sexto Cap XVII. Málaga, 1600.

more Moriscos flocked to the rebel cause and the uprising gained new strength.

Felipe II was conscious of these problems with the campaign, especially as Mondéjar's enemies were regularly informing on him to the King. In March 1569, Felipe turned to his half-brother, Don Juan de Austria (a mere 22 years of age) to direct his armies in suppressing the rebellion. The experienced Mondéjar and los Vélez were placed under this royal youth's overall command. The war, which initially had seemed like a local difficulty, had spread beyond the Alpujarras. The Christian forces were now strongly reinforced. They comprised infantry and supporting cavalry and artillery. These forces were a mix of seasoned veterans (including Italian *tercios*) of the regular army as well as militia forces raised from the cities. While the Christian forces had overwhelming might and the advantage in conventional warfare, the rebels gained some advantage in the mountains. There they knew their terrain, were able to choose impregnable positions and live off the land. They also had the support of latter-day fighters for the Islamic faith, some Turkish and North African soldiers who had landed on the Mediterranean coast. As always, the Spanish were very aware of the Turkish danger and placed a fleet to patrol the coasts and interdict any reinforcements.

The armies of Don Juan and his commanders fought hard through the Alpujarras and in the regions to the east, meeting fierce resistance. To the west, in the Málaga region, Moriscos in the Axarquía had also risen. In June 1570 the rebels had assembled from the surrounding districts and set up on the heights of the Peñón de Frigiliana. The Christian forces (including the feared tercio of Naples) moved to the

Above: tiles in Frigiliana. One, left, depicts 'tercios' disembarking. In June 1570 these attacked the Morisco forces on the peak of the Peñón de Frigiliana (right, Moriscos assembling to go to the peak) defeating them and leaving many dead.

Below: Don Juan de Austria. Felipe II appointed Don Juan, his half-brother, to command the Spanish armies in suppressing the rebellion.

Right: this seventeenth-century artillery manual demonstrates how to bombard an enemy fortification. Don Juan attacked the Morisco enclave of Galera (north-east of Baza) in January 1570. However, when the Christians discharged their heavy artillery at the defences here, it was initially to no great effect, as the walls of packed mud of the outer ring of houses were able to absorb the cannonballs.

area and launched an attack on the Moriscos, who lacked firearms and could only fight back with arrows and stones. The battle was intense and ranged over the nearby ridges and gullies. After many assaults, the Christian forces won, leaving 2,000 Moriscos dead, with the remainder put to flight.

As the war progressed, the Morisco ranks became riven by dissension. Aben Humeya had fallen out with his lieutenants. Personal differences arose along with suspicions that he was negotiating the handover of the Alpujarras to the Christians to further his own interests. In October 1569, a group of plotters, including one Aben Aboo, set out to intercept him at his headquarters in Láujar de Andarax. Luis de Mármol, in his contemporary account, hints darkly that Humeya was a sexual libertine; the assassins found him '*sleeping between two women.*' Whatever the truth, the intruders strangled Humeya. Aben Aboo was named as the new king and continued the war against the Christians.

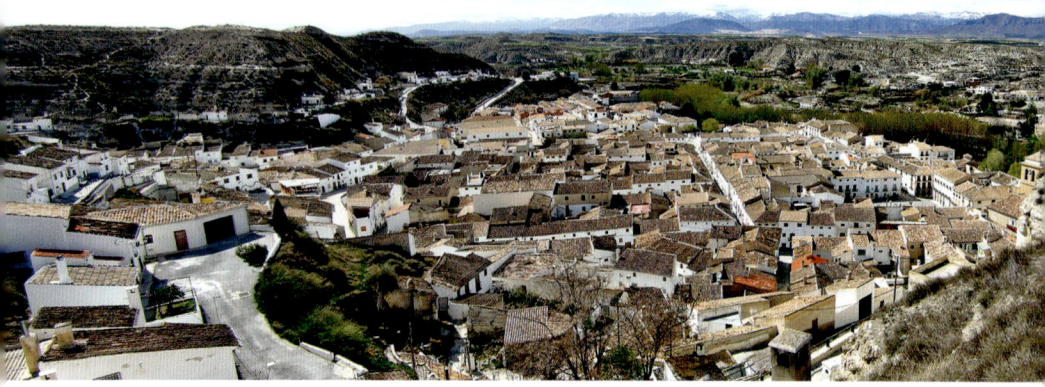

In October 1569 Felipe II ordered the waging of total war: in fire and blood. Don Juan demonstrated this amply when he attacked Galera (35 kilometres north-east of Baza) in January 1570. This encounter resulted in the greatest atrocity of this sanguinary war. Galera was a medium-sized town in the Granadan *altiplano* (high plain), with tightly packed houses built around a small ridge. Contrary to the principles of guerrilla warfare, several thousand rebels had allowed themselves to be corralled within this fixed location, now under siege by a conventional army. Don Juan's army amounted to over 12,000 men. The Christians duly discharged their heavy artillery, to no great effect, as the walls of packed mud of the outer ring of houses were able to absorb the cannonballs. It took weeks of fierce fighting to take the town, which fell at the beginning of February 1570. Thousands of Moriscos had lost their lives, including 400 women and children slaughtered by direct order of Don Juan after the capture of the town. The final punishment was biblical: the town was razed to the ground and the land was salted (under the direction of none other than our chronicler Luis de Mármol Carvajal, who was present at the siege, in a quartermaster role).

The rebels continued to fight across the region, but by now the Christian forces had the upper hand. Some of the rebels began to negotiate surrender. Others retreated higher into the mountains using caves for shelter. The Christian forces used fire to smoke them out and many were asphyxiated. Resistance reduced rapidly and by November 1570, the war was effectively over. In the west, around the Serranía de Ronda and the Sierra Bermeja, there were later instances of resistance, which were put down by the end of 1570.

Above: modern Galera, rebuilt since the original town was razed in February 1570, after its capture by Don Juan's army. The bloody aftermath of the surrender was in compliance with the order by Felipe II to wage total war: in fire and blood. © Tony Redmond.

Expulsion of Moriscos from Granada

The way was clear to complete the removal of all the Moriscos of Granada. There had been some evictions during the course of the rebellion, as the Spanish forces captured territory. Now, the main wave of expulsion began in November 1570. This was aimed, not only at those who had rebelled and surrendered, but at all Moriscos, including those who had peacefully carried on their daily life. The operation had been planned months before. Underlying it all was the need to maintain order and also to keep the productive economy of the Moriscos, lucrative source for the treasury (taxes on the Moriscos paid for most of the cost of maintaining the large Christian army, garrisoned to suppress revolt). Thus, in turn the vacuum had to be filled and the territory repopulated. The machinery of state swung into place with grim determination. A special office, the *Consejo de Población*, was set up in Granada to manage the process. The Kingdom of Granada was split up into seven zones. Moriscos in each zone were to assemble at designated points. They were then marched off in large groups, each escorted by a detachment of soldiers. They were dispersed widely, to Extremadura, other parts of Castile and western Andalucía (in other words, well away from the Mediterranean coast). The marches were cruel for the old and infirm, particularly as some of the refugee columns heading north encountered winter snows. On reaching the designated destinations, the intention was that the Moriscos were to be dispersed within the surrounding districts. In several cases, many stayed within the *morerías* (the Mudéjar quarter) of the Castilian cities. The last Moriscos remaining in the Albaicín were ejected to meet their Castilian fate by the end of 1570. Moriscos expelled from that emblematic hilltop *barrio* (suburb) of Granada arrived in Pastrana in Guadalajara province of Castile-La Mancha – they named the new barrio they settled in 'the Albaicín'.

A royal decree was issued ordering the confiscation of all the possessions and lands of the Moriscos for having rebelled. In all, it has been estimated that around 80,000 Moriscos were expelled from the Kingdom of Granada. This meant the effective end of Muslim Granada. The only vestige of Muslims remaining in the Kingdom of Granada were some Morisco slaves that belonged to powerful and important Christian families. A few others remained behind as experts to maintain the irrigation system, and to continue running the sugar mills and the silk industry. There also remained a new class: those principal families of the Moriscos who had succeeded in integrating fully into Christian society. Indeed some of these succeeded in avoiding the eventual expulsion of Moriscos from Spain which began in 1609.

As the stream of Moriscos left Granada, in turn there was an incoming stream of colonists – an estimated 35,000. Most came from other locations in Andalucía such as the provinces of Seville, Córdoba

Left: the impressive castle at Calahorra (50 kilometres to the east of Granada), seat of the Marques de Cenete. He was not enamoured with King Felipe II who had decreed the expulsion of the Moriscos from the Kingdom of Granada to other parts of Spain, following the Second War of the Alpujarras. The loss of his industrious tenants reduced the income of the Marques by 75%.

and Cádiz. Some came from the regions in Extremadura, Valencia and Toledo. A few were from within the Kingdom of Granada itself, transferring from poor land to the fertile plains of the Granadan Vega. Most of these land-hungry people were neighbours, who agreed to transfer en masse. There were fiscal incentives to make the transfer, including reduction of taxes. For those who would make the transfer to more difficult areas such as the mountainous Alpujarras (rather than the fertile plains of the Granadan Vega) there were more inducements. In some cases the scene facing the colonists was not easy: there was damage from the recent war – the lands also had been left uncultivated for some time. Bands of Morisco rebels ranged in the mountains – as we will see later. The new settlers also had to suffer the corruption of rapacious officials and the military. Some of the colonists promptly returned to their original lands when faced with this prospect. However, most remained in their new territory, as they had moved to escape from extreme poverty and the poor lands of the Meseta Central. They persevered and mastered the new techniques such as irrigation. It took many decades before they reached an equilibrium. In the meantime, the economy suffered. It was primarily due to the loss of the Moriscos, talented and productive people, but also due to the fact that the initial repopulation numbers were lower than those of the expelled. It is estimated that by 1591 the population of the Kingdom had dropped by at least a third over the preceding three decades. Some villages remained abandoned. The *Señores*, the lords, who had been granted large expanses of lands after the taking of Granada, suffered with the departure of their Morisco tenants – which led to friction between them and King Felipe II. One account tells that the income of the Marques de Cenete, whose seat was the castle of Calahorra, was reduced by up to 75%.

After the expulsion, production of silk fell by around 25%. To maintain the extensive silk weaving and dyeing industry in the city of Granada, silk had to be imported from other locations such as Murcia and Valencia. The extensive sugar refining industry on the Granadan

Right: a portrait of the Archbishop of Granada, Pedro de Castro y Quiñones. He is holding a lead 'sacred book'. A series of these was found in the caves of Sacromonte. Ostensibly they were written by Arabic-speaking Christians during the Roman era, describing the early martyrs and Christian tenets. The church authorities, led by the archbishop, accepted them as genuine. Sent to the Vatican, they were condemned as erroneous. It is generally accepted that these had been forged at an earlier date by Moriscos living in Granada who were attempting to square the circle: to describe a Christianity within which Islamic precepts could fit. © Museo de la Abadía del Sacromonte.

coast (in places such as Salobreña and Almuñécar), had been mainly in the hands of the Moriscos. This was to the benefit of Genoan merchants, who took control after the expulsion. The city's demographics changed radically after the expulsions of 1569-1570. By 1600 the population was approaching 40,000, all Christian (including those leading Muslim figures who had managed to become Christians and Castilianize themselves).

A few rebels still remained in the Alpujarras. Aben Aboo was at the head of a group of 400 who hid along the heights of the Sierra Nevada. However, one of these, a disgruntled rebel, had negotiated with the Christians to secure his own safety and in March 1571, in a mountain cave, he killed Aben Aboo. The last 'King of Granada' had an inauspicious end. His body was salted and sent off to Granada where it was paraded in the streets.

During the final decade of the sixteenth century, the discovery in the caves of Sacromonte of a series of books proved to be a poignant coda to the Morisco century in the city. This was a series of 22 packets of small lead discs, inscribed in Arabic. As news spread, they caused a sensation: ostensibly they were written by Arabic-speaking Christians during the Roman era, describing the early martyrs, as well as essential tenets of the faith. One book gave information about a disciple of Santiago (the Apostle Saint James). The church authorities, led by the Archbishop of Granada, Pedro de Castro y Quiñones, accepted them as genuine and representing authentic ancient Christian texts. They included a definition that *'God is One. There is no God but God, and Jesus is the Spirit of God'* – acceptable both in Christian and Islamic terms. The books were sent to the Vatican for examination. Pope Innocent XI in 1682 condemned them as containing erroneous doctrine. It was to take until the year 2000, when the then Cardinal Ratzinger (later Pope Benedict XVI), allowed the lead books to be returned to Granada. They now rest in the archives of the Abadía of Sacromonte. The generally accepted explanation of the books that these had been forged at an earlier date by Moriscos living in Granada (expelled from the Peninsula by the time of the discovery of the books) who had despaired of the intolerable situation they found themselves in. It was an attempt to square the circle: to describe a Christianity within which Islamic precepts could fit.

Felipe III and the expulsion of the Moriscos from Spain

In 1598 Felipe III came to power. He is remembered as different from his authoritarian and hard-working father, Felipe II. He was described as weak, vacillating and rigidly pious. The King and his courtiers, as well as the Council of State, must take the primary responsibility for that major exercise in ethnic cleansing of the seventeenth century: the expulsion of the Moriscos.

As the new century dawned, the pressures for expulsion were building with greater intensity. Within the church, there were those who argued that assimilation had not worked and expulsion was the solution. At a meeting in January 1608, the Council of State unanimously agreed to expel the Moriscos from Spain.

The decision was kept secret. It took over a year to make the detailed preparations. It had been decided to expel the Moriscos of Valencia first. These were the most concentrated, the most populous, many living in mountainous regions and seen as posing the most danger during the expulsion exercise. A fleet of Italian galleys was assembled clandestinely in Mallorca to await the call to Valencian ports. The decree of expulsion was published by the Viceroy in Valencia in September 1609. The Moriscos in each locality were given three days to arrive at specific gathering points whence they would travel to the embarkation ports. The ships would then transport them to North Africa. They could bring what they could carry. The remainder of their belongings could not be hidden or destroyed, under pain of death for all the people of the village in question. There was some opposition but most of the Moriscos of Valencia went to their exile quietly, stoi-

Below: Felipe III, who came to power in 1598. In January 1608, he and his Council of State decided to expel the Moriscos from Spain.

Above: the embarkation of the Moriscos at the port of Grau, Valencia, 1613. Painting by Pere Oromig. The Moriscos of Valencia were the most populous in Spain. It was decided to expel these first, a task completed by the middle of 1610. The expulsion of all the Moriscos in Spain was complete by February 1614. © Colección Fundación Bancaja, Valencia.

cally accepting the inevitable. Ships shuttled back and forth to Oran, an enclave under Spanish rule on the North African coast. On arrival at Oran, the Moriscos were rapidly deposited across the frontier. The first transfers began at the beginning of October 1609. Most went by sea but a few took the land route to France. By the middle of 1610, all the Moriscos of Valencia had been rounded up and expelled from the kingdom, an estimated 120,000 people.

Now it was the turn of other parts of Spain. This posed less danger for the State than the expulsion in Valencia, there were fewer Moriscos and they were more dispersed and less likely to cause trouble. Several edicts of expulsion were published in January 1610 covering Granada, Andalucía, Murcia and the rest of Castile. In February 1614, the Council of State reported to Felipe III that the expulsion had been completed.

Where did the Moriscos go? A small number settled in European countries and many went to Constantinople. However, the overwhelming majority of Moriscos went to the Maghreb. There had been a centuries-old tradition of emigration by Andalusis to the southern continent. The terrain in many parts of the Maghreb was similar, as was the culture and, of course, the religion. Many had gone there after the great expansion of Castile during the Reconquista of the thirteenth century. As the Christian pressure on al-Andalus was maintained, the steady stream of refugees continued. The fall of Granada resulted in a sharp increase in the number moving to the Maghreb. Quite a few

Moriscos went to Tunisia, which was under the Turkish rule of the Uthman Dey. He took an enlightened attitude, viewing this influx of capable people as an opportunity for development of the country. A substantial number of Moriscos went to the territory of present-day Morocco. They were very talented and brought a great number of skills to the local economy. Their influence is remembered in today's Morocco, especially their music, cuisine, ceramics, architecture, agriculture and irrigation. North Africa's gain was Spain's loss. As in the earlier expulsion of the Jews, Spain lost a host of industrious and skilled people. This was particularly marked in the parts of the country that had high numbers of Moriscos. Most estimates of the total number of expelled Moriscos put the figure at 300,000. The expulsion was later described by Cardinal Richelieu as '*the most barbarous act in human annals*'. Humanity has managed to outdo this barbarity over the following centuries. Nevertheless, this expulsion was truly a savage finish to the long history of al-Andalus.

Granada in the centuries that followed

During the second half of the sixteenth century Felipe II decided to make Madrid his capital. Granada descended into a provincial existence, no longer experiencing the attention that it gathered during the glory days of the Catholic Monarchs and Carlos V. As the centuries rolled on there was little development, as attempts at establishing

Above: Plataforma de Granada, 1613. This map of Granada by Ambrosio de Vico was commissioned by the Archbishop of the city, Pedro de Castro y Quiñones. It shows Granada and its transformation from the original Muslim city over the century following the conquest. © Museo de la Abadía del Sacromonte.

Above: James Cavanagh Murphy's 1816 view of Granada. The Alhambra is seen on the heights of the Sabika Hill, with, symbolically, a cross of the now dominant religion in the foreground.

industry across the Kingdom of Granada did not succeed. When Napoleon's forces invaded the Iberian Peninsula at the beginning of the nineteenth century, the city was occupied by the French. They set up in the Alhambra in January 1810. The complex provided a convenient barracks and they stayed there for over two years. Buildings were used for storage. Historic wood panels were removed for firewood. The Patio de los Leones was dug up and a garden planted. As the troops retreated they blew up towers around the defensive walls. Rubble from the destruction wrought by the French occupation remained in the upper part of the Sabika Hill until restoration began in the 1930s.

Foreign visitors visited Granada after the Reconquista. The earliest was the German polymath and geographer, Hieronymus Münzer, who visited Granada and the Alhambra, and described the city in that era. Another German traveller, Christoph Weiditz, passed through Carlos V's realm in 1529 and captured the dress and customs of the Moriscos of Granada in his illustrated book *Das Trachtenbuch des Christoph Weiditz von seinen Reisen nach Spanien*. Centuries later, James Cavanagh Murphy, an artist from Ireland, arrived to compile engravings of the Alhambra at the beginning of the nineteenth century. The Alhambra palaces were, of course, most suitable for the art of engraving – allowing the beautiful geometric lines to be finely elaborated and appreciated. Murphy was an architectural draughtsman, born in Cork, who first encountered Muslim architecture when he visited Portugal in

Left: A plate in the early nineteenth-century book by the architect Owen Jones shows the Sala de Dos Hermanas. The Alhambra palaces were most suitable for the art of engraving. These engravings allowed the beautiful lines and decoration to be finely elaborated and appreciated. The illustrations of the Alhambra that featured in this and many other nineteenth-century books were the inspiration for the contemporary enthusiasm to incorporate 'Moorish' architecture in grand buildings across Europe.

Below: statue of Washington Irving in the Alhambra Woods. His 'Tales of the Alhambra' promoted a romantic, if fanciful, narrative of exotic Nasrid life.

1789. A further visit to the Peninsula resulted in his *Arabian Antiquities of Spain*, of 1816. The illustrations of the Alhambra that featured in this and many later nineteenth-century books were the inspiration for the contemporary enthusiasm to incorporate 'Moorish' architecture in grand buildings across Europe.

The American writer Washington Irving arrived in the city in 1829 and his books generated widespread international interest in Granada and its wonders. His *Tales of the Alhambra* promoted a romantic, if fanciful, narrative of exotic Nasrid life. The Victorian British traveller, Richard Ford, visiting here, took a dyspeptic attitude to the Spanish people in his book *Handbook for Travellers in Spain*, of 1845. However he was enthralled by the Alhambra, although he described it as being

Right: Jarron de las Gacelas (Vase of the Gazelles). This large vessel dates from the fourteenth or fifteenth century. Many of these vases were used to decorate the Alhambra palaces. There is a series of these decorative 'Alhambra vases' (based on a traditional storage jar) in museums around the world. This masterpiece of Nasrid ceramic art shows two striding gazelles, set against a blue background, adorned with gold arabesques. There is a central band with an inscription which translates 'good fortune and prosperity'. The colours of the vase are white, gold and cobalt blue. It has a lustre finish, obtained by firing the vase several times. © Museo de la Alhambra.

Right: an illustration of a scene in the Alhambra in an 1874 book on Spain by the French illustrator, Gustave Doré. It shows a group of men, in a variety of contemporary dress, inspecting the Vase of the Gazelles at close hand. The left-hand ornamental handle is shown intact, as opposed to its present-day state as shown above

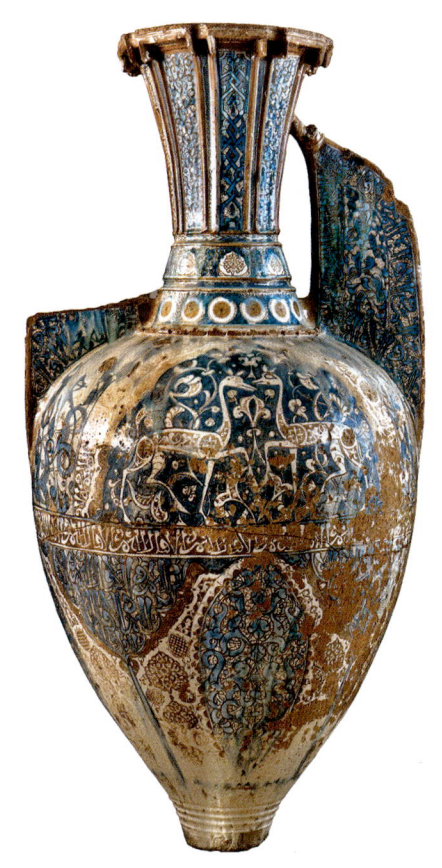

Gate of the Vivarrambla
GRANADA

Left: an engraving from David Roberts' 'Picturesque sketches in Spain taken during the years 1832 & 1833'. It shows the Puerta de Bibrambla in a dilapidated state. This was demolished in the period 1873 to 1884 and the pieces stored in the provincial museum.

Right: the Alhambra has suffered many indignities. This engraving by Gustave Doré shows the behaviour of some nineteenth-century tourists. They chipped off pieces of the stucco decoration to take home as souvenirs, several of which are in the collections of a number of eminent museums in western Europe.

Below: in 1933 the Puerta de Bibrambla was reconstructed in its present location in the Alhambra Woods.

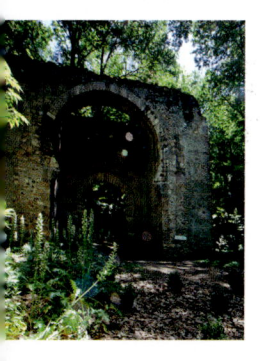

in a sorry state: the Alcazaba was used as a prison for galley-slaves; the court of one of the palaces was disfigured by *'invalids, beggars and convicts'*. The Alhambra was very much part of a nineteenth century 'Grand Tour' for well-heeled gentlemen. Visitors ranged from Benjamin Disraeli to the romantic French writer Vicomte de Chateaubriand. Some of the visitors took to chipping off parts of the decorative stucco and tiles in the Alhambra as souvenirs. This, regrettably, is the basis of some of the fragments of the art of Nasrid Alhambra now found in many eminent museums across the western world.

After a steep decline in the early half of the nineteenth century, a pro-active *Ayuntamiento* (City Council) began a phase of construction across the city, which created the basis of modern Granada as we know it today. It demolished many monasteries, now empty after the religious had been expelled in an earlier wave of anti-clericalism. The

On the Daro Granada
D Roberts 1834

Left: a vista long gone – 'Up the Darro' by David Roberts. This 1830s view shows the river, surrounded by buildings as it flowed through the city. The bridge in the background linked the Corral de Carbón with the Alcaicería (textile souk). In the mid-nineteenth century, it was decided to canalise part of the river Darro, and build a new street over it. After 30 years of construction, the first section from the Plaza Nueva was opened in 1884.

Below: in 1936, after the outbreak of Civil War, the army garrison took over Granada. The city became a Fascist island in the surrounding Republican sea. The poet Frederico García Lorca was murdered near Alfacar outside the city, near this memorial. His grave has not yet been located.

outer suburbs of the city had been built in the Vega after the Reconquista, to a rectangular plan and were relatively spacious. The older heart of the city, still with the narrow winding streets of Nasrid times, now came to the attention of the city fathers. To improve circulation, it was decided to canalise part of the river Darro, and build a new street over it. After thirty years of construction, the first section from the Plaza Nueva was opened in 1884. The old houses alongside were demolished, replaced by solidly bourgeois structures. Continuing with the objective of improving circulation, the Gran Vía de Colón was constructed by 1900, cutting through the houses of the old city and breaking the link between the old Medina and the Albaicín.

The poet and playwright Frederico García Lorca was born in 1898 on the outskirts of Granada (at Fuente Vaqueros, near Santa Fe, where in 1491 the Catholic Monarchs had established their siege camp). However, Lorca was anything but enamoured by his native city. He regarded the fall of Islamic Granada as a tragedy: *'an admirable civilisation and a poetry, astronomy, architecture and sensitivity unique in the world – all were lost, to give way to an impoverished, cowed city…a wasteland populated by the worst bourgeoisie in Spain today'*. That same bourgeoisie was part of the coalition of military, landowners and the Catholic Church, amongst others, who backed Franco during the Civil War. At the outbreak of the war in July 1936, the Nationalist military rose up and seized garrisons in Spanish cities. In Granada, the garrison initially vacillated, resisting demands from the Ministry of War in Madrid to arm the Republican militiamen. A few days later, a colonel led the troops to occupy the city, in the name of Franco and his generals. The Albaicín resisted for several days. Granada became a Fascist island in the surrounding Republican sea. The Nationalists quickly got down to work. Lorca had the misfortune to be paying a brief visit to the city just after the outbreak of the war. This native-born poet was soon arrested, put on a lorry and shot in the hills between Alfacar and Viznar. He was buried there, in an area which now contains the mass graves of thousands of the *desaparecidos*. Paradoxically, his murder, a consequence of cruel intolerance, took place in close proximity to a practical yet elegant example of Muslim civilisation. His grave (its exact location is still not known at the time of writing) is on a pine-clad hill overlooking the exquisitely-engineered Acequia de Aynadamar of eleventh-century Zirid Granada, which weaves along the contours of the hills, to bring the cool mountain water from the Fuente Grande to the Albaicín. Coincidentally, Lorca wrote a poem in *Sueño* in 1919 about a spring: *'my heart rests there, beside the cold spring'*.

Before 1492 Granada had been capital of its own Nasrid kingdom. After its capture in 1492, it was the biggest city in that new entity, Spain. The city did not fare well in the centuries that followed. It did

Left: a night-time view of the river Darro by the Carrera del Darro, down below the Alhambra and the Sabika Hill. With a large student population and tourists flocking to visit the Alhambra, Granada nowadays is a bright modern city.

not grow as fast as other cities of Spain. Now it is a mere seventeenth (ranked by population) amongst Spanish cities. However Granada nowadays is a bright modern city. One of the jewels in Granada's crown is its historic University, one of the largest in Spain. The city's permanent population of over 240,000 is augmented by the student population of well over 60,000. This adds a vivacity, youthfulness and intellectual life. Tourists flock to the city, principally to savour and appreciate the wonderful heritage of the Alhambra. The Alhambra is now well managed, maintained and expertly renovated by the Patronato de la Alhambra y Generalife. The Legado Andalusí foundation, based in the city, seeks to recover the heritage of al-Andalus and disseminate its story of tolerance, creativity and ingenuity.

Chapter 4
The Alhambra

The Alhambra is one of the jewels of world heritage. Described as the finest example of a medieval Muslim palace, this is located, not in the Islamic Middle East, but in southern Europe. Its setting is dramatic – located high on the Sabika Hill, above the bustling city of Granada. The walls of this compound, interspersed with many towers, line the edge of a steep gorge on the northern side. Looking at the crenellations and the towers, it presents a formidable and imposing defensive façade. It is hard to imagine the wealth of wonders within: the palaces of delicate architecture and elaborate decoration. When you enter the Alhambra for the first time be prepared for a shock, it is almost a sensory overload. Rest assured, you have never seen anything like this. Within the walls and towers, there is a sprawling complex of graceful Islamic palaces, a Christian palace of stern symmetry, archaeological works in progress, hotels, shops, and now, the heaving mass of iPhone-toting, selfie-taking, modern tourists.

There is some vagueness as to what was in the locality of Granada before Roman times. Certain Roman and Visigothic remains have been found. There are references to a small castle here, the *qalat al-hamra* (or red castle) on the Sabika plateau from the end of the ninth century. This is an obvious strategic point, a great location to dominate the Vega to the west while nestling in the high mountains of the Sierra Nevada which provide a defensive backdrop.

The Zirids developed the fortification here. It provided defence in conjunction with the principal fortress (referred to as the *Alcazaba Qadima*) down in their new city of Granada. These rulers of the taifa built the protective walls which linked the walls around the medina and the Alcazaba Qadima via the Puente del Qadí over the river Darro, with the line of walls reaching to a castle on top of the Sabika Hill. This fortification was rebuilt and enlarged by the Jewish vizier to the Zirid Amirs, Samuel Ibn Naghrela.

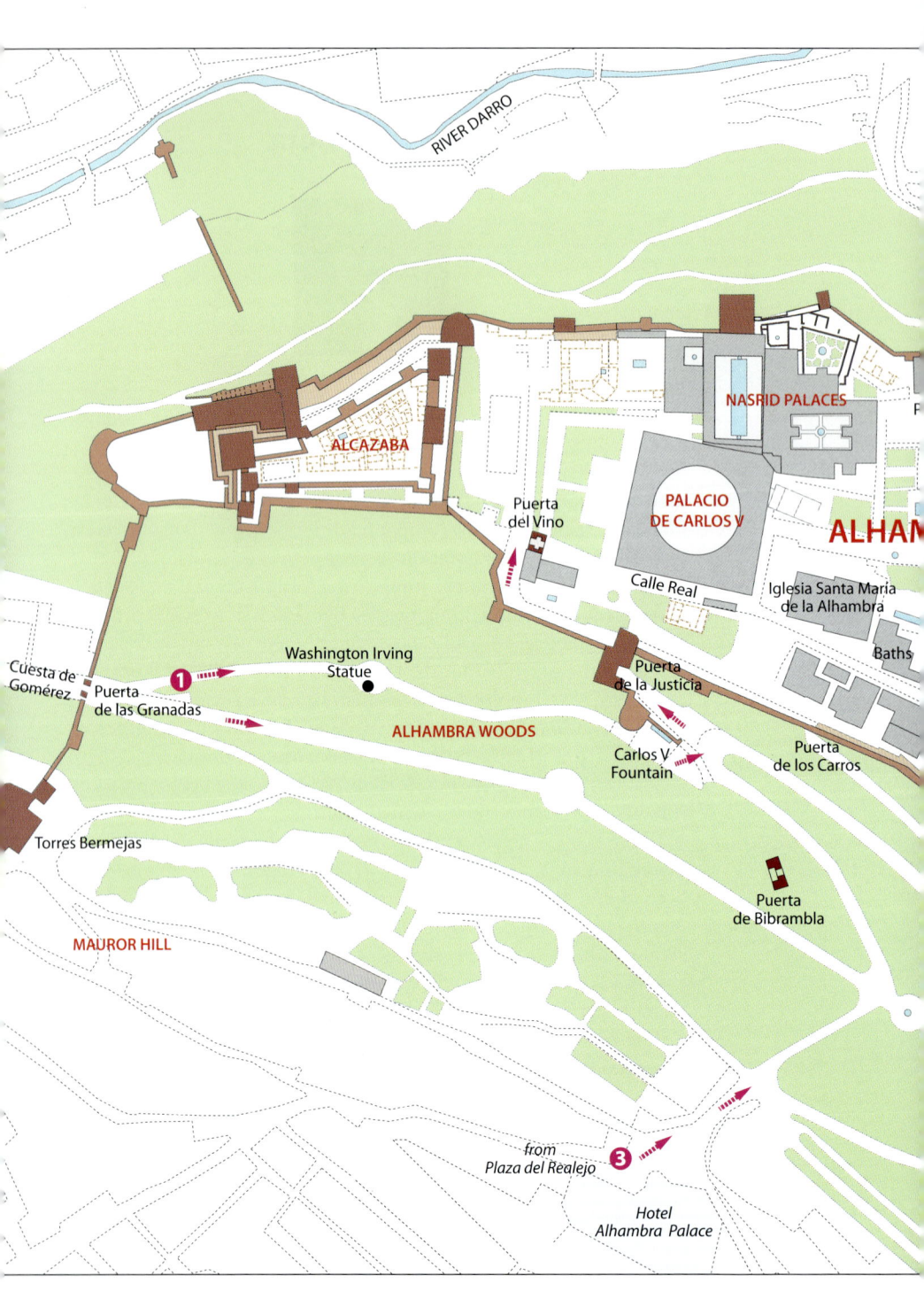

RIVER DARRO

NASRID PALACES

ALCAZABA

Puerta
del Vino

PALACIO
DE CARLOS V

ALHA

Calle Real

Iglesia Santa María
de la Alhambra

Baths

Cuesta de
Gomérez

Puerta
de las Granadas

Washington Irving
Statue

Puerta
de la Justicia

ALHAMBRA WOODS

Carlos V
Fountain

Puerta
de los Carros

Torres Bermejas

Puerta
de Bibrambla

MAUROR HILL

from
Plaza del Realejo

Hotel
Alhambra Palace

N

GENERALIFE

Cuesta del Rey Chico

Gardens

Albercón

Open-Air Theatre

PARADOR

acio de encerrajes

UPPER MEDINA

Acequia Real

Entrance Pavilion

P

In 1238 when the founder of the Nasrids, Ibn al-Ahmar, arrived in Granada, he chose this outstanding location on the Sabika Hill for his seat of power. He immediately began to develop his military fortress over the previous constructions on the Sabika Hill. In time the Alhambra expanded and became the royal palace-city. At its heart were the royal palaces. It was also the seat of government, with administrative offices, barracks, a mint and accommodation for the palace functionaries. In addition there were the basic facilities necessary for palatine city life: a mosque, baths, workshops and shops.

What you see in the Alhambra today is a mix of the old and the new. There has been much modification over the years. From the Catholic Monarchs onwards, those in power did not refrain from alteration when they felt like it. Examples include the demolition of a Nasrid palace to make way for the Convento de San Francisco and the addition of the Carlos V Palace. However, we are exceedingly lucky that the Catholic Monarchs essentially enjoyed and appreciated the Alhambra and its wonders; and that they did not destroy the complex. In the centuries that followed the Alhambra suffered benignly from being ignored – apart from the brief interlude when it was used as a barracks for French troops. Towers were destroyed as French troops retreated in 1812, but luckily a corporal neutralized some of the charges

Above: a panoramic view of the Generalife and the Alhambra, high over Granada, with the Sierra Nevada in the background. Ibn al-Ahmar (Muhammad I), founder of the Nasrid dynasty, chose an outstanding location on the Sabika Hill for his palace and seat of government.

and the extent of destruction was reduced. The Alhambra was abandoned during the nineteenth century. One might say that being left to the gypsies and sheep to wander within probably saved it.

Some of the restoration work in the last century has suffered from the curse of archaeological rehabilitation: it represents the vision of the particular archaeologist – which may or may not be correct. (Archaeologists have an essential advantage in their professional work – there is nobody around who can contradict them as to what existed centuries or millennia ago.) There had been some heavy-handed rehabilitation over several decades. However, despite many vicissitudes, the Alhambra has survived to today with a good deal of it intact, in a form that we can walk though and experience the unique world of the Nasrid rulers and their court.

One wonders how the amirs of the Kingdom of Granada could have conceived of constructing something with the magnificence of the Alhambra, surrounded as they were by a such a doleful legacy of assassination. At that time, the medieval world, both Christian and Muslim, was a place of intrigue and dispute. However, particularly uneasy sat the Nasrid crown. The Nasrids outrivalled all others for violent change, with only a few amirs dying peacefully in their beds. Over the 250-year course of the Kingdom of Granada the rulers were routinely

Left: the Puerta de las Granadas (Gate of the Pomegranates). This gate, attributed to Pedro Machuca (architect of the Palacio de Carlos V), was built in 1536. Approached from the Cuesta de Gomérez, it is an entrance to the Alhambra Woods, which leads onwards to the Alhambra.

overthrown and assassinated. As one wanders through this, the finest example of Islamic architecture in the world, one wonders how these rulers could have had the disposition amongst this mayhem to finance, to select architects and master craftsmen and to create this brilliance. It is also a wonder that the Alhambra palaces are the airy open buildings that they are, rather than being defensive bunkers for the rulers, always fearful of assassins.

The preceding chapters of this book tell the story of the Kingdom of Granada; its origins, the evolution after the fall of the Almohads; its period of (sometimes savage) splendour, and its rapid fall. Key to all of this and at the heart of the story is the Alhambra palace complex. This is a unique time-capsule of a long-lost world. Here, as you walk through the Nasrid palaces and other buildings of the Alhambra complex, you can discover the complex tale of the rise to prominence of the Nasrids. It is possible within the Alhambra to understand how the Islamic presence in Europe was preserved for 250 fraught years, as illustrated by one of most sublime examples of architectural expression in the world.

Note: the various palaces and other parts of the Alhambra complex have had many names over the centuries. The names as presented

Below: surmounted by three pomegranates, symbol of Granada – the Puerta de las Granadas.

Above: the Carlos V fountain, with a bastion in the background. Designed by Pedro Machuca, the decoration includes Carlos' motto 'plus ultra'.

Below: the Puerta de Bibrambla, originally part of the Nasrid city walls. It was demolished and in 1933 the remains were reconstructed here in the Alhambra Woods.

here are those used in the Alhambra by the Patronato de la Alhambra y Generalife. The descriptions of the sights that follow are more or less in the sequence that a visitor might encounter them on entering the Alhambra Woods from the Plaza Nueva and as visitors proceed through the Alhambra complex.

The Alhambra Woods

The usual way to reach the Alhambra is via Plaza Nueva in the heart of Granada, ascending the Cuesta de Gomérez, where you pass a variety of souvenir shops, the most interesting of which are those selling hand-crafted guitars. The ascent continues as one encounters the monumental gate, the Puerta de las Granadas (Gate of the Pomegranates). This gate, attributed to Pedro Machuca (architect of the Palacio de Carlos V) is surmounted by three stone pomegranates, symbol of Granada. The gate was built in 1536, with the intention of offering a suitably dramatic entrance for Carlos V, who could continue to his imperial residence in the Alhambra. Pass through to enter the Alhambra Woods, which provides a welcome expanse of greenery in the heart of the city. However, in Nasrid times the area around the Sabika Hill, for defensive purposes, was generally bare of such vegetation. Starting with Carlos V, trees were planted in this area. Centuries later, these were added to by the Duke of Wellington (better known for his brusque military manner than for his environmentalism), after his victory in the Peninsular War. He ordered a veritable forest of horse

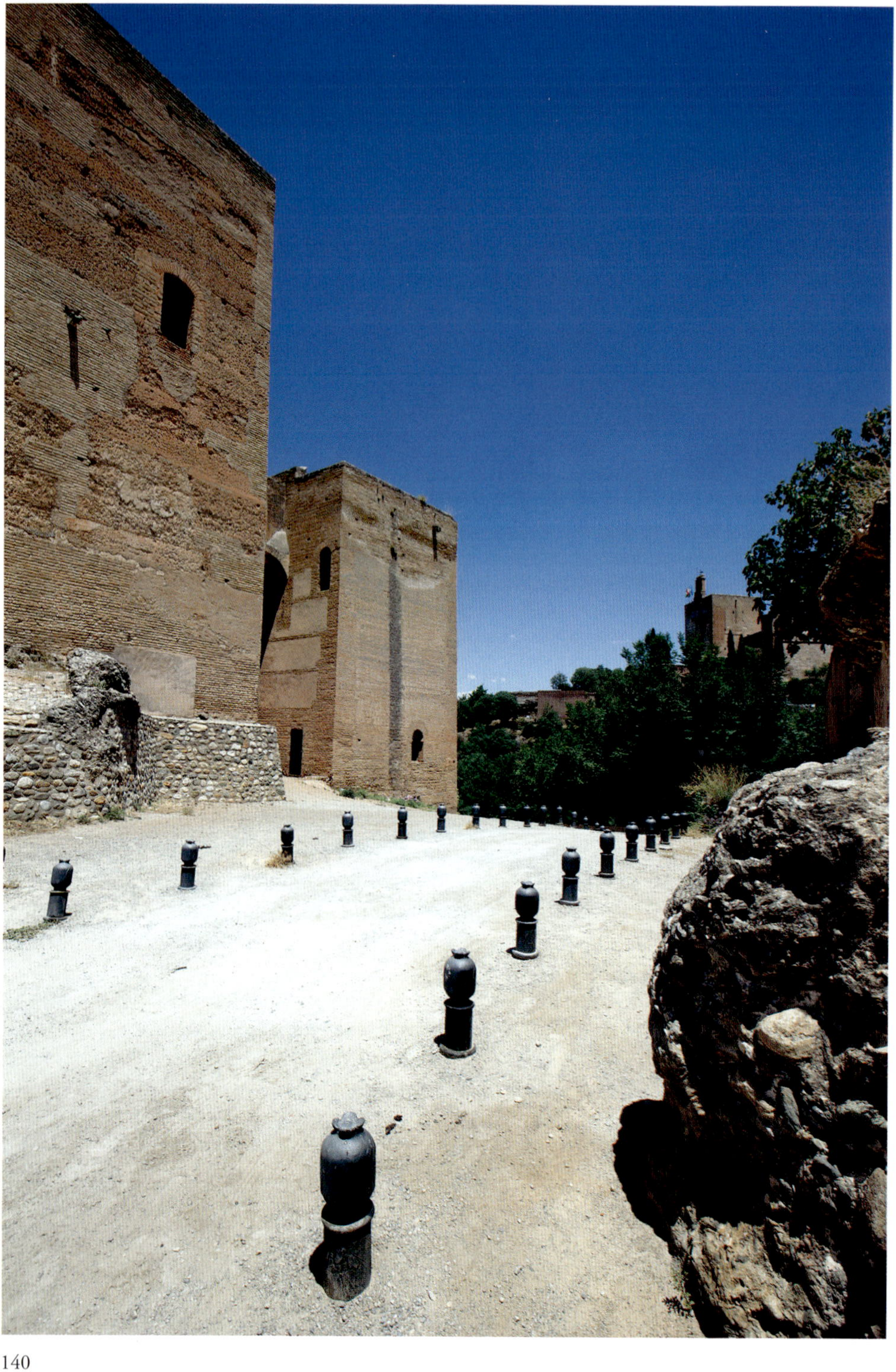

Left: the Torres Bermejas, with a view of the Torre de la Vela in the Alcazaba at the Alhambra in the distance. The three towers here at the western crest of the Mauror Hill were built on earlier fortifications by the Nasrid founder, Muhammad I, at the same time as he established himself in the Alcazaba.

chestnuts, elms and other species to be planted here in green profusion.

Take the left path for the direct route to the Alhambra. You pass by the Washington Irving statue. More climbing and, as you pass the walls of the Alhambra on the left, you reach the Carlos V fountain. Designed by Pedro Machuca, this monumental fountain has extensive decoration, which includes Carlos' motto '*plus ultra*' ('further beyond', and now the national motto of Spain). It also had practical functions: it forms part of the retaining wall for the Puerta de la Justicia and provided drinking water for the horses of the Emperor's cavalry.

If, after passing through the gate, the Puerta de las Granadas, you instead take the central path, you continue along a long avenue. Half-way along on the left you see, almost hidden in the undergrowth, the Puerta de Bibrambla. Here you can quietly observe a gate in the characteristic style of al-Andalus with its horseshoe arch. This is a historic gate, part of the walls encircling Nasrid Madinat Gharnata. Like the rest of central Granada, the Plaza de Bibrambla underwent major reconstruction during the nineteenth century. By 1884 the arch was in poor condition and was demolished and stored in a museum. In 1933 the remains were reconstructed here in the woods.

The Torres Bermejas.

On entering through the Puerta de las Granadas, the right hand track will take you up to the Torres Bermejas (Red Towers). It is a quiet location – tourists rarely visit here. It is worth the steep climb to observe this example of solid Nasrid defensive architecture. Follow the rightmost path, then make a sharp right to climb the path which leads to the three towers, at the western crest of the Mauror Hill, overlooking the Vega. Muhammad I built these towers, possibly on the foundations of earlier defences, at the same time as he built the Alcazaba. A wall snakes down the small valley to the Puerta de las Granadas and then runs upwards to connect with the Alcazaba walls. There are good views of the Alcazaba, with the flags fluttering over the westernmost tower, the Torre de la Vela. After 1492, the Torres Bermejas were much altered internally. The middle tower has a prominent bastion for artillery – a splendid platform to smite one's enemies all around. There was a prison and a military barracks here up to the middle of the last century.

Towers

Currently there are 29 towers spaced around the walls of the Alhambra. Most are Nasrid, but a few were added after 1492. Some of the original towers have been destroyed, most notably those on the southern walls, in the evacuation by the French troops from the Alhambra in 1812 when they placed their gunpowder charges and blew

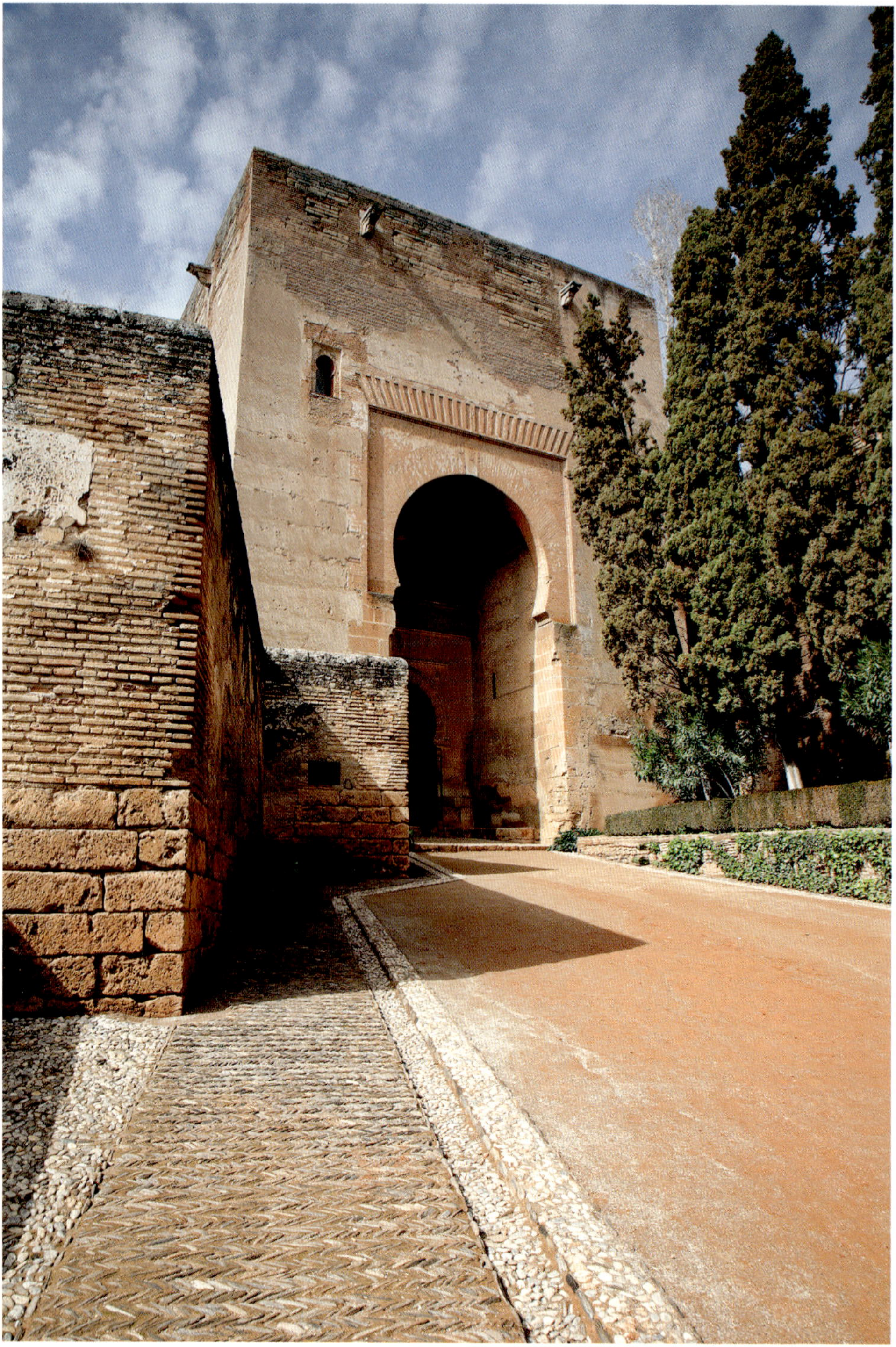

Above: over the arch of the Puerta de la Justicia, a hand symbolises the five pillars of Islam.

Above right: the cranked entrance of the Puerta de la Justicia, a defensive measure common to gates in all al-Andalus. On entering, one has to take a sharp turn right, and then take a left turn. This prevented attackers from charging directly inside.

Left: the Puerta de la Justicia, a principal entrance to the Alhambra. The gate was ordered by Yusuf I in 1348.

Below: the key above the interior entrance arch, a symbol of faith.

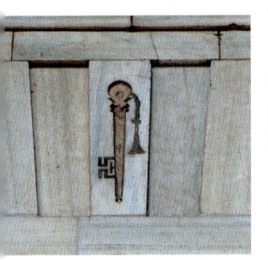

up many of these. Most have been rebuilt. Circular bastions can be seen attached to many towers. In Christian times, with the advent of artillery, these provided better resistance to cannonballs. The space on top of these bastions also allowed the defenders to mount their cannon. Towers, like the Torre del Agua on the eastern end, had specific functions. This tower was located adjacent to the aqueduct where the Acequia Real entered the Alhambra – and guarded this highly strategic feature. As we shall see later, there is an opportunity to visit some of the towers on the northern walls after one heads from the Partal area in an easterly direction towards the Generalife.

Puerta de la Justicia

As you pass the Carlos V fountain, take a sharp turn left. Here is the Puerta de la Justicia (Gate of Justice), a majestic entrance to the Alhambra, with the gate towering above the long approach ramp. The gate was built by decree of Yusuf I in 1348. In accordance with Islamic custom, it has a cranked entrance. On entering, one has to take a sharp turn right, and then take a left turn. This prevented attackers from charging directly inside. High on the towering façade, in the keystone of the external arch, there is a hand, symbolising the five pillars of Islam. Another symbol is a key above the interior entrance arch, which denotes faith.

A little further on to the east is the Puerta de los Carros, the current entrance for vehicles. This was a later insertion from 1526, part of the project to construct the Palacio de Carlos V. Take care if you enter here as there is quite a lot of traffic.

As you walk into the Alhambra complex, the Palacio de Carlos V comes into sight, with the Alcazaba fortifications to the west. Between the Alcazaba and the palace can be seen the Puerta del Vino. This gate

Left: the main entrance to Madinat Al-Hamra was via the Puerta del Vino. It is thought to date from the reign of Muhammad III (r. 1302-1309), although there were later improvements, as evidenced by the inscription on the stone plaque on the western side referring to Muhammad V.

Below: a key symbol above the arch on the western side of the Puerta del Vino.

was the main entrance to Madinat al-Hamra, the city built on the Sabika Hill adjacent to the Nasrid palaces. The gate was within the overall complex, so, unlike others, it was a straight (not cranked) gate, allowing through access. There was of course an alcove for guards, who controlled access (and lived above the gate). It is thought to date from the reign of Muhammad III (r. 1302-1309), although there were later renovations, as evidenced by the inscription on the stone plaque on the western side referring to Muhammad V. Here too above the arch is the key symbol, signifying faith.

Medina

Madinat al-Hamra was the city, adjacent to the palaces, which developed from the middle of the thirteenth century over the 250 years of Nasrid rule. Note that this was an entirely distinct entity from the city down below, Madinat Gharnata. Here, on the Sabika Hill, were

Right: a westward view down the Calle Real. The Palacio de Carlos V is on the right, with, just visible, the Puerta del Vino in the background.

all the essentials of everyday city life. Central to all was the mosque. Then among the streets and narrow alleyways there were markets, workshops, houses, as well as baths. The nobility, the servants and the administrators of the kingdom lived here in Madinat al-Hamra. Today, the area of the medina has a rather scattered look. Portions remain in private hands. There are hotels and shops. It also houses the administration of the Alhambra, the Patronato de la Alhambra y Generalife. In addition, within the walls is a plethora of archaeological remains, many with low foundations denoting the Nasrid buildings that once stood here. Work is ongoing and new discoveries are being made, which further unlock the history of Madinat al-Hamra.

The core of this is the Calle Real which runs from the Puerta del Vino in an easterly direction. The line of the street more or less follows the line of the Acequia Real. This water channel, which entered the complex from the eastern end, running in a westerly direction, was

Left: bronze lamp from the Alhambra mosque. It was made in the workshops of the Nasrid court and was donated to the mosque by Muhammad III (r. 1302-1309). The lamp has four graduated spheres, below which is a large pyramidal piece. It has an inscription on the the lip of the lower rim which includes: 'in the name of Allah, the Merciful, the Compassionate, bless our lord Muhammad and his people'. After the conquest this lamp was confiscated and taken to the palace of Cardinal Cisneros at Alcalá de Henares. © Museo Arqueológico Nacional. Photograph: Ángel Martínez Levas (N.I. 50519).

central to the layout of the city, as it provided the essential water supply to the entire complex.

Pass the Carlos V building on the left (with excavations of a Nasrid house across from its southern façade), and next is the church of Santa María de la Alhambra. The mosque of the Madinat al-Hamra (dating from the reign of Muhammad III, 1302-1309), was on this site. After 1492 the mosque was immediately converted into a church on the or-

Right: the baths, or hammam, of the mosque. Built at the same time as the adjacent mosque, the baths suffered partial destruction during the sixteenth century, but they have been reconstructed around those elements which remained. The rooms are illuminated by star-shaped windows in the ceiling.

ders of Fernando and Isabel. The present church was built after 1581, when the older building, in ruins, was demolished.

Next are the baths of the mosque. Baths, or the *hammam*, are a fundamental part of Islamic tradition, which includes ablution before praying. These were built at the same time as the mosque next door. This suffered some destruction during the sixteenth century, but has been reconstructed around those elements which remained. One can visit the baths today. Here are the cold and hot rooms, separated by horseshoe arches, and illuminated by star-shaped windows in the ceiling.

Left: the low walls denoting the location of the buildings of the Palacio de los Abencerrajes. The palace was probably built at the beginning of the fourteenth century and is thought to belong to the powerful family of the Abencerraje.

On the right is a block of shops and galleries and next on the Calle Real to the left is the Hotel America. The rooms of this nineteenth-century hotel are much in demand, this location being as close to the Alhambra palaces as one can stay.

On the right is the Palacio de los Abencerrajes. Now it is a maze of low walls which show the location of the many buildings within. An adjacent tower on the southern walls had been flattened by the demolitions by the French troops as they evacuated in 1812. It was to take until the 1930s for the rubble to be removed and excavations carried out, which revealed the remains of a large and important palace. The palace, probably built around the beginning of the fourteenth century, is thought to have belonged to the powerful Abencerraje family.

Continuing our journey, we reach the former Franciscan monastery, Convento de San Francisco (now a parador, part of a chain of Spanish luxury hotels, usually located in heritage sites) to the left. This monastery had been built over the site of a Nasrid palace, on the orders of the Catholic Monarchs. In addition to the hotel now providing a civilised and elegant location to have welcome refreshment, it is worth visiting the public rooms here. One can see elements of the fine Nasrid stucco decoration, which have been integrated into today's parador. The building, which had fallen into a ruinous state, was restored in the late 1920s. Inside, you can see the marble slab commemorating the temporary resting place of the Catholic Monarchs, before they were interred permanently in the purpose-built Capilla Real in the city below. Recent excavation work in the garden area has uncovered the remains of the palace baths.

The roadway past the parador continues through the area known as the Secano of the Upper Medina, interspersed with many trees

Right: a view through a door leading to a courtyard of the parador (previously the Convento de San Francisco). In the background can be seen the temporary resting place of the Catholic Monarchs, before they were interred permanently in the purpose-built Capilla Real in the city down below.

Right: stucco decoration in the parador. This is a vestige of the original Nasrid palace, over which the Convento was built soon after the conquest.

Left: the aqueduct over the Cuesta del Rey Chico. This carried the water for the Acequia Real, which supplied the water for the Alhambra complex. Behind is the Torre del Agua. The tower, which had guarded this essential part of the Alhambra's infrastructure, was in ruins after the French destruction of 1812 and has been reconstructed.

and gardens established during the 1930s. Between the roadway and the parador buildings are low walls, the remains of a network of houses and workshops, punctuated by narrow streets. The tannery, the remains of which can be seen adjacent to the eastern end of the parador, was located near the Acequia Real, as it needed large volumes of water. All of this workshop area would have provided the luxury goods necessary for the Nasrid court. Further on are remains of Nasrid houses. This whole quarter again suffered in 1812 as the French troops retreated – it was destroyed. It was only in the middle of the twentieth century that the area began to be restored.

Towards the end of the walkway of the upper Medina, is the Torre del Agua (Water Tower) on the easternmost section of the walls. At the side of this can be seen the red-brick channel of the Acequia Real, which supplied the water for the Alhambra complex. The tower, which had guarded this essential part of the Alhambra's infrastructure, was destroyed by the French in 1812 and has been reconstructed. Continue along the path where one can cross the bridge (constructed in the 1970s) over the Cuesta del Rey Chico. From this modern bridge, look south and you can see the aqueduct, still intact, which carried the

Above: the might of the large and powerful Holy Roman Empire is manifest in the Palacio de Carlos V.

Below: the Battle of Pavia is depicted on the façade of the Palacio. This battle, fought in 1525, was a decisive victory for the Spanish and Imperial armies of Carlos V over his French enemy.

Acequia Real across the divide to the Alhambra complex, by the side of the Torre del Agua. Once across the bridge, it is decision time: turn left for the Generalife or turn right for the exit by the ticket office.

Palacio de Carlos V

Entering the Alhambra via the Puerta de Justicia, one sees immediately the imposing palace Palacio de Carlos V. As one approaches the entrance to the Nasrid palaces, it certainly makes a statement. This is different in every conceivable way from the grandeur and delicacy of the Nasrid architecture that is all around. Metaphors abound: the delicate architecture of a small Islamic kingdom in the southern Peninsula meets the brawn, the power of the unimaginably large, extensive and powerful Holy Roman Empire.

The story of the palace starts in 1517 with the arrival in Spain of a young man from Flanders. He was the new ruler of Castile and Aragón (and later in 1519, he became Carlos V of the Holy Roman Empire). Initially he could not speak Spanish and brought his Flemish courtiers with him. In 1526, following his dynastic marriage to Isabel of Portugal in Seville, he arrived in Granada. Carlos lodged in the Alhambra, where he made alterations, creating royal apartments. Seeing this as a suitable location for a grand palace, which would reflect the grandeur of his Holy Roman Empire, he ordered the construction of his palace here. Renaissance architecture had spread from Italy

Above: within the square exterior is a circular courtyard, with an imposing façade made up of two galleries, supported by 32 columns. The stone used for these is a reddish conglomerate from Loja.

Left: the main entrance, at the centre of the western façade of the Palacio.

Right: a stone relief on the western façade. This allegorical scene symbolises peace. Victories in the centre each hold a laurel branch and the imperial emblem, the Pillars of Hercules. At the base, angels set fire to piles of armaments. Carlos V seemingly desired universal peace, albeit under his rule.

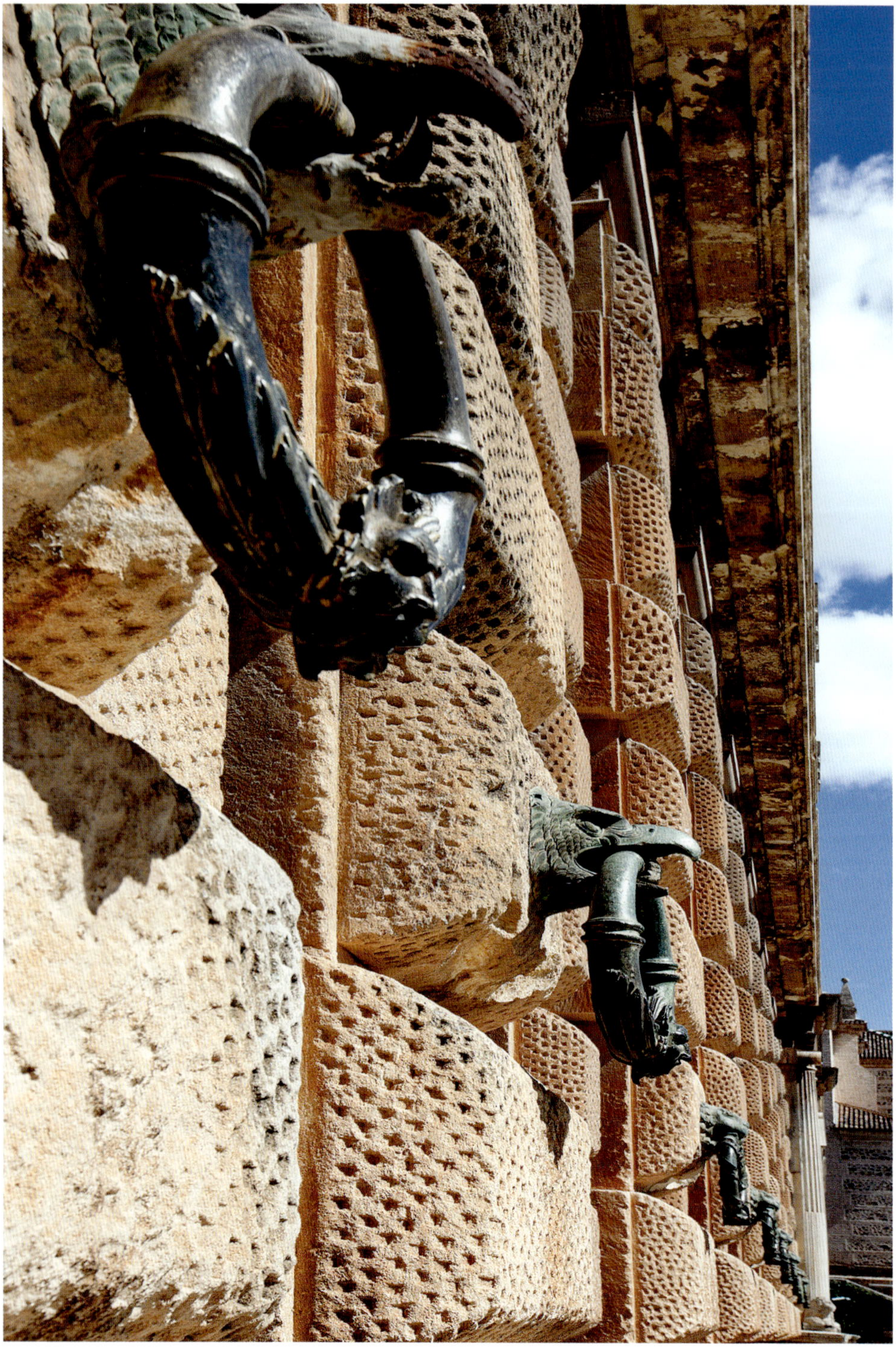

Right: a curving staircase leads to the upper gallery of the Palacio.

Left: in the Italian style, there is rustication of the stone in the lower section of the façade. Fixed to this are bronze eagles' heads, each of which holds a large ring, decorated with a lion's head.

over the previous century. For Carlos, this embodied the classical antiquity of Roman times, perfectly in line with his perception of the Holy Roman Empire. And so the design of his new palace was in that style, developed by the Spanish painter, sculptor and architect, Pedro Machuca, who had studied in Italy under Michelangelo. The building was funded by a portion of a tax levied on the unfortunate Moriscos. This square building (63 metres long on each side) was commenced in 1527. Within the square exterior is a circular courtyard, with an imposing façade made up of two galleries, supported by 32 columns. It was originally intended by Machuca to be a commanding portico to the Nasrid palaces, but that is not how it came to pass. Work proceeded intermittently for nearly a century and was stopped with the roof still unfinished (the roof was only completed in the twentieth centu-

Above: map of the Alcazaba.

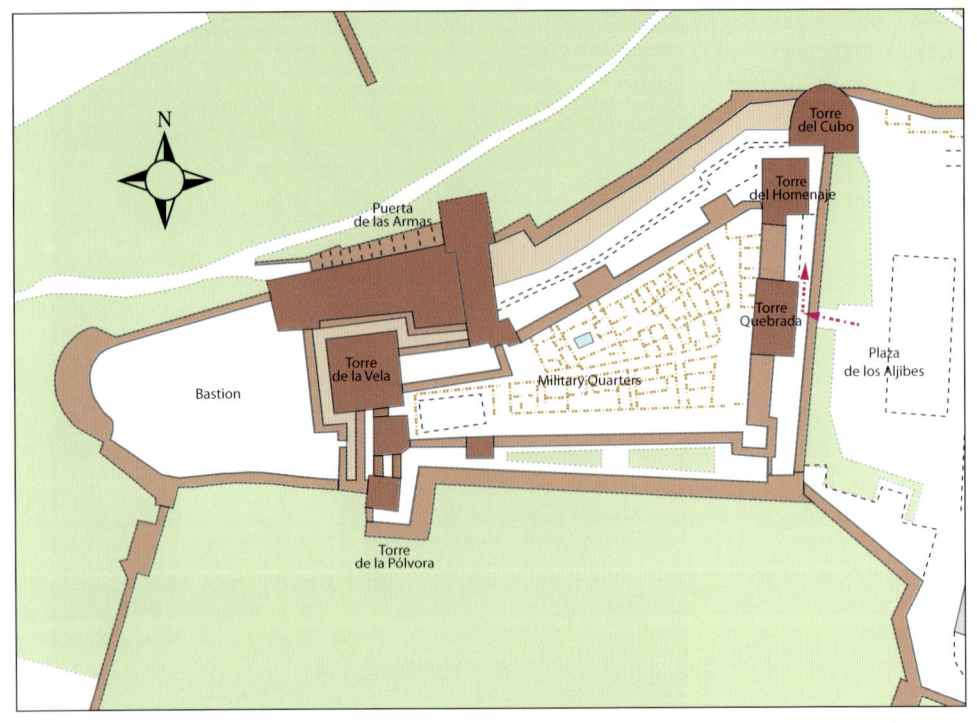

ry). The writer Robert Irwin has perhaps the wisest words to conclude on the palacio: *'There is a long literary tradition disparaging Charles V's palace. In fact it is a fine, imposing building, but on the wrong site.'*

Alcazaba

The Alcazaba (citadel) is a separate block within the Alhambra complex, to the west of the Palacio de Carlos V. It is entered by the gate at the base of the Torre Quebrada, from the open area in front, the Plaza de los Aljibes. This was the first Nasrid structure to be built on the Alhambra site. Muhammad I ordered the erection of a new fortification here, where a Zirid stronghold had previously existed. It was a perfect defensive location, on the western end of the plateau on the Sabika Hill, overlooking the deep valley of the river Darro to the north, and to the south, the valley between it and the Mauror Hill. Towers were added on existing foundations, altered as necessary. The walls were reconstructed. The Alcazaba was a military city, distinctly separate from what was to become the rest of the Alhambra palace-city. Within the triangular walls were quarters for the Amir's elite guard. Nowadays, the centre of the Alcazaba is an open-air space. The archaeologists have been at work and laid out the low walls indicating where the various buildings of the military encampment were. You can see the foundations of the various elements: living quarters, baths, and

Right: a view of the walls and towers of the Alcazaba, from the Plaza de los Aljibes. The entrance door can be seen at the foot of the central tower, the Torre Quebrada.

a bakery. Other elements for the garrison are here: dungeons; storerooms for provisions and weapons. An aljibe (cistern) was the destination of the Acequia Real (royal waterway), the water channel that Muhammad I ordered to be built to bring the clear waters of the river Darro, intercepted at a dam around six kilometres upstream. Dotted around the Alcazaba are various towers of some solidity, including: the Torre del Homenaje (to the north); Torre de la Vela (overlooking the present-day city, where the Catholic Monarchs' flag was raised in January 1492) and the Torre de la Pólvora (Gunpowder Tower), to the south. When the Christians took over the Alhambra, the walls were strengthened. This was a defence against the new technology of the time – heavy massed artillery, now the game changer in siege warfare. In turn artillery platforms were built to allow the defending cannons to be positioned. The Torre del Cubo, built during the Christian era, at the base of the Torre del Homenaje, provided both defence against bombardment as well as being a platform for artillery. The Puerta de las Armas (at the Torre de las Armas, with its large projecting platform

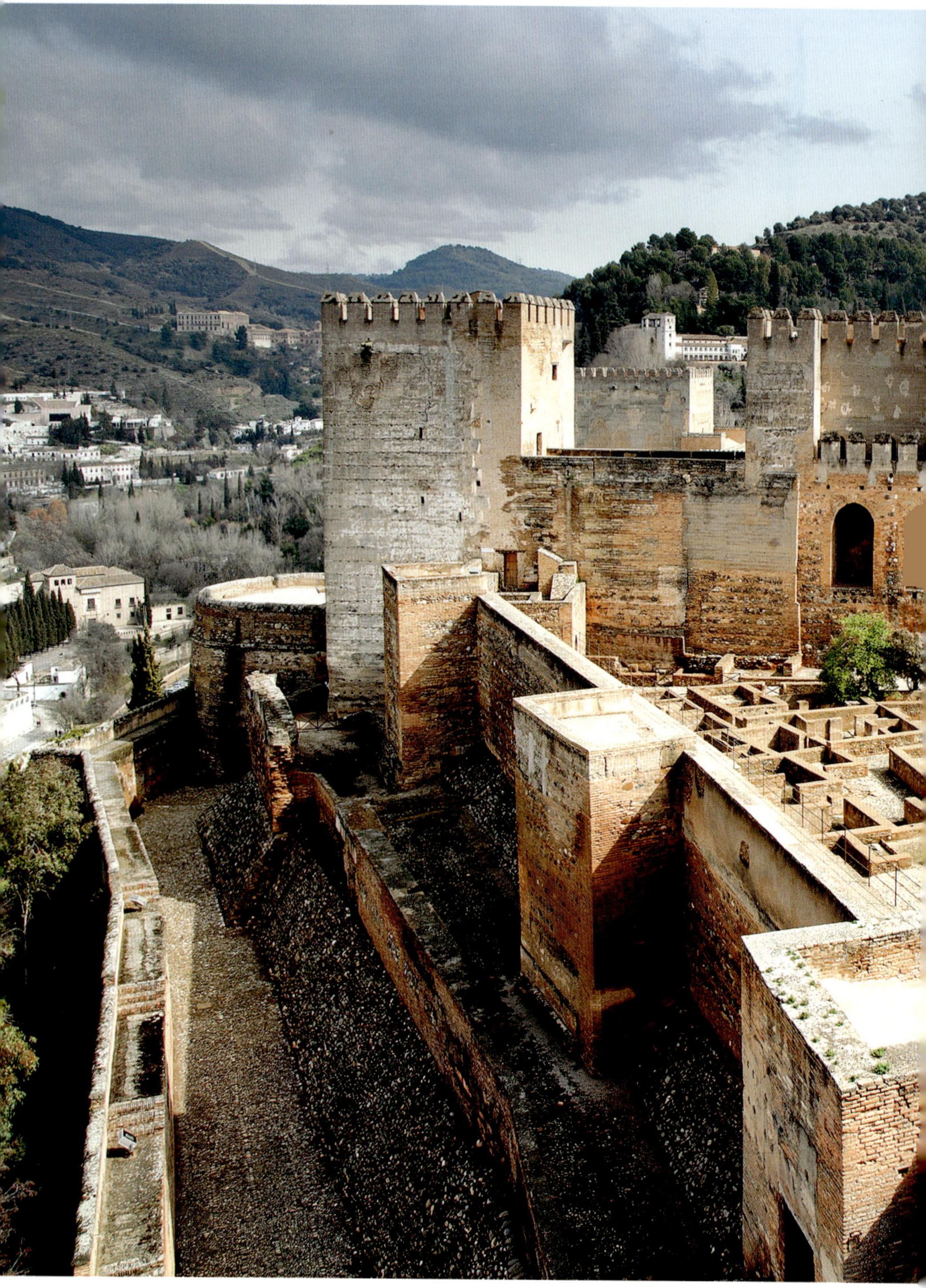

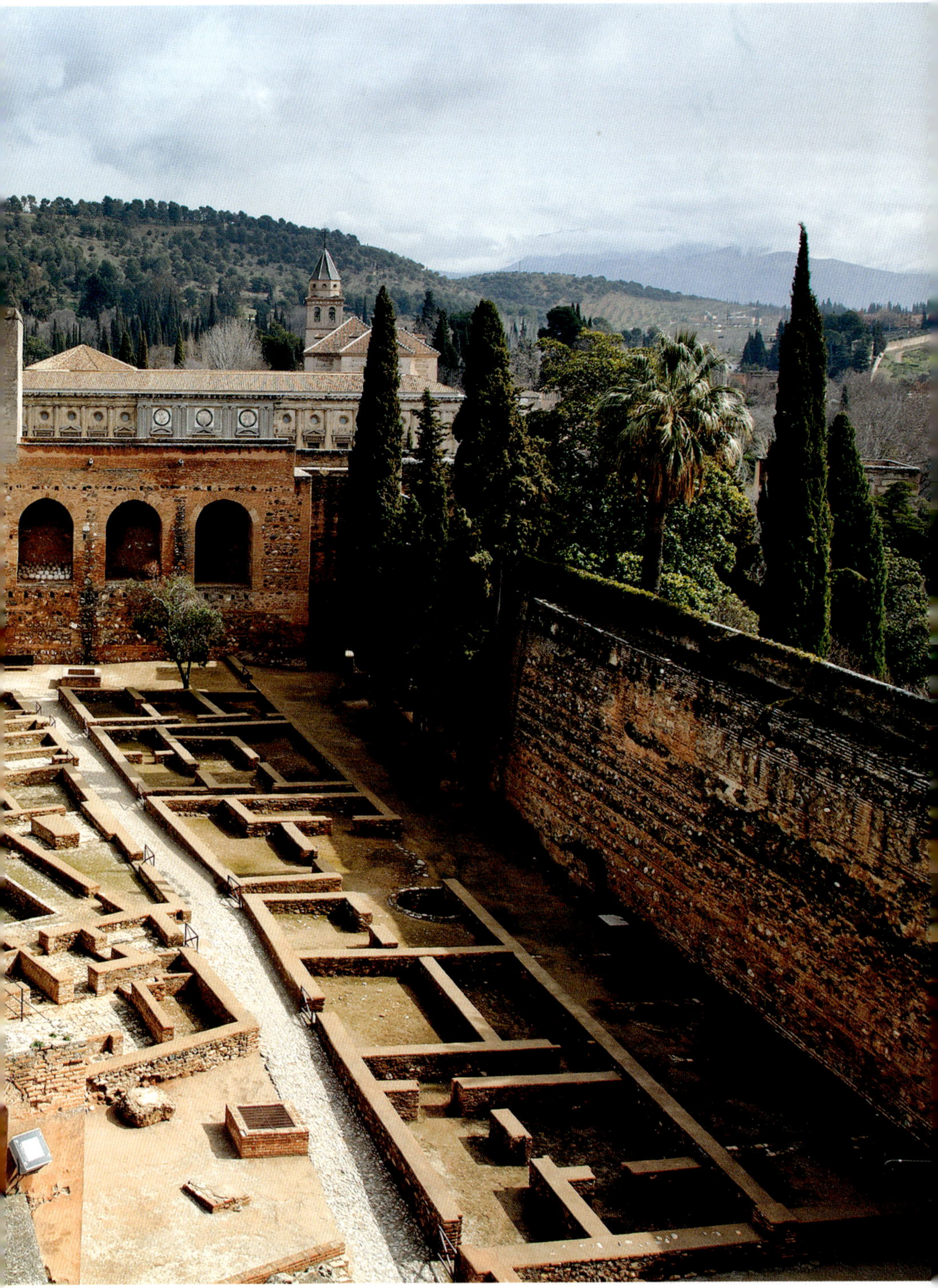

Previous page: the Alcazaba was a military city. Within the triangular walls were quarters for the Amir's elite guard. The low walls seen here indicate the layout of the various buildings of the military encampment.

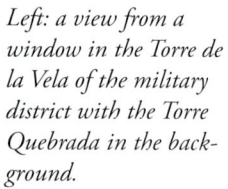

Left: a view from a window in the Torre de la Vela of the military district with the Torre Quebrada in the background.

Left: the Torre de la Pólvora (Gunpowder Tower). The defensive wall begins here and runs down the valley to connect with the Torres Bermejas on Mauror Hill (these towers are seen on the right, in the background).

Right: the Torre de la Vela. This tower was one of the original fortifications built by Muhammad I. It has a commanding view of the city below. In January 1492, the standard of the victorious Catholic Monarchs was raised here.

Right: a view eastwards along the northern walls of the Alcazaba. There are three walls. From left: the general perimeter wall; a middle wall and the high defensive wall interspersed with projecting towers. In the background is the Torre del Homenaje, with the Torre del Cubo projecting at its base. The latter was built during the Christian era. Its circular shape was designed to provide better resistance to artillery fire.

161

Left: map of the Mexuar area.

providing excellent views over the Albaicín) was one of the original gates of the Alhambra, providing direct access to and from the city below.

The Nasrid Palaces

Here is a series of palaces, each associated with the individual amirs who built them during the centuries of the Nasrid dynasty. Three distinct palaces are connected but independent of each other. These are: the Mexuar; the Palacio de Comares and the Palacio de los Leones. Further on, set apart from these, is the Palacio de Partal. Nasrid palaces consisted of a set of buildings grouped around a courtyard. They alternate between what were originally areas where subjects and

Left: the Patio de la Mezquita and, somewhat obscured by trees, the Patio de Machuca. The patio within has a pool with many indentations at each end.

Above: the Sala de Mexuar, the main hall of the palace. It was originally constructed by Isma'il I (r. 1314-1325) and modified by his great-grandson Muhammad V. This room has had many modifications, during both the Muslim and Christian eras. The Amir's throne was located here at one stage. The high wooden railing dates from the room's later use as a Christian chapel when it was used for a choir.

functionaries could meet the rulers and private areas for the family of the Amir. All these palaces had different axes and were separate.

Mexuar

The Mexuar is the oldest among the set of Nasrid palaces that have been conserved and are now on display. This location is now the official entry point to access the Nasrid palaces. Before one enters, two courtyards can be seen to the left. In the first, Patio de la Mezquita, one can see the foundations of what were administration buildings, which opened onto a courtyard. The second courtyard, the Patio de Machuca, is adjacent to the Torre de Machuca. These were called after Pedro Machuca, the architect of the Palacio de Carlos V, who lived here. Much modified during Machuca's time, the patio has an atypically shaped pool (with many indentations at each end) in its centre and is surrounded by trees. As one enters the Mexuar proper, one can see to the right an entrance from the Palacio de Carlos V which gave access to the Nasrid palaces.

Left: polychromatic stucco decoration above a column in the Sala de Mexuar

Right: the small courtyard of the Cuarto Dorado (Golden Chamber). It has a fountain with a central basin (a replica) in fluted marble. The façade of the Palacio de Comares can be seen in the background.

Below: the decoration of the walls in the Sala de Mexuar is a mélange: it ranges from the original Nasrid stucco to, as seen here, tiles inserted with the personal motto 'plus ultra' of Carlos V and his symbol of the Pillar of Hercules.

Go down a corridor and enter the Sala de Mexuar, the main hall of the palace. It was originally constructed by Isma'il I (r. 1314-1325) and modified by his great-grandson Muhammad V. This room has had many modifications, during both the Muslim and Christian eras. The Amir's throne was located here at one stage. There is a high wooden railing, which dates from the room's later evolution to a Christian chapel when it was used for the choir stall. The decoration is a mélange: it ranges from the original Nasrid stucco to the new tiles inserted with the imperial coat of arms (motto: *plus ultra*) as well as those of the Christian Governors who used the upper level of the Mexuar building as a residence.

Next proceed through a narrow entrance into the small courtyard of the Cuarto Dorado (or Golden Chamber). Again, this section has been much remodelled. Three arches frame the portico, facing the exquisite central basin (a replica) of a fountain in fluted marble. The coffered ceiling of the portico was originally Nasrid, but was painted over with gold decorative motifs after the Christian conquest. During the fourteenth century, the rulers received their subjects here. (The narrow doorway was a means for the guards to control access).

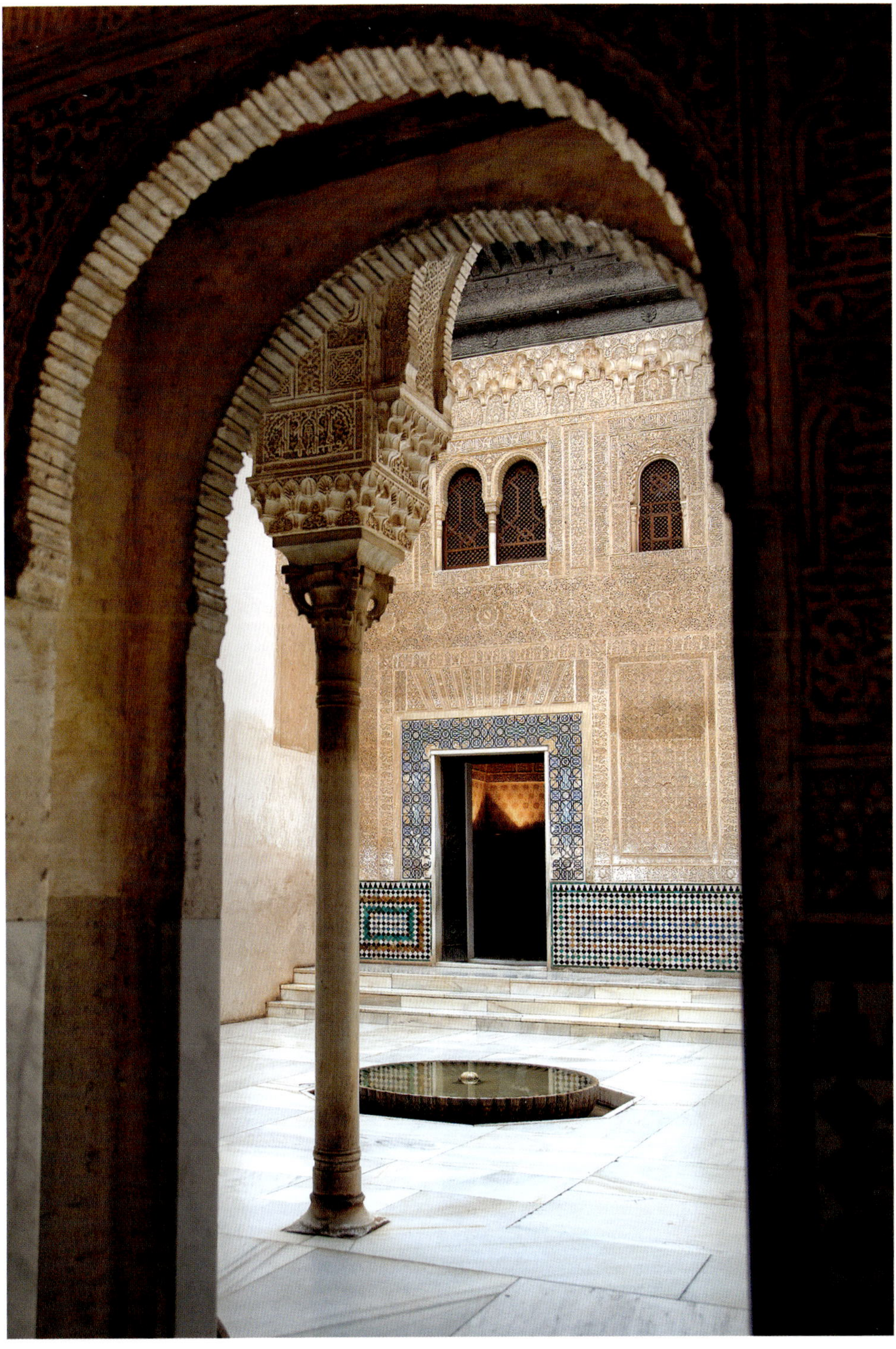

Left: map of the Palacio de Comares.

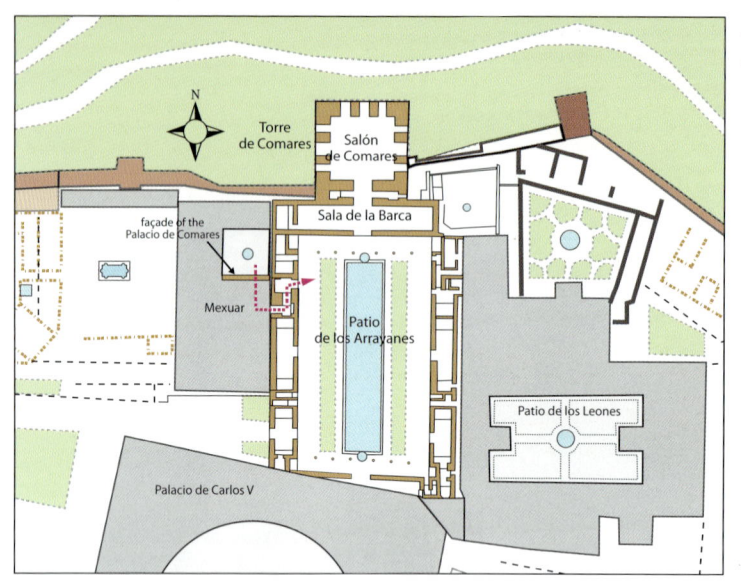

Palacio de Comares

Now turn around in the courtyard of the Cuarto Dorado and observe the façade of the Palacio de Comares. The façade marks the separation between the public and private spaces, and leads to the adjacent Palacio de Comares. This palace was commissioned by Yusuf I. The exquisite stucco-work and azulejo tiles were installed by Yusuf's son Muhammad V to commemorate a famous success – in 1369 he took the port of Algeciras, regaining once again control of the Strait of Gibraltar.

Beyond the façade one steps into what was a private area. The passageway has a double bend, again the basic Islamic security feature of the times, allowing guards to intercept any intruders. After a labyrinthine passage, one enters into daylight at the side of the wide and well-proportioned expanse of the Patio de los Arrayanes (myrtles). This is a classic layout of Islamic architecture where water is the central feature – the exquisite buildings are reflected in the waters of the pool. The rectangular pool is flanked by a line of myrtle bushes. It is a characteristic plant of Nasrid Alhambra – the Spanish name, *arrayán* comes from the Arabic *al-rayhan*, meaning aromatic. The oil of the myrtle gives off a pleasant fragrance when one rubs the leaves. In their original form, these myrtle beds were sunk so that the plants did not interfere with the views of the carefully-planned proportions. In front of the porticos at either end are fountains set in circular basins that supply the water via a channel to the central rectangular pool. The levels are aligned so that the water 'pauses' before entering the pool, ensuring that there are no ripples to disturb this experience of sublime serenity. One of these fountains is in the northern portico in front of

Right: the ceiling at the entrance to the Palacio de Comares. This wooden latticework is typical of the Islamic geometric style and has gilding and motifs which date from the end of the fifteenth century when the Catholic Monarchs came to reside in the Alhambra.

Right: decoration of a wall in the Palacio de Comares. The decorated stucco features a dado of epigraphic verses, with, in the centre, a small shield inscribed with the Nasrid motto ('the only conqueror is God'). It is crowned by a 'tree of life', a common symbol in Islamic art and architecture. Below the dado are azulejo tiles, with a wonderful geometric design made up of small multi-coloured ceramic pieces.

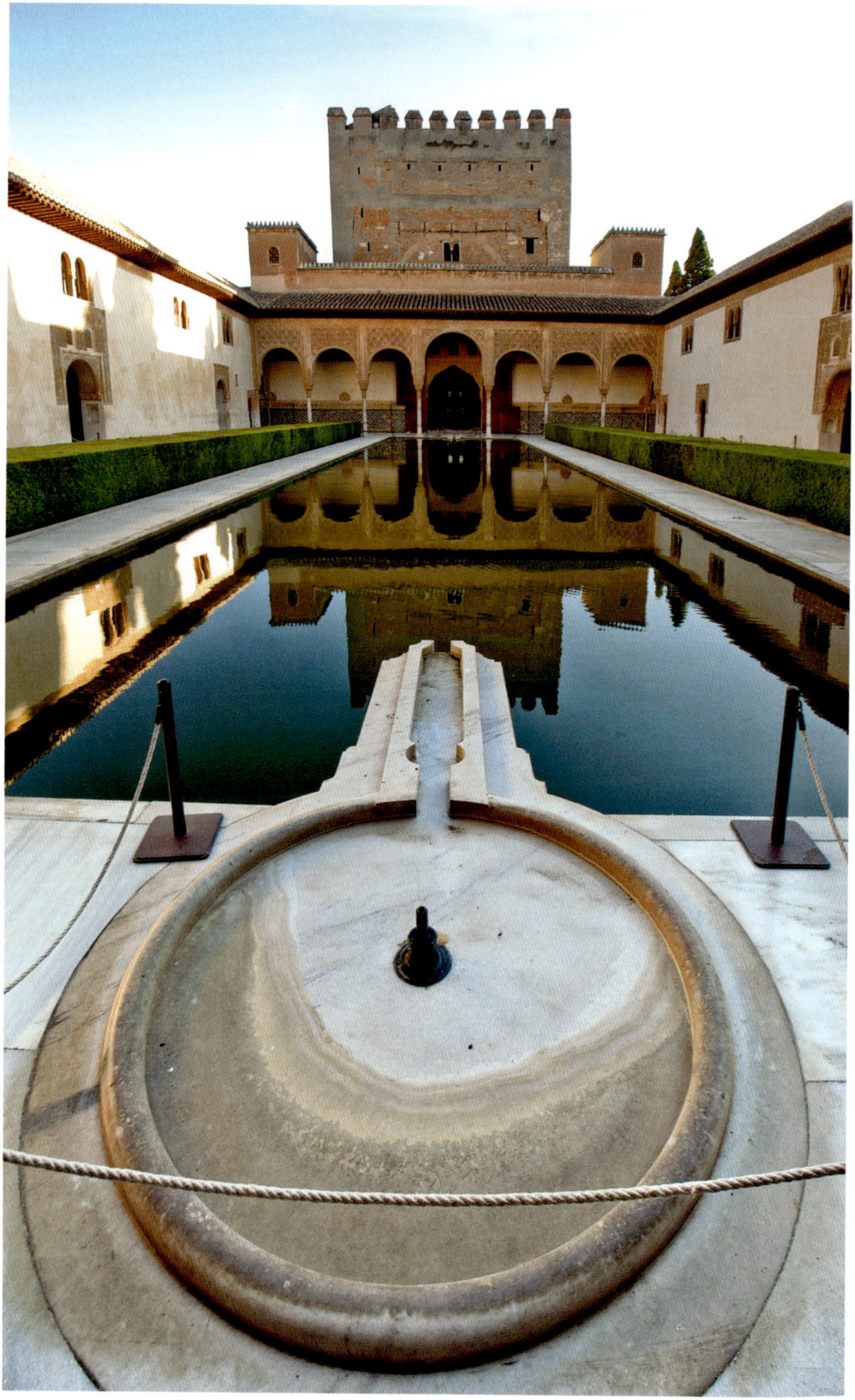

Left: with the Torre de Comares in the background, the wide and well-proportioned expanse of the Patio de los Arrayanes (Patio of the Myrtles). In their original form, the myrtle beds were sunk so that the plants did not interfere with the views of the pool's carefully-planned proportions. This is a classic layout of Islamic architecture where water is the central feature — the exquisite buildings are reflected in the waters of the pool.

Right: polychrome decoration with Kufic inscription in the Palacio de Comares.

Right: framed by the entrance arch of the Salón del Trono and the columns of the portico, looking south to the Patio de los Arrayanes.

the Sala de la Barca (the antechamber to the Salón del Trono). One of the inscribed texts refers to this inner space of thrones as a tent for the Amir, with an outer canopy unfolded. The name 'barca' comes from the Arabic: *al-baraka*, the blessing, a motif that appears frequently in the inscriptions on the walls. The threshold walls contain highly embellished niches, which held decorated vases.

Encompassed within the Torre de Comares, the Salón del Trono (also known as the Hall of the Ambassadors) is a cubic-shaped structure which accomplishes what it was intended for – to convey a feeling of the majesty of the Amir, by virtue of the palatial architecture. With its soaring majestic ceiling, one can feel that there is an intersection between earthly and supernatural power. Epigraphic decorations all around emphasise this, with quotations from the Koran. Here one can

Above: the Salón del Trono (also known as the Hall of the Ambassadors). It has a soaring ceiling and superbly decorated walls and imparts a feeling of the majesty of the Amir. With three windowed alcoves, this was a throne room and an audience chamber.

appreciate the glory of Nasrid power. The ornamentation is sublime: 8,017 different timber interlinked sections make up the polychromatic ceiling; the stucco decoration on the walls and the azulejo tiles that line the lower walls. This was a throne room and an audience chamber. There are three windowed alcoves, which look out over the river Darro and the Albaicín to the north. The windows originally had stained glass, which was destroyed in a 1590 explosion of gunpowder stored in the room. The Amir sat on his throne in the central alcove. To his front he could meet his subjects – or he could look backwards and view his domain. This indeed was the very epicentre of the Kingdom of Granada.

There are several explanations of the name 'Comares'. One is that the second element comes from the Arabic word *'arsh*: which can mean either 'tent' or 'throne'. Another is that it was named after the Gomares Berbers from the Gomara Mountains in North Africa. The throne room was originated by Yusuf I, but he never saw it completed as he was assassinated in 1354. It was finished by his son Muhammad V. The stucco decoration was one of the final parts of construction – Muhammad V's name is recorded in the plasterwork.

The southern pavilion of the Palacio de Comares is a mirror image of the northern pavilion, the Sala de la Barca, across the Patio de los Arrayanes. Most of this southern pavilion was torn down to make way for the imposition of the Palacio de Carlos V in the early 1600s. The three-story façade was maintained to provide what is in effect a theatrical backdrop, which still preserves the original appearance of the pavilion facing the patio. However, the full-on view of the façade is marred by the Carlos V Palacio roof, looming above. It is worthwhile to pause at this southern façade. Turn around, look northwards and appreciate the view as it was intended in Nasrid times: the careful proportion of the patio with the reflection of the Torre de Comares in the pool.

Each of the Alhambra palaces had a *hammam* or baths. There is indeed one for the Palacio de Comares. It is located between it and the Palacio de los Leones, although the baths are not open to the public at present. It is a shame that they cannot be seen – they are wonderfully decorated inside. Quite apart from personal hygiene, baths have a religious function in Islamic society. They allow a Muslim to be in a state of ritual purity in order to perform prayer. This baths complex was illuminated by polygonal skylights. It had warm and cold rooms, a changing room and a furnace. After the conquest they were referred as the 'Royal Baths'. Carlos V, when he stayed here in the 1520s, used the hammam, but had an immersion bath, in the Western style, placed in the hot room. He also had his imperial motto, *plus ultra* (by now, seeming to be very ubiquitous in the Alhambra!) included among the azulejos on the wall.

Below: a niche in the threshold at the entrance to the Salón del Trono. It is framed by stucco with inscribed metaphorical verses offering hospitality. Flower vases (alternatively jars of perfume or water) were placed here.

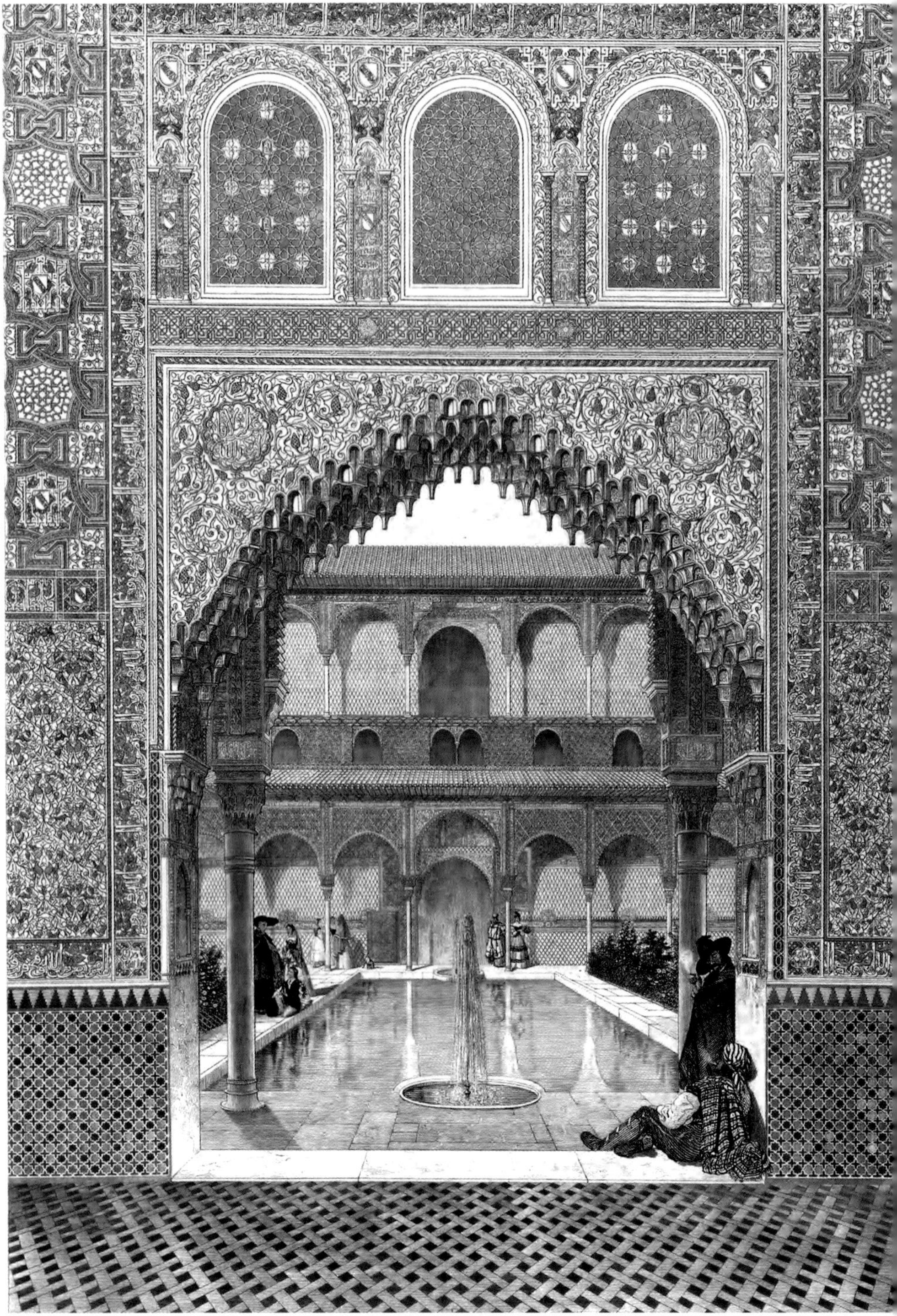

Left: an early nineteenth century view of the Patio de los Arrayanes, from the book by Owen Jones 'Plans, Elevations, Sections and Details of the Alhambra.'

Right: James Cavanagh Murphy's engraving 'The Hall of the Baths'.

Right: polychromatic decoration in the baths, or hammam, of the Palacio de Comares.

173

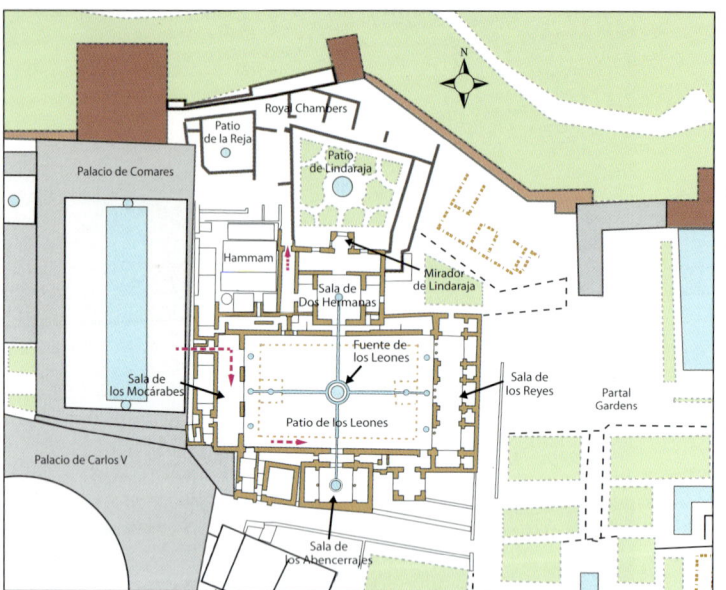

Right: the Patio de los Leones, with, in the centre, the fabled lions of the Fuente de los Leones. The courtyard has a porticoed gallery around its perimeter. The gallery is made up of rich arcades of carved stucco resting on a forest of slender marble columns. It was commissioned by Muhammad V and enlarged during his second reign (1362-1391).

Left: map of the Patio de los Leones.

Palacio de los Leones

This palace (of the lions) was commissioned by Muhammad V (who reigned intermittently over the period 1354-1391). Possibly the greatest amir of the Nasrid Dynasty, he ruled wisely and was responsible for many magnificent buildings. Muhammad had several reigns. He was deposed but returned to power: the Leones complex was enlarged during his second tenure (1362-1391). Currently one accesses the palace directly from the Palacio de Comares via the Patio de los Arrayanes. The palaces were joined together as part of the alterations made under the Catholic Monarchs, who were engaged in creating their 'Royal Palace'. However, in their original form these palaces comprised two distinctly separate sets of buildings. The Palacio de los Leones was reached by entering from a royal street. The palace complex consists of two terraces at different levels, enclosing a rectangular courtyard, in the centre of which is that most emblematic symbol of the Alhambra, the Fuente de los Leones or Fountain of the Lions. It is thought that the palace was essentially residential. One possibility is that the affairs of state and public events were then conducted in the adjacent Palacio de Comares. In the main halls on each side of the Palacio de los Leones, the leisure activities, festivities, feasting, poetry readings and musical events of the Amir and his family took place.

Currently one enters through a door on the western side, from the adjacent Palacio de Comares. The route allows one to circumnavigate the patio, and visit each of the various rooms off it. If you are lucky enough to see the courtyard early in the day with fewer tourists, pause and enjoy the spectacle. This is one of the most magnificent buildings

Following page spread: the most emblematic symbol of the Alhambra, the Fuente de los Leones. Here a basin (made from a single block of marble) sits, apparently supported by 12 stylised lions. These are outward-facing with spouts in their mouths. All of the lions, like the basin, are carved from white Macael marble. A carved band of calligraphy runs around the edge of the basin, with verses by the vizier Ibn Zamrak in praise of Muhammad V, who commissioned the fountain. It includes: 'for are there not in this garden marvels that God has made unrivalled in their loveliness…'

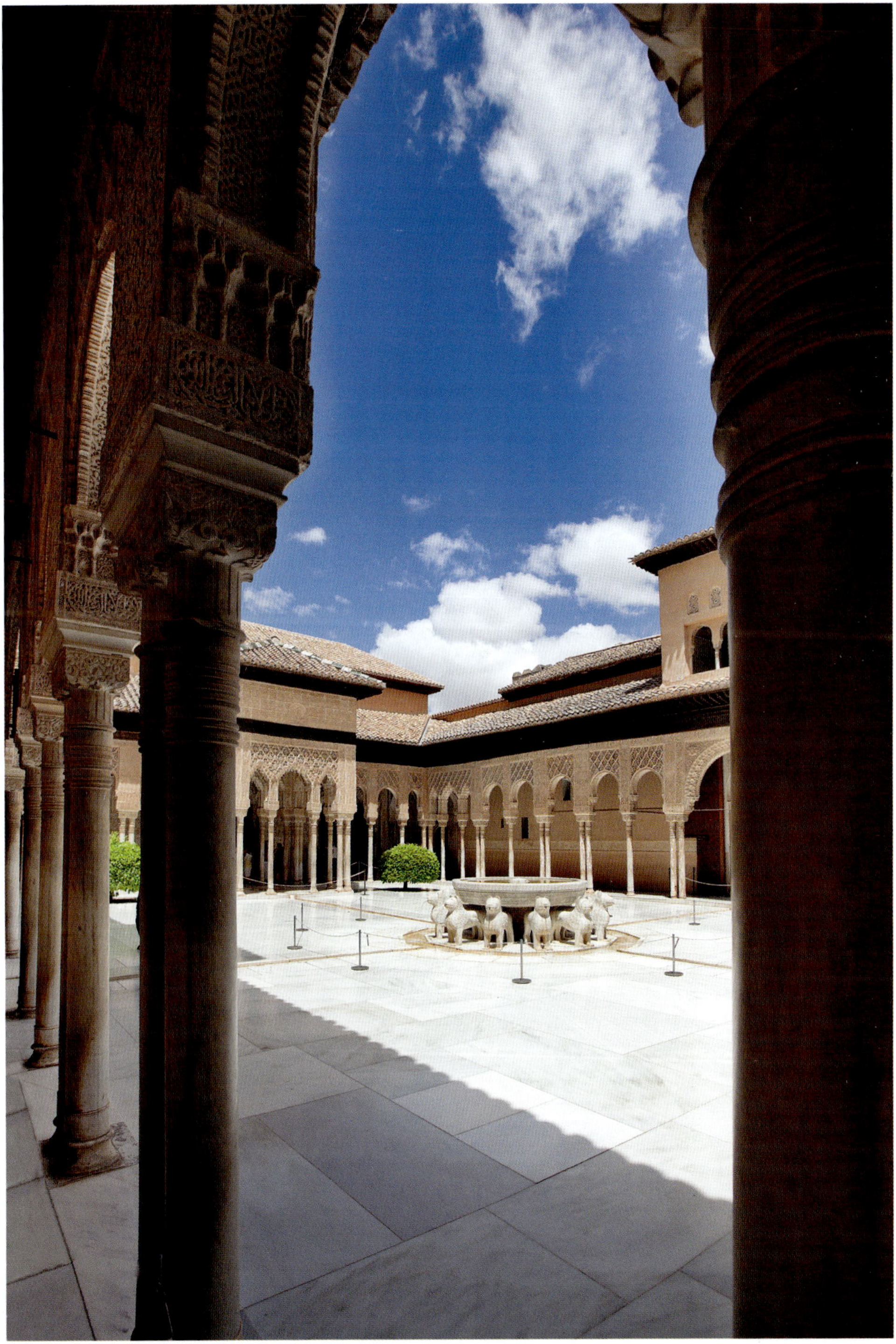

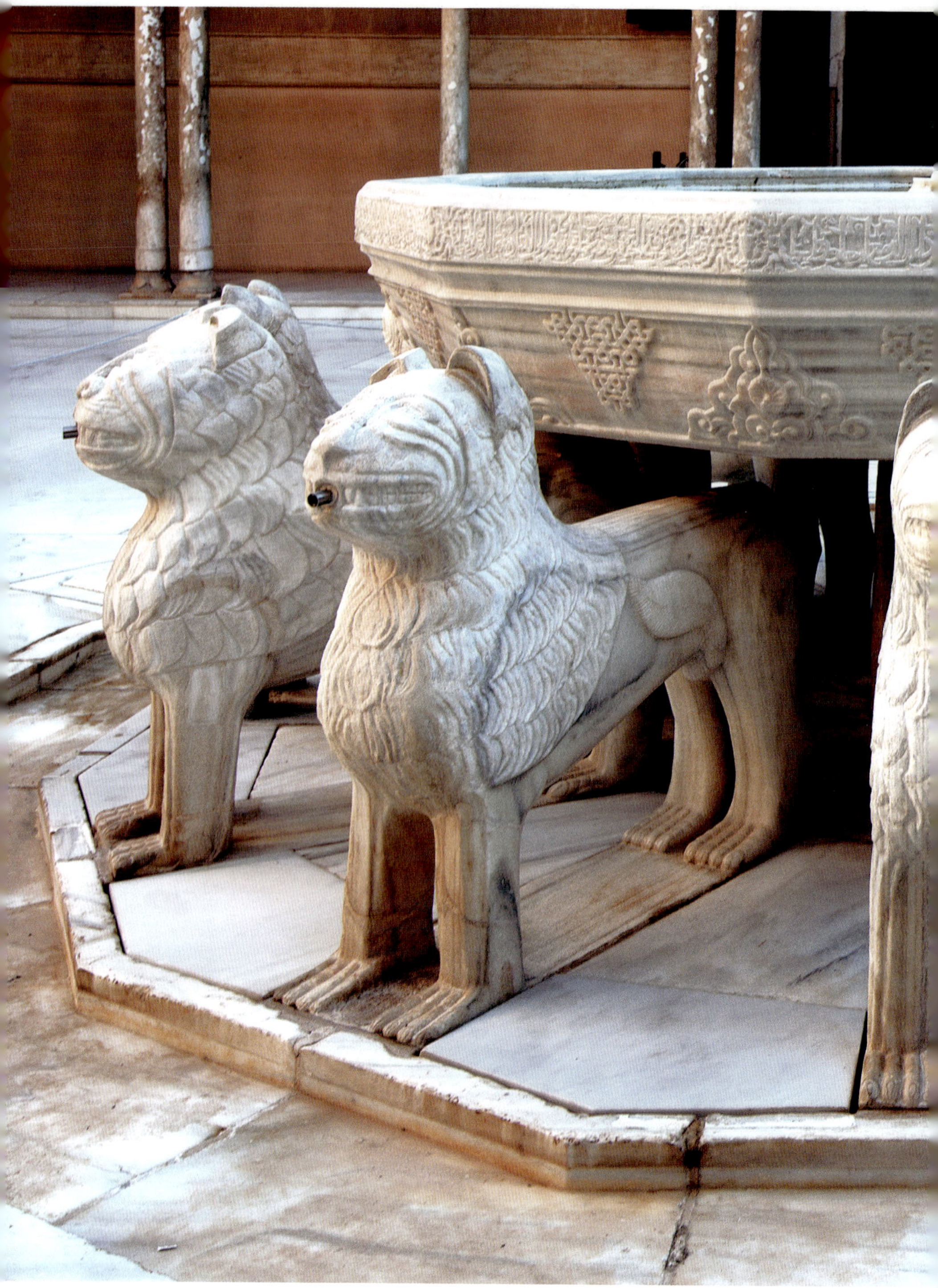

177

Left: a mesmerising sight. The lions, in the centre of the patio, framed by the delicate stucco decoration and arches of the portico.

Below: a reminder from the decorated wall of the Palacio de los Leones that alterations and renovations have been made here over the centuries. Set in stucco amidst inscriptions in Arabic is the symbol of Carlos V, with his motto of 'plus ultra'.

in the world. Surrounded by delicate stucco decoration and arches of the portico, it has a mesmerising effect. If architecture is frozen poetry, this is the poetry of the spheres.

The courtyard has a porticoed gallery around its entire perimeter. These are made up of rich arcades of carved stucco resting on slender marble columns. The columns, either singly or in pairs, are ringed with a variety of stylised carved capitals. White marble, used for both the columns and the lion statues in the centre of the patio, was quarried in the Macael area of Almería. On each of the narrower sides, there is a square porticoed pavilion, with a decorated domed ceiling. At the midpoint of each side of the courtyard, a circular fountain is embedded in the pavement, where water gently flows in a channel to the focal point of the courtyard, the Fuente de los Leones. Here a basin (carved from a single block of marble) sits, apparently supported by 12 stylised lions. The practice of using animal forms in fountains was common in the previous era, that of the Umayyads in al-Andalus. Here the sculptors cleverly used the natural veins in the marble to

Above: the coffered wooden ceiling of one of the two square pavilions in the patio.

emphasise the fur and other delicate features of each lion. A poem, written by the vizier and poet Ibn Zamrak, is inscribed on the outside edge of the basin. It includes the following verses, eulogising the fountain, the lions and the Amir (of course employing the flattery of elevating him to the next rank, that of Caliph):

'Blessed be the One who granted Imam Muhammad the wonderful ideas for ornamenting his mansions,
For are there not in this garden marvels that God has made unrivalled in their loveliness…
Water and marble seem to be one in manifestation, and we do not know which of the two is flowing,
Do you not see how the water spills into the bowl, but the secret spouts conceal it immediately?
Is it not, in fact, like a white cloud that pours its surging water onto the lions,
And looks like the hand of the Caliph, who in the first light of dawn bestows his favours on the lions of war?'

Walk counter-clockwise around the patio, and you encounter four major halls. The first is Sala de los Mocárabes (Hall of the Stalactite Ceiling), located on the western side. Most likely this was part of a living quarters. The roof here was destroyed in the explosion of a neighbouring powder magazine in 1590. There are still remnants of the original 'stalactite' ceiling, but most of the ceiling is a plain plaster vault dating from the early eighteenth century.

The Sala de los Abencerrajes is located next, on the south side of the patio. This square hall has an exceptional ceiling: it consists of an eight-pointed star-shaped mocárabe design (made up of prisms, with lower concave pieces). It is a symphony in three-dimensionalism. In the centre of the hall is a fountain, with red staining within its marble. In the early nineteenth century, Washington Irving disseminated the tale (which resonates still, much loved by tour guides) that the family of courtiers and intriguers, the Abencerrajes or Banu Serraj were slaughtered here – this was their blood. Thus the hall gained its name from the family. Alas the truth is more prosaic: the red staining arises from the ferruginous content of the stone.

The Sala de los Reyes (Hall of the Kings) is on the east side of the patio. There are a series of rooms on its eastern side, adjacent to a rectangular hall. This, the main hall, has three mocárabe ceilings.

Above: poetry in three dimensions – the ceiling in the Sala de los Abencerrajes. The mocárabe dome has the shape of an eight-pointed star.

Right: James Cavanagh Murphy's engraving of the Sala de los Abencerrajes, from his book of 1816. Reflecting the difficulty of making a drawing from later memory, his engraving is a little out of scale and the flat detailing does not capture the fine delicacy of the mocárabe dome.

Right: the fountain in the Sala de los Abencerrajes. The staining is alas, not the blood of the slain Abencerrajes as the romantic legend has it – rather it is merely due to ferruginous veins in the marble.

181

Restoration is currently being undertaken on the vaulted wooden-framed ceilings, damaged due to lack of ventilation in the surrounding upper level. The three vaults are painted with a rich and detailed series of court scenes. The vaults were created with timber spars shaped like those of an upturned boat. Pine planks were nailed on the inside of these spars, using timber pins. Leather was stretched on the concave shape of the planks. Paint was applied using the tempera method and then a coat of varnish. These paintings offer an opportunity to visualise the life of the rulers of the Alhambra. The ceiling of the middle hall depicts a static scene: what could be a group, possibly the Amir and his viziers, seated at a gathering or council. They are dressed in Nasrid clothing. Each carries his *jineta* sword, implying that they were persons of high station. The other two ceilings show more animated

Above: ceiling in the Sala de los Reyes. A group is depicted, possibly the Amir and viziers, seated at a gathering. Dressed in Nasrid clothing, each person carries a jineta sword, conveying his importance. © Archivo y Biblioteca del Patronato de la Alhambra y Generalife.

tableaux: a variety of scenes, courts, romances and combat between Muslims and Christians. There is controversy over the origin of these paintings, as figurative art had not been generally used in al-Andalus. However Nasrid Granada was an open economy and thus accessible to outside cultural contacts: there would have been trade across the Mediterranean in agricultural produce and especially in the highly-valued silk. Thus there would have been influences from city-states such as Genoa and Venice. One eminent art historian has speculated that the paintings were executed by Muslim artists (who may have been exposed to European artistic traditions) despatched by the Castilian king, Pedro (the 'Cruel', r. 1350-1369), who had excellent political relations with the Amir, Muhammad V. Pedro was an admirer of Islamic art and architecture, as evidenced by his stunning Alcázar in Seville, built by Muslim craftsmen, many from Granada.

Continue counter-clockwise around the patio and, on the northern side, we come to the Sala de Dos Hermanas (the Hall of Two Sisters). This modern-day name denotes the two slabs of marble placed in the centre of the floor. This was the principal chamber of the Palacio de los Leones. Entrance to this hall from the patio was up steps and via an entrance doorway. The magnificent original doors from this entrance can now be seen in the Museo de la Alhambra. On the floor in the middle is a fountain, from which water flows to the Patio de los Leones. Look up, and experience the celestial ambience. The roof of the Sala de Dos Hermanas is the most exquisite ceiling of the Alhambra – and indeed of the Islamic world. It is an octagonal mocárabe dome with glittering 'stalactite' decoration – there are a reported 5,416 individual pieces. These comprise seven different types of prismatic shapes, all made of stucco. The cupola is octagonal, with two elevated windows in the plane of each of the eight sides. Windows at the base of the octagon allow sunlight to penetrate into the hall. This results in a rich multi-faceted array of light and shadow that varies, depending on the light filtering in at different times of day. All around the walls is a dado composed of hand-made azulejos, in alternating patterns. Above the dado is stucco inscribed with verses written by the vizier-poet Ibn Zamrak that extend around the room. Comparing the splendour of the room to that of a garden, it includes:

'I am a garden adorned with magnificence; behold my beauty and you will understand me.

Through the generosity of my lord Muhammad this is the greatest thing that ever has been or in the future.'

This is complemented by the panorama of panelled stucco decoration on the walls above. Pass now through an ante-room, the Sala de los Ajimeces. This rectangular hall has an elegant mocárabe vault. The name comes from the two mullioned windows (*ajimez*, a window with a dividing column.)

Now we come to the Mirador de Lindaraja (viewing point of Lindaraja). One possibility is that the name comes from the Arabic '*ayn dar Axa*' or 'eyes of the abode of Aixa'. The Mirador contains the most beautiful decoration of this palace. Here are geometric stucco decorations and epigraphs. The window is framed under a mocárabe arch. The dado has azulejos made up of colourful and differing star patterns. This balcony was originally open to the air and was a perfect spot to observe the Albaicín with, in the foreground, a garden orchard that extended to the walls of the Alhambra. Ibn Zamrak composed a suitable verse for the scene (it encompassed the usual modicum of flattery, promoting Muhammad V to a Caliph):

Right: an upwards view of the mocárabe dome in the Sala de Dos Hermanas. It is composed of 5,416 triangular and prismatic-shaped stucco pieces. There are eight points in the central star. It is surrounded by 16 smaller domes that sit over latticed windows, allowing light to illuminate the hall.

Right: the structure of the Sala de Dos Hermanas. A drawing by the nineteenth-century architect, Owen Jones, of the cross-section and plan of the dome.

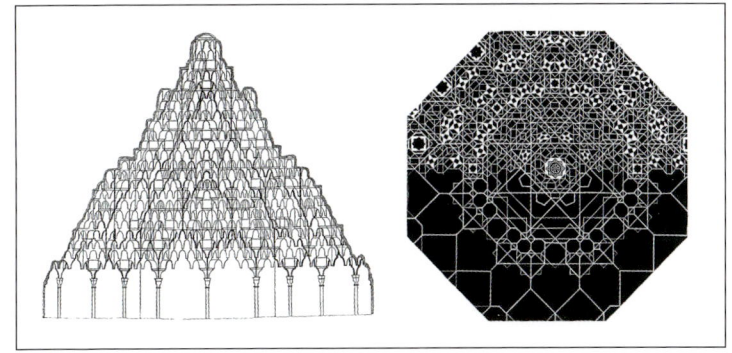

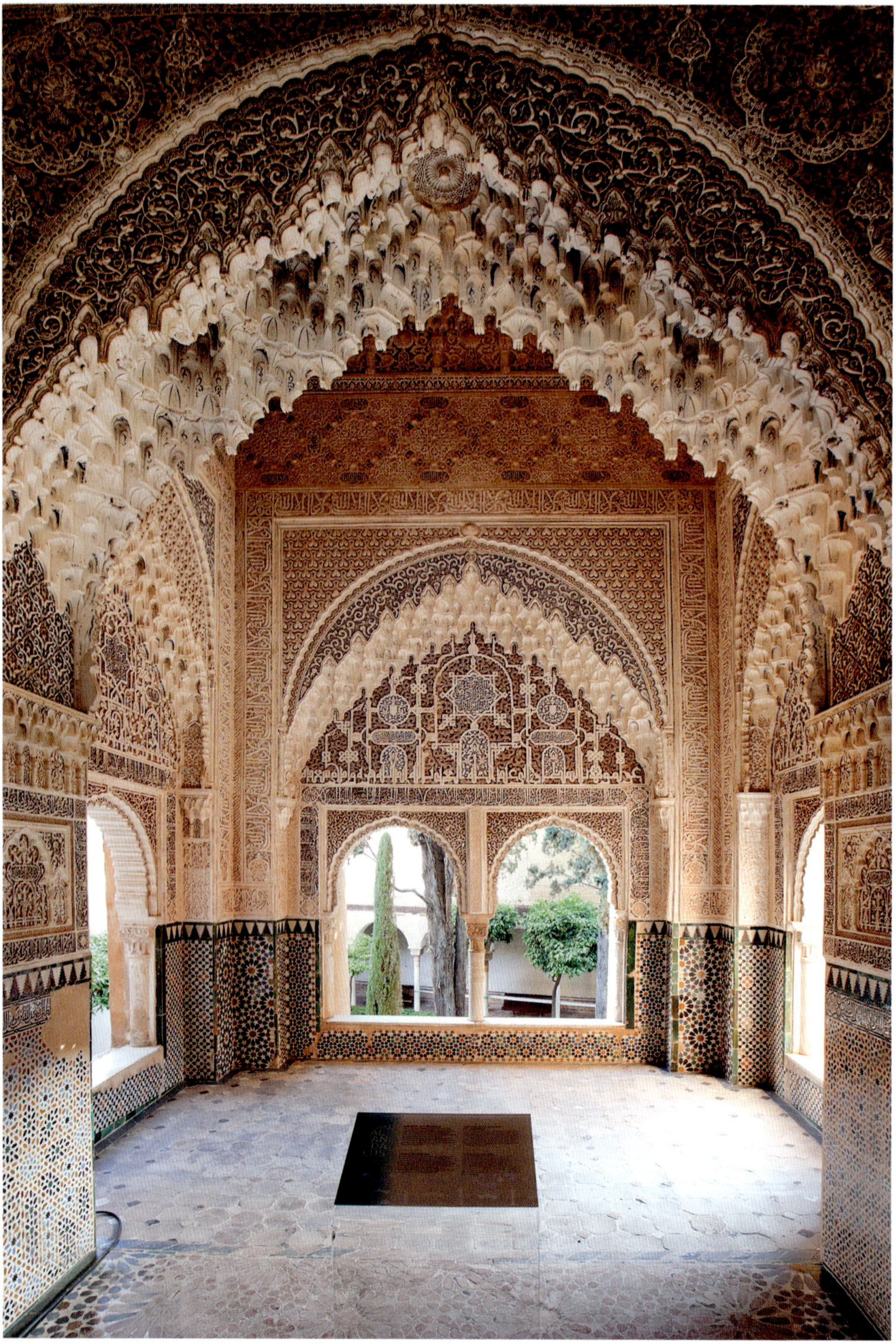

Left: the Mirador de Lindaraja. This beautifully-decorated balcony was originally open to the air. It was a perfect spot for the Amir to observe the Albaicín in the distance below. The view was blocked when, in 1528, Carlos V built his residential apartments around the lower garden.

Right: a hip-joint chair or 'jamuga' in wood and leather. The leather is embossed with the Nasrid shield. The marquetry decoration includes eight-pointed stars in ivory and triangular silver figures, framed by wooden octagons. Did the Amir view his domain from the Mirador de Lindaraja, sitting in such a chair? © Museo de la Alhambra.

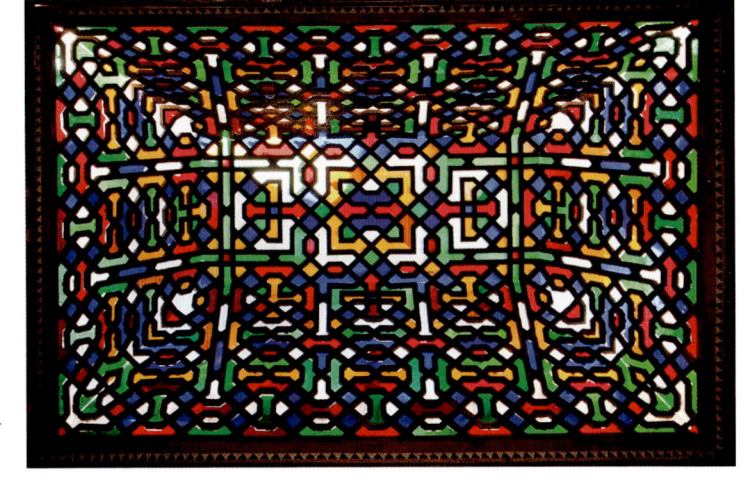

Right: the glass ceiling of the Mirador de Lindaraja – the only example of stained glass still in the Alhambra.

Left: the sparsely decorated room in the Emperor's Chambers, commisioned by Carlos V, where Washington Irving stayed when he lived in the Alhambra in 1829. He is commemorated here by a plaque over the door.

'In this garden I am the soothing eye filled with happiness and the pupil of this eye is in all righteousness, my lord…
Through me he views the capital of his realm, each time he is seated on his caliphal throne.'

In 1528, Carlos V built his residential apartments around the lower garden, thus abruptly blocking it.

Exit the Sala de Dos Hermanas, leaving behind the exquisite architecture of the Nasrid centuries. Now, in effect, you enter the spare world of late medieval northern Europe. In June 1526, Carlos V arrived in Granada along with his wife Isabel of Portugal. Though first cousins, they had married in the Alcázar in Seville just three months before. On arrival in the Alhambra, Carlos was so impressed by its magnificence that he decided that this could be the principal seat of his empire. In addition to decreeing the construction of a great palace nearby, he ordered that royal quarters be immediately provided. This series of rooms, the Emperor's Chambers, was built, remodelling the gardens between the Palacio de Comares and the Palacio de los Leones. An open-air gallery which connects the rooms was built. It provides a balcony that gives good views of the Albaicín and Sacromonte. The walls of the rooms one now encounters, in contrast to the palaces, are stark, although there are finely decorated wooden coffered ceilings in Flemish style. One account relates that Carlos' wife, Isabel, was frightened of the regular earth tremors that were occurring then in Granada and that she withdrew to the Monastery of Saint Jerome (the first monastery to be built after the conquest) in the lower city. Three centuries on, the American author Washington Irving had steadier nerves. He stayed in the Emperor's Chambers when he lived in the Alhambra in 1829 (as commemorated by a plaque to his memory).

Descending to ground level you pass through the small courtyard, dating from the middle of the seventeenth century, called the Patio de

Below: the Patio de Lindaraja, which is located below the Mirador de Lindaraja.

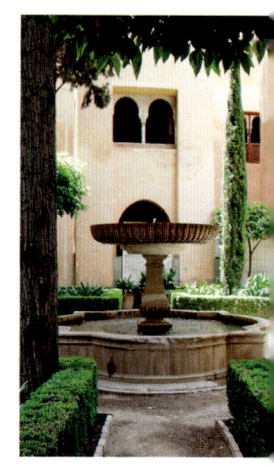

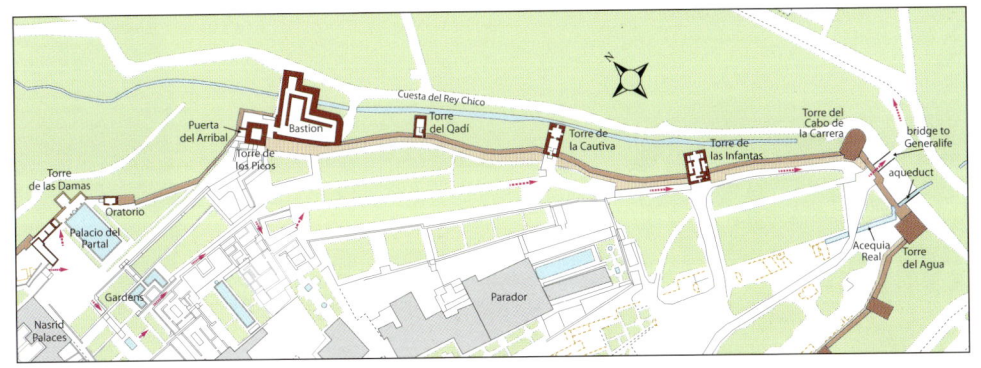

Above: map of the Partal and the Northern Towers.

la Reja (named after the overhanging ironwork balcony) with its small central fountain. Next is the Patio de Lindaraja. This was created by the three bays of the Emperor's Chambers and sits below the Mirador de Lindaraja.

The Palacio del Partal

Continue into the Jardines del Partal, the open air in this garden area giving perhaps an opportunity to catch one's breath after the intense experience of the Nasrid palaces. Here there are terraces, gardens and another palace, the Palacio del Partal. With a good imagination you can visualise how this location once was: it comprised of streets, a mosque and cemetary, gardens and villas of the Nasrid elite.

The layout of ascending terraces of the gardens has similarities to that employed in the palace city of Madinat al-Zahra in Córdoba of the tenth century. Prominent in this area is the Palacio del Partal. This consists of a tower, the Torre de las Damas (the Tower of the Ladies), with a frontal portico of five arches, which looks over a large rectan-

Right: a view from the patio of the Palacio del Partal.

gular pool. The palace was built early in the history of the Alhambra – it dates from the reign of Muhammad III (r. 1302-1309). Here one can enjoy a basic tenet of Nasrid architecture: the employment of water. The reflections of the tower and portico on the pool give depth and enjoyment to the scene. To the right of the Palacio is a building, now known as the Oratorio, which dates from the reign of Yusuf I (r. 1333-1354). This is not generally accessible to the public, but within is a room decorated with stucco, and containing a *mihrab* (a niche indicating the direction of prayer). Reflecting the tangled history of the Alhambra, much of this area was in private hands after the Christian conquest. It was only over the past two centuries that the land was acquired by the State. During the first half of the twentieth century, when the landscaping was done, there was much archaeological excavation here and the foundations of original buildings were identified. The Palacio del Partal was ceded to the state only in 1891, by its owner, a German. However the original wooden ceiling had been removed by the owner and it now resides in the Pergamon Museum in Berlin.

Now, you have a choice, depending on your stamina (and to fully appreciate the Alhambra, it really deserves to be visited over several days). The easy option is to head directly away from the Partal in a southerly direction and exit from the palace complex, into the general area known as the Medina.

Above: the Palacio del Partal. This consists of a tower, the Torre de las Damas, with a frontal portico of five arches, which overlooks a large rectangular pool. The palace was built during the reign of Muhammad III (r. 1302-1309).

Right: a view westwards along the northern defensive walls. The Torre del Qadi is on the right. To the left, in the background, is the Torre de los Picos. Just visible is one of the masonry corbels that project at corners, which give the tower its name of 'picos'.

The Northern Towers

Alternatively one can continue in a easterly direction, towards the Generalife. Pass along the landscaped walkway and one reaches a series of towers. As well as having a defensive function several of these towers had residential quarters. The Torre de los Picos gets its name from the masonry corbels that project at the corners. It is distinctive also by its merlons (the upright sections of the parapets). It was first built in the reign of Muhammad II, and there have been many subsequent alterations. It controls a gate, the Puerta del Arribal, which opens onto the

Above: a view from the Torre de los Picos of the walls and its bastion. This tower guarded an important gate, the Puerta del Arribal, which allowed access to the Cuesta del Rey Chico and onwards to the Generalife or to the Albaicín.

Left: an ornamented vaulted ceiling in the Torre de los Picos.

Right: the Torre de las Infantas. In his stories about the Alhambra, Washington Irving wrote about the legend of the three princesses in this tower

Cuesta del Rey Chico track (which leads from the Alhambra down to the river Darro and onwards to the Albaicín.)

The Torre del Qadí (the Tower of the Judge) had a purely defensive function, hence it is smaller. Like the other towers it divided up the walkways along the walls into discrete patrol sections for the guards. The construction of the Torre de la Cautiva (the Tower of the Captive) is attributed to Yusuf I (r. 1333-1354) who developed many fine buildings in the Alhambra. It is plain on the outside, but within are delightfully decorated rooms. The Torre de las Infantas (the Tower of the Princesses) also has typical Nasrid rooms within. Washington Ir-

Left: map of the Generalife.

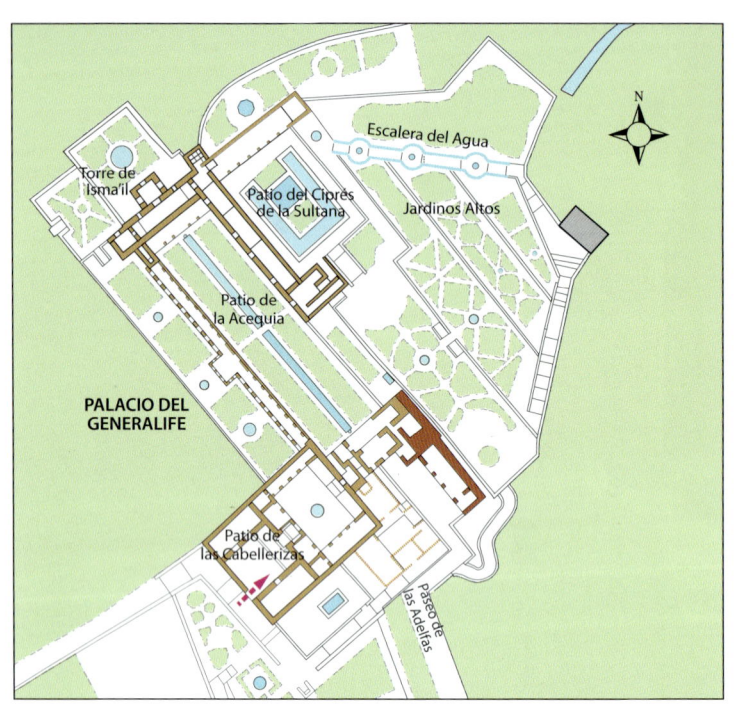

ving spun the legend of the three princesses of this tower in his *Tales of the Alhambra*. The Torre del Cabo de la Carrera (the Tower of the End of the Street) is the easternmost of the northern towers. This tower was added in 1502 under the Catholic Monarchs. It is still awaiting full reconstruction – it is one of the series of towers demolished by the French troops during their retreat from the Alhambra in 1812.

The Generalife

Cross a modern bridge over the Cuesta del Rey Chico and one enters the grounds of the Generalife. In Nasrid times it was common for the Amirs (and the rich and prominent) to have *almunias*, estates with a villa and agricultural lands, dotted around the Granadan Vega. The Generalife (one theory is that the name comes from *yannat al-arif*, 'garden of the architect'), being the nearest to the Alhambra, was the principal country estate of the Amir. This afforded a retreat where he could relax with his family. It was still close enough to the Alhambra that urgent affairs of state could be quickly attended to. In addition to being a royal residence, there were a number of market gardens and orchards within the grounds. The first buildings here are thought to date from the reign of the second Amir of the dynasty, Muhammad II (r. 1273-1302) – there were many modifications by later rulers.

The gardens have been renovated many times over the centuries. First one passes the open-air theatre, which is a wonderful venue for

Above: looking down from the Sacromonte, a view of the Generalife, set against the majestic backdrop of the Sierra Nevada. The Generalife was the principal country estate of the Amir. This afforded a retreat where he could escape from the cares of state in the nearby Alhambra and relax with his family.

the Granada International Festival of Music and Dance, held each June. Next are the gardens which date from the 1930s onwards. Here are avenues of cypresses with a central pool and fountain. (There are many fountains in the Generalife!) Next is a rose labyrinth. As you proceed, you can catch good views of the Alhambra, with, in the foreground, the *huertas* (gardens) sloping down to the track of the Cuesta del Rey Chico. As well as supplying the Alhambra, the Acequia Real (the royal waterway) brings water to the Generalife and its gardens.

One enters the Palacio del Generalife by means of two contiguous courtyards. Within the first (the Patio de las Cabellerizas, or Patio of the Stables) there are benches which were used by horsemen to dismount in olden days. They used to enter by an ancient route into the complex directly via the huertas from the Cuesta. Pass up steps through an entrance whose portal is topped by a key motif, a symbol of faith. Enter the second courtyard with its central fountain surrounded by orange trees. Next walk through an angled and ascending passageway to encounter one of the splendid sights of the Generalife, the Patio de la Acequia. The channel, the Acequia Real, has a starring and central role as it runs down the long, rectangular-shaped courtyard. It encompasses all that is wonderful about Nasrid architecture. This was a space where water, fountains and plants form a tableau of relaxation and nature. The senses are still assaulted: as well as the visual sense, one can enjoy the sounds of water and smell the plants.

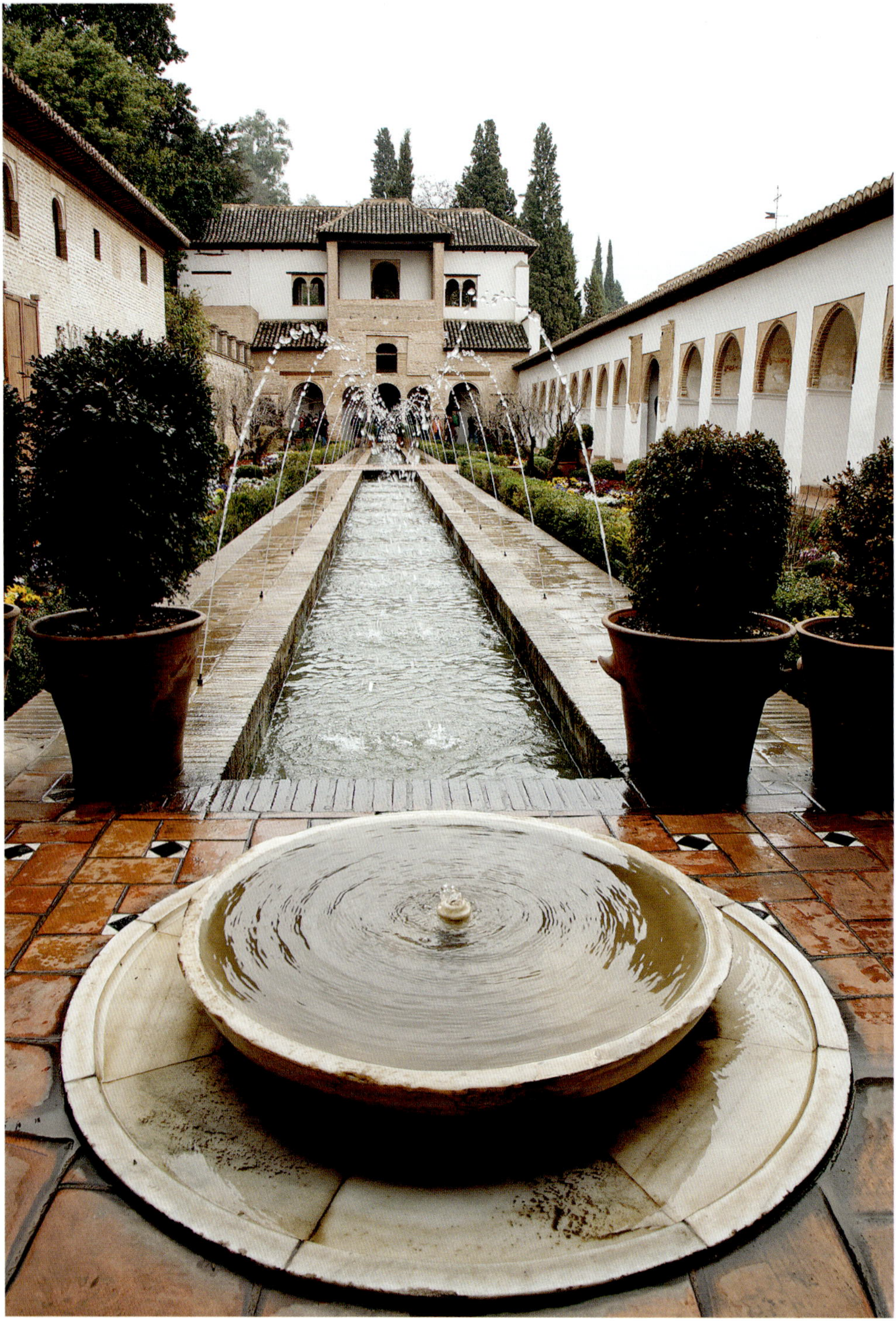

Above: the mirador in the pavilion of the Torre de Ismaʾil.

Right: polychromatic stucco decoration in the Generalife.

Left: the Patio de la Acequia. This long, rectangular-shaped courtyard encompasses all that is wonderful about Nasrid architecture. Originally this is was a closed private space where water, fountains and plants form a tableau of relaxation and nature.

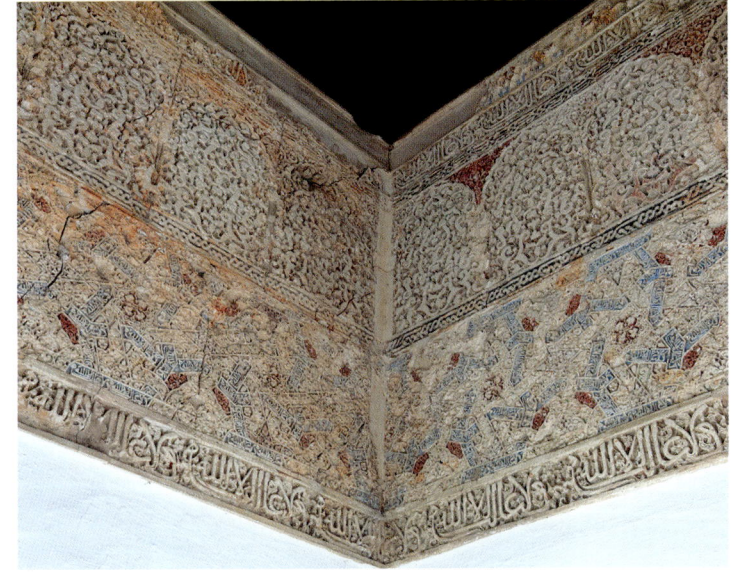

Left: The pillars of the arches on the façade of the northern pavilion are supported by mocárabe capitals. This pavilion constituted the principal rooms of the royal residence in the Palacio del Generalife.

Above: the delightful sound of running water. The Escalera del Agua (water stairway) has four sections and three landings, the hand rail on each side is a channel through which the water runs down.

Right: the Patio delCiprés de la Sultana, with its U-shaped pool. A plaque by the cypress tree tells the legend that the wife of Boabdil supposedly had a tryst by the cypress tree here with a member of the Abencerraje family.

Left: farewell to the Generalife – the long avenue of the Paseo de las Adelfas, with its arch of oleander, cypress and myrtle.

Originally the plants to the side were set in sunken sections so as not to impede the view. The angled water spouts that present an arcade of falling water are a later addition. In Nasrid times the sound of water trickling from the fountain and running along the channel would have been a delicate sufficiency.

The pavilion at the north end, which constituted the principal rooms of the royal residence, preserves wonderful ornamentation. Here, in the ceiling, is a superb wooden vault with interlaced decoration. The pillars of the five arches on the façade are supported by mocárabe capitals. The Torre de Isma'il in the middle, whose mirador gives views over the Albaicín, was commissioned by Isma'il I in 1319, in celebration of his victory over the Castilians in the Battle of the Vega. Next, accessed via a stairway, is the Patio del Ciprés de la Sultana, with its U-shaped pool, much modified from the original layout. You can read the plaque by the cypress tree: according to romantic legend the Sultana, or wife of the Amir, Boabdil, supposedly had a tryst with a *caballero* of the Abencerraje family – which resulted in a massacre of the menfolk of the clan.

Onwards up the stairs to the Jardines Altos, the upper gardens, which are a landscaped series of nineteenth-century gardens. The Escalera del Agua (water stairway) provides an opportunity to see an interesting original feature, encompassing the Nasrid appreciation of water as an art form. In this stairway with four sections and three landings, the hand rail on each side is a water channel. The water runs down the channels, again fed by the ever-munificent Acequia Real. Renovations during the nineteenth century are thought to have demolished a royal oratory at the top of the stairway.

The Paseo de las Adelfas runs through the gardens from the upper palace area and leads eventually to the exit (by the ticket office). It gets its name from the oleander shrubs that line the pathway along with cypresses and myrtles.

General Information

How to get to the Alhambra
(*See routes on map, pages 134-5*)

On foot
1. The most usual: from the Plaza Nueva in the heart of Granada. Walk up the Cuesta de Gomérez. At the end of the street enter though the Puerta de Granadas and into the Alhambra Woods. Continue climbing on the left-hand track. On reaching the Fuente de Carlos V, turn left and enter the Alhambra complex via the Puerta de la Justicia (if you already have obtained your ticket – if not, continue to the Entrance Pavilion). Entrance to the Alcazaba is via the Torre de Quebrada, from the Plaza de los Aljibes. Entrance to the Nasrid palaces is via the Mexuar, to the north of the Palacio de Carlos V.
2. Direct to the Entrance Pavilion: from the Paseo de los Tristes cross the bridge (Puente del Aljibillo) over the river Darro. Take the Cuesta del Rey Chico upwards. The track ascends steeply and continues through the ravine between the Generalife and its gardens on the left and the defensive walls and towers of the Alhambra on the right. After the track becomes level you pass under two small bridges and arrive near the Entrance Pavilion.
3. Steep, but picturesque: from the Plaza del Realejo, to the south of the Alhambra, walk up the Cuesta del Realejo. After the Alhambra Palace Hotel, turn north then to the right along the road that leads to the Entrance Pavilion.

Public transport
The C3 bus (every eight minutes) is best to the Alhambra, from the central Plaza Isabel la Católica. The C4 bus also leaves from there and passes the Alhambra (every 30 minutes).

By car
From the A44 take exit 132 for the southern ring road, the A395 (signs for Ronda Sur/Sierra Nevada/Alhambra). Pass through a tunnel, keeping in the left lane. At the roundabout, take the second exit and head uphill along Avenida Santa María de la Alhambra for around one kilometre. The official car parks are along the Paseo de la Sabika, within walking distance of the Entrance Pavilion (and ticket office).

Buying tickets
As there is great demand it is advisable to purchase your tickets well in advance. Advance tickets can be bought online (www.alhambra-tickets.es) or by phone: from Spain dial 902 888001; from abroad: +34 958 926031. Tickets purchased online or by telephone can be picked up at: La Caixa Bank ATMs; the automatic ticket machines at the Alhambra Entrance Pavilion; or downtown at the Alhambra ticket office in the Corral de Carbón, Calle Mariana Pineda. Tickets for that day's visit can be purchased directly at the ticket office located in the Entrance Pavilion.

Entry times
Note: things change. Consult www.alhambra-patronato.es for the most up-to-date information.

The Alhambra is open all year round, except 25 December and 1 January.

Daytime visits
15 March – 14 October: 08:30 – 20:00
15 October – 14 March: 08:30 – 18:00

Night-time visits
Consult www.alhambra-patronato.es for details.

The best time of year to visit
Granada and the Alhambra are best visited during the spring and autumn. The summers are hot, reaching an average highest temperature of 32ºC in August. As Granada is at over 700 metres altitude, the winters are cold, with an average lowest temperature of 1ºC in January.

Chronology

19 BC	Romans consolidate their control over the Iberian Peninsula, thus establishing their province called Hispania.
AD 409	German tribes invade the north-west of Hispania and range all over the Peninsula. In 569 King Leovigild consolidates Visigothic rule.
622	The Prophet Muhammad, accompanied by his followers, moves to Medina in the Arabian Peninsula.
681	Islamic forces, having conquered North Africa, reach the Atlantic Ocean.
711	An army led by Tariq bin Zayed lands at Calpe (now known as Gibraltar, or Jebel Tariq).
720	Most of the Iberian Peninsula (except the mountainous regions of Cantabria and the Pyrenees) is under Islamic control. The new entity is called al-Andalus.
750	In Damascus, the Umayyad Caliph is overthrown by the Abbasid clan. An Umayyad prince, Abd al-Rahman, flees and arrives in al-Andalus in 755. With the aid of followers, including Syrian soldiers settled near Elvira (present-day Granada), he seizes power the following year.
784	Abd al-Rahman orders construction of the Great Mosque of Córdoba.
912	Abd al-Rahman III comes to power in Córdoba. He battles with three threats: the Fatimids of North Africa; the Christians to the north and the continuing rebellion of Ibn Hafsun. In 929 Abd al-Rahman III declares himself Caliph.
961	On Abd al Rahman III's death, his son al-Hakam II becomes Caliph. He extends the Great Mosque of Córdoba, its third extension.
1002	Almanzor dies. His sons seize power in turn. After an attempt by one to be designated Caliph, uproar and civil war ensue.
1031	Al-Andalus flies apart. Over 30 taifas (or party states) are formed. A Berber, Zawi bin Ziri, sets up in Elvira. He abandons Madinat Elvira and establishes himself in a new location, present-day Granada. The Zirids develop Madinat Gharnata, installing defensive walls and fortifications.
1090	A fundamentalist group, the Almoravids, takes over from the weak and decadent taifa rulers. The Taifa of Granada is the first to be seized.
1160	A new fundamentalist group, the Almohads, seizes power in al-Andalus.
1212	A coalition of Christian forces assembles and decisively defeats the Almohad army at Las Navas de Tolosa.
1238	Ibn al-Ahmar is invited by the people of Granada to rule them. This is the beginning of the Nasrid dynasty.
1246	Ibn al-Ahmar, now Muhammad I, signs a treaty with Castile, gaining years of stability. He orders the construction of the Alcazaba on the Sabika Hill.
1273	Muhammad II takes over on his father's death. A confused period of strife ensues, with Marinids (from North Africa) and the Castilians vying to take over the Strait of Gibraltar.
1333	Yusuf I ascends the throne. He embarks on major contruction works in the Alhambra including the towers of Machuca and Comares; the Hall of the Ambassadors, and in central Granada, the Madrasa.
1354	Muhammad V comes to the throne. He continues with the construction of great buildings. With a peace treaty in place with Castile, it is a period of prosperity and some of the finest buildings in the Alhambra are built. Muhammad is deposed several times. This pattern has became a characteristic of the Nasrids. In the years that follow each Nasrid ruler is either deposed or assassinated.
1469	Isabel of Castile marries Fernando of Aragón (they are later to be known as the Catholic Monarchs).
1482	Continuing their determined campaign against the Kingdom of Granada, the army of the Catholic Monarch's captures Alhama de Granada. In the years that follow, they methodically seize towns throughout the Kingdom of Granada.
1487	Granada's second city, Málaga, is captured after a long siege. The capture of Muslim territory accelerates.
1491	The siege of Granada begins.
1492	The ruler of Granada, Boabdil, surrenders to the Catholic Monarchs, having signed 'capitulations' which grant rights to the Muslims of Granada.
1499	The Muslims of Granada stage a small revolt after the breaking of the capitulations. Subsequently, all Muslims are told to convert or be expelled. Mass forced baptisms ensue, creating *Moriscos* (Muslims who become baptised Christians, under Christian rule).
1500	Mosques across Granada are converted to churches. As new Christian buildings are constructed, usually in a characteristic Renaissance style, Granada begins to lose its distinctive Muslim features.
1526	Construction of the Palacio de Carlos V in the Alhambra (part-funded by a tax on *Moriscos*) begins.
1570	An uprising by *Moriscos*, principally in the Alpujarras, is put down. All *Moriscos* are expelled from the Kingdom of Granada to other parts of Spain.
1609	King Felipe III decides to expel all *Moriscos* from Spain. The expulsion begins in Valencia, is extended to other parts of Spain and is completed by 1614.
1810	French troops occupy the Alhambra, then neglected and in decline. On abandoning the position in 1812, they destroy several of the defensive towers.
1829	The American author Washington Irving arrives in Granada and writes *Tales of the Alhambra*. This and other books spark an interest in the Alhambra. Visitor numbers increase throughout the late nineteenth century.
1884	Much of the river Darro is covered over. Continuing urban improvements remove other vestiges of Muslim Granada.
1936	Granada comes under Nationalist control during the Civil War. Many left-wing supporters (including Frederico García Lorca) are rounded up and shot.
2016	The Alhambra continues to be restored, as it has been over the years. Since 1984 it has been recognised as a UNESCO World Heritage Site and has developed into a major tourist attraction. Visitors throng the streets of Granada and savour the essence of the city and its jewel on the Sabika Hill.

Glossary

Abencerrajes   A powerful family in the Kingdom of Granada during the fifteenth century, much given to intrigue amidst the dynastic upheavals of the Nasrid Court.

Acequia   Water channel.

Al-Andalus   Islamic Spain and Portugal. Originally it extended over most of the Iberian Peninsula, but progressively was reduced so that by the middle of the thirteenth century it was confined to the Kingdom of Granada, more or less the territory of present-day Andalucía.

Alcazaba   Castle or citadel.

Alfaqui   Person versed in Islamic law.

Aljibe   Cistern or well.

Almohads   Fundamentalist group founded at the beginning of the twelfth century in the High Atlas Mountains of Morocco and which overthrew the Almoravids. They ruled in al-Andalus up to their defeat by Christian forces at the Battle of las Navas de Tolosa in 1212, after which they went into decline.

Almoravids   Fundamentalist group that emerged from south of Morocco, founding Marrakech in 1062. They expanded to al-Andalus, seizing power from the *taifa* rulers, then reeling under pressure from the Christian kingdoms. The Taifa of Granada was the first to be seized in 1090.

Almunia   A country estate with gardens and a farm.

Amir   A ruler or commander.

Banu   Banu or Beni from Arabic, 'sons', or 'family of'. Hence its use as 'ben' in many Spanish placenames; Benidorm; Benicassim; Benalidad, etc.

Caliph   The successor (of the Prophet) and both spiritual and temporal ruler.

Fatimids   Shia dynasty that ruled much of North Africa from the beginning of the tenth century for around three centuries. The name comes from Fatima, daughter of Muhammad.

Fuente   Spring or fountain.

Hammam   Baths.

Jihad   Striving for religious and moral perfection. It can involve waging a holy war in the name of God against unbelievers.

Jineta   Highly decorated sword from Nasrid Granada. The name is related to the Spanish for horseman, '*jinete*'.

Kufic   An early form of Arabic script. Used in ornamental inscriptions in the Alhambra.

Madrasa   Islamic school of learning.

Mihrab   Niche in mosque indicating the direction of Mecca, and thus of prayer.

Mocárabe   'Stalactite ceiling' made up of a multitude of prismatic pieces, cut into concave shapes at the bottom.

Moors   A term commonly used, in the context of Spain, to denote Muslim inhabitants of al-Andalus. However, it is inaccurate, as most of the Muslim Andalusis were descended from the original inhabitants of the Iberian Peninsula (who had converted over the centuries), with only a minority originating from the Maghreb or further to the east.

Morisco   Iberian Muslim who was forced to become a baptised Christian, living under Christian rule.

Mozarab   Iberian Christian living under Muslim rule.

Mudéjar   Muslim living under Christian rule, after the Reconquista.

Muwallad   Christian living in the Iberian Peninsula who had converted to Islam.

Nasrids   The last dynasty of al-Andalus. Founded by Ibn al-Ahmar in 1238, it ruled the Kingdom of Granada until 1492.

Noria   A waterwheel.

Qadí   Judge who adjudicates on the basis of Islamic law.

Reconquista   Reconquest: denoting the capture by the Christian kingdoms of the territory of al-Andalus, over the centuries up to 1492. The term 'reconquest' implies the rightful taking back of the Iberian Peninsula, which 'belonged' to the Christian Visigoths, from the Muslims who had captured it in AD 711.

Taifas   A series of around 30 statelets which were founded in al-Andalus after the break-up of the Umayyad Caliphate in Cordoba in 1030. *Taifas* survived until the end of the eleventh century, i.e. until the arrival of the Almoravids.

Tapial wall   Mixtures of soil, compressed in layers, used to construct walls. In the Alhambra, the local conglomerate soil, mixed with lime, was used to construct the defensive walls.

Umayyads   This dynasty ruled in Damascus from AD 661. Following their overthrow by the Abbasid clan in 750, a surviving member, Abd al-Rahman, fled to al-Andalus and seized power in 756. The dynasty lasted in al-Andalus until 1030.

Vega   A plain. The Vega of Granada stretches from the Sierra Nevada and ranges along the basin of the river Genil, as far as Loja, a distance of nearly 60 kilometres.

Vizier   A high-ranking official of the Amir.

Zirids   A Berber dynasty, originating in North Africa. They established the Taifa of Granada (1013-1090).

Illustration Credits

All photographs and maps are by Michael B. Barry © 2016 plus old engravings from the author's collection, with the exception of the following:

Images on the specified pages are courtesy and copyright of the following (abbreviations for top, bottom, left, middle, right, respectively, are: t, b, l, m, r):
Archivo y Biblioteca del Patronato de la Alhambra y Generalife: 61, 182-183
Capilla Real de Granada: 86b, 102
Catedral Basilica del Pilar, Cabildo Metropolitano de Zaragoza: 52
Catedral de Córdoba: 10b
Fundación El Legado Andalusí: 16t
Fundación Bancaja: 123
Metropolitan Museum of Art, New York/Artstor: 47t, 80
Museo Arqueológico de Córdoba: 15b, 41t
Museo Arqueológico de Granada: 17t, 82b, 84t
Museo Arqueológico Nacional, Madrid: 89t, 146
Museo de Almería: 14, 40b,
Museo de Jaén: 28 br
Museo de la Abadía del Sacromonte: 121, 124
Museo de la Alhambra: 53, 72, 127t, 187t
Museo de Zaragoza: 99t
Museo del Ejército, Toledo: 90
Museo Lázaro Galdiano, Madrid: 57
Museum With No Frontiers/Discover Islamic Art: 38
Patrimonio Histórico-Artístico del Senado, Madrid: 41b, 96
Tony Redmond: 18
Visita Arjona/Antonio Salas Sola: 44t
Wikimedia Commons: 68 – Luis García/ Zaqarbal/Museo Arqueológico Nacional; 79t – Storkk/Royal Monastery of San Lorenzo de El Escorial; 85t – Gun Powder Ma/Lee Sie; 99b – MaiDireLollo/www.fuenterrebollo.com; 105b – The Yorck Project/Alte Pinakothek, Munich; 116b – Tiberioclaudio99/Convent of Las Descalzas Reales, Madrid; 122 – Escarlati/Museo del Prado.

Bibliography

The following are recommended in the first instance:

For more detail on the Alhambra:

'Official Guide: the Alhambra and the Generalife', Patronato de la Alhambra y Generalife.

For more detail on al-Andalus, the Kingdom of Granada and Spanish history:

Barry, M. B., 'Homage to al-Andalus, the Rise and Fall of Islamic Spain', Andalus Press, Dublin, 2016.

Elliott, J. H., 'Imperial Spain, 1469-1716', Penguin, London, 2002.

García de Cortázar, F., 'Atlas de Historia de España', Editorial Planeta, Barcelona, 2005.

Harvey, L. P., 'Islamic Spain 1250 to 1500', University of Chicago Press, Chicago and London, 1990.

Kennedy, H., 'Muslim Spain and Portugal', Longman, Harlow, 1996.

Other sources:

'Arquitectura de al-Andalus', Editorial Comares, Granada, 2002.

'Granada and the Alhambra', Ediciones Miguel Sánchez, Granada, 2005.

'Historia de Andalucía', Diario 16 Andalucía/Editorial Planeta, Barcelona, 1992.

'Itenerario Cultural de Almorávides y Almohades', Legado Andalusí. Granada, 2003.

'Route of the Caliphate', Legado Andalusí, Granada, 1998.

'Route of the Nasrids', Legado Andalusí, Granada, 2001.

'Ruta de los Almorávides y Almohades', Legado Andalusí, Granada, 2006.

'Ruta de Washington Irving', Legado Andalusí, Granada, 1999.

'The Alhambra and Granada in Focus', Edilux, 2006.

'The Encyclopedia of Islam', E. J. Brill, Leiden; Luzac, London.

Aranda Doncal, J., 'Los Moriscos en Tierras de Córdoba', Publicaciones del Monte de Piedad y Caja de Ahorros de Córdoba, Córdoba, 1984.

Barrios Rozúa, J. M., 'Guia de la Granada desaparecida', Editorial Comares, Granada, 2006.

Barrucand, M., Bednorz, A., 'Moorish Architecture in Andalusia', Taschen, Cologne, 2002.

Barbour, N., 'Morocco', Methuen, London, 1965.

Becerra, E. R., 'Igualeja Despues de la Expulsion de los Moriscos', Editorial la Serranía, Ronda 2005.

Brazales, J. C., Uzal, A. O., 'En Busca de la Granada Andalusí', Granada 2002.

Brett, M., Fentress, E., 'The Berbers', Blackwell, Oxford, 1997.

Burckhardt, T., 'La Civilizacion Hispano-

Arabe', Alianza Editorial, Madrid, 2001.

Cavanagh Murphy, J., 'The Arabian Antiquities of Spain', Cadell & Davies, London, 1816.

Clevenot, D., Degeorge, G., 'Ornament and Decoration in Islamic Architecture', Thames & Hudson, London, 2000.

Coleman, C., 'Creating Christian Granada', Cornell University Press, 2003.

Collins, R., 'Early Medieval Spain', St. Martin's Press, New York, 1995.

Cuello, A. M., 'Mil Años de Madinat Ilbira', Legado Andalusí, Granada, 2014.

Cuenca Toribio, J. M., 'Historia General de Andalucía', Editorial Almuzara, Madrid, 2005.

Davillier, Baron, 'L'Espagne', Librairie Hachette, Paris, 1874.

De Mármol Carvajal, L., 'Historia de la Rebelión y Castigo de los Moriscos del Reino de Granada', Editorial Arguval, Malaga.

Encinas Moral, A., L., 'Cronologia Historica de al-Andalus', Miragueno Ediciones, Madrid, 2005.

Fanjul, S., 'La Quimera de al-Andalus', Siglo XXI de España Editores, Madrid, 2005.

Fletcher, R., 'Moorish Spain', University of California Press, Berkeley, 1993.

Ford, R., 'A Handbook for Travellers in Spain', John Murray, London, 1845.

Garcia-Arenal, M., 'La Diáspora de los Andalusies', Icaria Editorial, Barcelona, 2003.

Gerli, E. M., 'Medieval Iberia, an Encyclopedia', Routledge, London, 2003.

Gomez Bayarri, J. V., 'La Valencia Medieval', Real Academia de Cultura Valenciana, Valencia, 2003.

Gonzalez Ferrin, E., 'Historia General de al-Andalus', Editorial Almuzara, Madrid, 2006.

Goodwin, G., 'Islamic Spain', Penguin, London, 1991.

Guichard, P., 'From the Arab Conquest to the Reconquest, The Splendour and Fragility of al-Andalus', Legado Andalusí, Granada, 2006.

Harris, K., 'From Muslim to Christian Granada', Johns Hopkins University Press, 2007.

Harvey, G., 'Gibraltar, a History', Spellmount, Staplehurst, 2000.

Harvey, L. P., 'Muslims in Spain, 1500 to 1614', University of Chicago Press, Chicago and London, 2005.

Irwin, R., 'The Alhambra', Profile Books, London, 2004.

Jacobs, M., 'Andalucia', Pallas Guides, London, 2006.

Jayyusi, S. K., ed., 'The Legacy of Muslim Spain', Brill, Leyden, 2005.

Janer, F., 'Condicion Social de los Moriscos de España', Ediciones Espuela de Plata, 2006.

Jones, O., 'Plans, Elevations, Sections and Details of the Alhambra', London, 1836-45.

Kamen, H., 'Spain 1469-1714, a Society of Conflict', Longman, London, 1991.

Kamen, H., 'The Spanish Inquisition, an Historical Revision', Phoenix, London, 2003.

Ladero Quesada, M. A., 'La Guerra de Granada', Los Libros de la Estrella, Granada, 2001.

Levi-Provençal, E., 'Histoire de l'Espagne Musulmane", Vol 3, Maisonneuve et Larose, Paris, 1999.

Morales, C., Molino, E., 'Reino de Granada, Tomo I, El Islam', Ideal, Granada, 1991.

Makariou, S., 'La Andalucía Arabe', Legado Andalusí, Granada, 2000.

Maranon, G., 'Expulsion y Diaspora de los Moriscos Españoles', Taurus, 2004.

Marcos Cobaleda, M., 'Los Almorávides, Arquitectura de un Imperio', Editorial Universidad de Granada, Granada, 2015.

Menendez Pidal, R., 'Historia de España', Vols. III, IV, V, VIII (1,2,3,4), IX, Editorial Espasa Calpe, Madrid.

Mileto, C., 'Rammed Earth Construction', CRC Press, London, 2002.

Moreno, E. M., 'Conquistadores, Emires y Califas', Critica, Barcelona, 2006.

Nicolle, D., 'Historical Atlas of the Islamic World', Mercury Books, London, 2003.

O'Callaghan, J. F., 'A History of Medieval Spain', Cornell University Press, Ithaca and London, 1983.

O'Callaghan, J. F., 'Reconquest and Crusade in Medieval Spain', University of Pennsylvania Press, Philadelphia, 2003.

Orihuela, A., 'Granada, entre Ziríes y Nazaríes', Legado Andalusí. Granada, 2003.

Ortiz, A. D., Vincent, B., 'Historia de los Moriscos', Alianza Editorial, Madrid, 2003.

Perez Higuera, T., 'Objetos e Imagenes de al-Andalus', Lunwerg, Barcelona.

Puerta Vílchez, J. M., 'Reading the Alhambra', The Alhambra and Generalife Trust/Edilux, 2010.

Requesens, C., 'Granada Insólita y Secreta', Editorial Jonglez, Versailles.

Robinson, F., 'Cambridge Illustrated History of the Islamic World', Cambridge University Press, Cambridge, 2005.

Rodríguez Sánchez, Á., Martin, J. L., 'La España de los Reyes Católicos', Editorial Epasa Calpe, Madrid, 2004.

Salmerón Escobar, P., 'The Alhambra, Structure and Landscape', Editorial Almuzara, Córdoba, 2007.

Torres Balbás, L., 'Artes Almorávide y Almohade', Instituto Diego Velázquez, Madrid, 1955.

Trillo San Jose, C., 'Agua, Tierra y Hombres en al-Andalus', Ajbar Colección, Granada, 2004.

Valdeon Baruque, J., 'Abderraman III y el Califato de Córdoba', Editorial Debate, Madrid, 2001.

Valdeon Baruque, J., 'La Reconquista', Editorial Espasa Calpe, Madrid, 2006.

Index

A

Abbasids 14
Abd Allah 23, 31-32, 35-6, 51, 88
Abd al-Rahman I 14-15, 17
Abd al-Rahman III 18-19, 31, 56, 59, 73
Aben Aboo 117-118, 121
Abencerrajes 76, 80-82, 88, 113, 148, 180-181, 199, 200
Aben Humeya 113, 115, 117
Abu Bakr 11
Abu Ya'qub 57
Abu Yusuf 55, 56
Acequia 17, 31, 32
Acequia Real 51, 143, 145, 150-151, 157, 195, 200
Aghmat 36
Al-Andalus 13-17, 19-24, 34-45, 51-52, 55, 59, 96, 123-124, 132, 141, 143, 178, 183
Alange 42
Alans 9
Alarcos 38
Albaicín 8, 29, 31-33, 40, 51-52, 72, 74, 76, 82, 90-91, 95, 99-100, 113, 119, 131, 162, 171, 184, 187-188, 192, 193, 200
Albercón 51
Alcaiceria 131
Alcalá de Henares 100, 146
Alcalá la Real 84
Alcazaba, Alhambra 48-49, 51, 60, 63, 77, 84, 90, 92-93, 96, 129, 133, 141, 143, 156-157, 160-161
Alcazaba Qadima, Granada 27, 29, 33, 49, 133
Alcázar, Toledo 58
Aledo 35
Alfacar 32, 131
Alfonso I 37
Alfonso VI 34-35
Alfonso VII 38
Alfonso VIII 40
Alfonso X 53-54, 56
Alfonso XI 61-62, 64, 66
Algeciras 22, 24, 55-56, 58-59, 61-65, 70, 166
Algeria 12, 23, 56
Al-Hakam II 20-22
Alhama de Granada 77, 87
Alhambra 48-49, 51, 53, 60-61, 65-66, 68-70, 72-73, 78, 80-81, 88, 90, 96, 99, 103-105, 108-109, 125-127, 129, 132-133, 136-139, 141, 143, 145-146, 148, 150-151, 156-157, 162, 166-167, 171, 173-174, 182, 184, 187-188, 190, 193-195
Aljibe 17, 31, 51, 157
Aljibe del Rey 32-33
Almanzor 21-22, 31
Almería 14, 20, 22, 24, 35, 40-42, 46, 48, 51-52, 59-60, 63, 73, 86, 90, 93-94, 178
Almohads 29, 34, 36-44, 48-49, 53, 55, 68
Almoravids 22, 29, 31, 34-38, 44, 49, 55
Almuñécar 7, 14-15, 17
Alpujarras 63, 81, 85, 94-96, 98-99, 101, 113-117, 120-121
Al-Zagal 88, 90-94
America 97
Andalucía 43, 119-120, 123
Andarax 98, 101, 117
Antequera 9, 54, 76-78, 86-89
Antequerela 78
Arabian Peninsula 11
Arabic 100, 111, 121-122
Arabs 13-14, 44
Aragón 37, 41, 47, 53, 57-60, 68-70, 82-84, 97-98, 105, 112, 151
Archidona 81
Arco de los Pesos 29-28
Arcos 22
Arjona 42, 44, 46-48
Artillery 60, 65, 76-77, 84-85, 87, 90-94, 116-118
Asturias 9
Atarfe 16-17
Atlantic Ocean 7, 12
Axarquía 88, 116
Ayesha 82, 88
Aynadamar irrigation channel 31-33, 75, 132

B

Badajoz 34, 42
Badis bin Habus 27, 28, 31, 32
Baetica province 8-10
Baetic Cordillera 46, 48
Baeza 52, 70
Balearics 36
Banu Asqilula 44, 46, 53-57
Bañuelo 29, 31
Banu Ghaniya 37
Barbate 13
Barcelona 15
Battle of the Higuerela 79-80
Battle of las Navas de Tolosa 41
Battle of Pavia 151
Battle of the Vega 60, 200
Baza 44, 93, 117-118
Berbers 12, 14, 21-23, 34, 36, 44, 62-63, 92-93
Béznar 113
Black Plague 65-66
Boabdil (Muhammad XII) 82, 88-96, 98-99, 199-200
Bobastro 18
Byzantines 11

C

Cádiz 7, 55, 120
Calahorra 120
Calatuyud 37
Calpe 12
Cambil 70, 90
Cantabria 13
Cantigas de Santa Maria 24
Capilla Real 100, 102-103, 108, 109, 148, 149
Capitulations 88, 96, 100
Carlos V 105, 108-109, 112, 124-125, 136, 138-139, 141, 143, 145-146, 151, 153, 156, 163-164, 171, 178, 187-188
Carlos V fountain 105, 139, 141, 143
Carmona 22
Cartagena 7, 9
Cártama 90
Carthage 7, 8
Casa de Cabildo 64, 103, 104
Casa de Zafra 103
Castile 21, 38, 41-45, 47, 48-49, 52-53, 56-61, 64, 66, 68, 70, 76-77, 79-84, 86, 97-98, 105, 110-111, 119, 123, 151
Catalonia 82, 112
Catholic Church 131
Catholic Monarchs 82-86, 88, 92-93, 95-97, 99, 102-105, 109-110, 124, 131, 136, 148-149, 157, 161, 167, 174, 194
Central Asia 14
Ceuta 54, 58-59
Charlemagne 15
Christian 15, 17-21, 28, 31, 34-35, 37-38, 41-43, 46-49, 53, 55, 57, 60-61, 63-64, 74, 76, 78, 82, 86, 89, 91-92, 94, 96-100, 102, 104, 108-112, 114-119, 121-123, 133, 137, 143, 157, 161, 163-164, 190
Civil War, Spanish 131
Coín 90
Columbus, Christopher 97-98
Comares 162, 164, 166-167, 169, 170-171, 173-174, 188
Consejo de Población 119
Constantinople 123
Convento de San Francisco 103-104, 136, 148-149
Córdoba 7-10, 13, 15, 17-23, 37, 41-46, 49, 52, 55, 72, 90, 120, 189
Corral de Carbón 63, 131
Cuarto Dorado 164, 166
Cuesta de Gomérez 138-139
Cuesta del Rey Chico 150, 192-195

D

Damascus 11, 14
Daroca 37
Darro river 24, 27, 29, 31, 40, 49, 51, 74, 131-133, 156-157, 171, 193
De Cárdenas, Gutierre 96
De Castro y Quiñones, Pedro, Archbishop 121-122, 124
De Cenete, Marques 120
De Cisneros, Francisco, Archbishop of Toledo 99, 101
De Granada Venegas, Pedro 94
De Guzmán, Alfonso Pérez 58
De Lara, Nuño González 53-54
De los Vélez, Marques 115
De Mármol Carvajal, Luis 98, 102, 117-118
De Molino, Cristóbal 115
De Mondéjar, Marques 115
Dénia 22
De Siloé, Diego 108, 109
De Talavera, Archbishop 100, 102
De Vico, Ambrosio 124
De Zafra, Hernando 103
Disraeli, Benjamin 129
Don Juan de Austria 116-118
Doré, Gustave 127, 129

E

Ecija 18
Edward, Black Prince 70
Egypt 11-12, 68
Elvira 8, 14, 16, 19, 23
Emperor's Chambers 188-189
England 64, 70
Enrique II 69-70
Enrique III 76
Enrique IV 82
Ermita de San Miguel Alto 74, 76
Ermita de San Sebastián 36

Escalera del Agua 199-200
Escorial 79, 80
Expulsion of the Moriscos 97, 101, 112, 119-124
Extremadura 119-120

F

Farax Aben Farax 113
Fatimids 19
Felipe II 110, 112, 115-116, 118, 120, 122, 124
Felipe III 122-123
Fernando II of Aragón 82-84, 88-91, 93, 100-101, 104-105, 112, 114
Fernando III 42-47, 52
Fernando IV 59-60
Fez 53, 55, 62, 68, 70, 98
Flanders 151
Ford, Richard 126
France 82, 123
Franche-Comté 105
Franco, Francisco 131
French occupation of Alhambra 125, 136, 141, 148, 150, 194
Fuente de los Leones 174, 178
Fuente Grande 32-33, 95, 131

G

Galera 81, 93, 118
Galicia 14
Gaul 9-10
Generalife 51, 61, 136, 139, 143, 145, 151, 182, 191-192, 194-195, 197-198, 200
Genil 17, 31, 49, 51, 80
Genoa 63, 183
Gibralfaro 66, 92-93
Gibraltar 12, 53-56, 58-59, 62, 66, 70, 79, 81
Giralda tower 39
Gomara region 92, 171
Gothic style 108-110
Granada 7-8, 17, 22-24, 27-29, 31-32, 35-44, 46-49, 51-54, 56-66, 68-70, 72-73, 76- 105, 108-111, 113, 115, 119-126, 129, 131-133, 136-139, 141, 151, 171, 183-184, 188
Gran Vía de Colón 131
Grau, Valencia 123
Great Mosque, Córdoba 19, 20
Guadalajara 119
Guadalete 13
Guadalhorce 18
Guadalquivir 7-8, 15, 42-43, 46-47, 53
Guadiaro 62-63
Guadix 9, 44, 53, 60, 68, 88, 89, 92-94

Guza 53, 55, 62, 63

H

Habus al-Muzaffar 24
Hafsids 41, 68
Hama, Syria 17
Hammudids 23
Hasding Vandals 9, 10
High Atlas Mountains 37, 38
Hisham II 20
Hispania 8, 9, 10
Holy Roman Empire 85, 105, 109, 151, 155
Huéscar 60, 86

I

Iberian Peninsula 7-8, 10-13, 15, 17, 20, 22-23, 31, 34-38, 41, 43, 46-47, 53, 55-58, 60, 62, 68, 73, 78, 82-84, 86, 96-98, 102, 109, 112-113, 122, 125-126, 151
Ibn al-Ahmar (Muhammad I) 44, 47-48, 51-53, 62, 136, 141, 156-157, 161
Ibn al-Khatib 58, 60, 66, 68, 70
Ibn Hud 41-44, 46
Ibn Naghrela, Joseph 24
Ibn Naghrela, Samuel 24, 51, 133
Ibn Tashufin 34-36
Ibn Zamrak 70, 73, 174, 179, 184
Iglesia de San José 31
Iglesia de San Juan de los Reyes 40
Iglesia de Santa María de la Alhambra 146
Iliberris 8-9, 14, 17, 23
Illora 91
India 14
Inquisition 97
Innocent III, Pope 41
Iraq 11
Ireland 125
Irving, Washington 126, 141, 180, 188, 193
Isabel of Castile 82-84, 86-88, 90, 93-94, 98-99, 103, 105
Islam 11, 14, 20, 35, 47, 82, 86, 97, 100, 102, 105, 109-112, 116, 121-122, 131, 133, 138, 143, 147, 151, 166-167, 169, 171, 183-184
Isma'il I 60, 163-164, 200
Isma'il II 68
Italica 9
Italy 108, 155

J

Jaén 23, 28, 41, 44, 46-48, 55, 60, 70
Jaime I 53
Jamuga 187
Játiva 22
Jerez 53
Jews 24, 51, 97, 124, 133
Jinete 62
Jones, Owen 49, 126, 173, 185
Juana, 'la Loca' 105
Juana, 'la Beltraneja' 82
Juan II 84

K

Kairouan 12
Koran 11, 47, 170
Koutoubia Mosque 39
Ksar el-Kabir 57

L

Lanjarón 85, 101, 115
Láujar 98, 101, 117
Lead disc books 121
Legado Andalusí 132, 200
León 21, 38, 41-56
Leovigild 10
Lerín, Count of 101
Levante 22, 35, 47
Libya 12
Loja 87-88, 91, 152
Lorca, Frederico García 131
Lorca 35
Louis XI 82
Lucena 15, 89-90
Lusitania 9

M

Macael 174, 178
Machuca, Pedro 108, 138, 139, 141, 155, 163
Madinat al-Hamra 144-145
Madinat al-Zahra 19-20, 49, 73, 189
Madinat Elvira 16-17, 29
Madinat Gharnata 23-24, 141, 144
Madrasa 62, 64-65, 103-104
Madrid 100, 124, 131
Málaga 18, 22-24, 46, 48, 52-53, 56-57, 63, 65-66, 68, 81, 86-93, 116
Mallorca 122
Mamelukes 68
Marinids 41, 53-59, 62-64, 68, 70, 73, 79
Maristan 70, 72
Marrakech 34, 36-37, 39, 41
Mauror Hill 141, 156, 160
Mecca 11
Medina 11
Medinaceli 21

Mediterranean 9, 23, 48, 63, 82, 84, 88, 97, 112, 116, 119
Mérida 8, 15, 42
Meseta Central 7, 43, 82, 120
Mexuar 162-164
Michelangelo 108, 155
Middle East 133
Minorca 42
Mirador de Lindaraja 184, 187-189
Moclín 90-91
Mojácar 86, 93
Monasterio de la Cartuja 110
Monasterio de San Jerónimo 188
Montefrío 91
Moriscos 103, 109, 111-125
Morocco 12, 34, 37-38, 53, 54, 59, 64, 79
Morón 22
Moscardó, Colonel 58
Mozarabs 18
Mudéjars 53, 98-103, 110-112, 119
Muhammad bin Tumart 38
Muhammad II 54-58, 191, 194
Muhammad III 58-59, 144, 146, 190
Muhammad IV 61-62
Muhammad IX 78, 80
Muhammad, Prophet 11
Muhammad V 63, 65-66, 68-70, 72, 76, 79, 144, 163-164, 166, 171, 174, 183-184
Muhammad VI 68
Muhammad VII 73, 76
Muhammad XI 81-82
Muhammad XI, 'el Chiquito' 81
Muley Hacén 78, 81-82, 87-90
Mulhacén Mountain 7
Münzer, Hieronymus 125
Murcia 7, 22, 35, 41-42, 48, 53
Murphy, James Cavanagh 60, 65, 125
Muslim 12, 15, 17, 22, 24, 34, 38, 41, 42, 43, 46, 47, 48, 51, 52, 55, 60, 64, 68, 69, 73, 80, 89, 92, 93, 94, 96, 97, 99, 100, 101, 109, 111, 112, 113, 114, 119, 121, 124, 126, 131, 133, 137, 163, 164, 171, 183, 184
Muwallads 17-18

N

Naples 93
Nasr 44, 59, 60
Nasrids 41, 43-44, 47, 49, 51-54, 56-61, 64, 66, 68, 70, 72-82,

207

84-86, 88, 90, 92, 96,
103-104, 108-110,
113, 126-127, 129,
131, 136-139, 141,
144-146, 148-151,
155-156, 162-164,
166-167, 171, 174,
182-183, 187-190,
193-195, 197, 200
Nasrid Palaces 151, 162, 163
Navarra 21
Netherlands 105
North Africa 10-12, 14, 19-24,
31, 34-36, 38, 41, 46,
48, 55-58, 63, 68, 78,
86, 92, 94-96, 98-99,
111, 122-124

O

Oran 95, 111, 123
Oratorio 190
Orgiva 115
Orontes river 17
Ottoman Empire 105, 112

P

Palacio de Carlos V 108, 138-
139, 143, 145, 151,
156, 163, 171
Palacio de Comares 65, 162,
164, 166-167, 169,
171, 173-174, 188
Palacio de los Abencerrajes
148
Palacio de los Leones 162, 171,
174, 178, 184, 188
Palacio del Partal 72, 143, 162,
189-190
Paseo de las Adelfas 200
Patio de la Acequia 195, 197
Patio de la Mezquita 162-163
Patio de las Cabellerizas 195
Patio del Ciprés de la Sultana
199-200
Patio de Lindaraja 188-189
Patio de los Arrayanes 65, 166,
169, 171, 173-174
Patio de los Leones 70, 125,
174, 184
Patio de Machuca 162-163
Patronato de la Alhambra y
Generalife 139, 145
Pechina 14
Pedro I, 'the Cruel' 66, 68-69,
183
Peñón de Frigiliana 116
Pergamon Museum, Berlin
190
Persia 14
Phillip, 'el Hermoso' 105
Phoenicians 7
Pillars of Hercules 153, 164
Pinos Puente 17
Plaza de Bibrambla 100, 110

Plaza de España, Seville 24
Plaza de los Aljibes 156-157
Plaza Nueva 131, 139
Portugal 38, 64, 70, 82, 93, 97,
105, 126, 151, 188
Puente del Qadí 27, 29, 31, 133
Puerta de Bibrambla 129,
139, 141
Puerta de Elvira 27, 29
Puerta de Fajalauza 75
Puerta de la Justicia 143
Puerta del Arribal 191-192
Puerta de las Armas 157
Puerta de las Granadas 138-
139, 141
Puerta de los Carros 143
Puerta del Vino 143-145
Puerta de Monaita 28-29
Pyrenees 7, 13-14

R

Real Alcázar, Seville 68-69,
184, 188
Reconquista 42, 52-53, 82, 84,
97-98, 123, 125, 131
Renaissance style 108-110, 151
Richelieu, Armand, Cardinal
120
Ricos Hombres 54
Rif Mountains 92
Rio Salado 64
Roderic, King 12
Roberts, David 129, 131
Romans 8-10, 13, 15, 17, 23,
133, 151, 155
Rome 9, 108
Ronda 18, 22, 58-59, 62, 68,
76, 86, 88, 90
Royal Chancellery 110
Royal Hospital 109, 110
Rute 70

S

Sabika Hill 27, 29, 48, 125,
132-133, 136, 139,
144, 156
Sacromonte 74, 121-122, 124,
188
Sagrajas 34-35
Sagunto 8
Sala de Dos Hermanas 184,
185, 188
Sala de la Barca 166, 171
Sala de los Abencerrajes
180-181
Sala de los Mocárabes 179
Sala de los Reyes 60-61, 180,
182
Sala de Mexuar 163-164
Salobreña 73, 76, 81, 94
Salón del Trono (also known
as the Hall of the
Ambassadors) 96,
169-171

Salón Rico 19
Sancho IV 56, 57, 58
Sanhaja Berbers 23, 34-35
Santa Catalina 44
Santa Fe 95, 131
Sardinia 82
Sassanian Empire 11
Secano 148
Second War of the Alpujarras
113-114, 120
Serranía de Ronda 102, 118
Seville 7, 22-24, 37-42, 44, 52,
54-55, 68-69, 105,
120, 151, 184, 188
Sicily 82
Sierra Bermeja 102, 115, 118
Sierra de Alfaguera 33
Sierra Elvira 16-17
Sierra Nevada 8, 23, 51, 121,
133, 136, 195
Siling Vandals 9
Silk industry 113, 119-120
Slaves 22
Spain 63-64, 83-84, 97-98,
105, 108-110, 112,
115, 119-120, 122-
124, 126-127, 129,
131-132
Strait of Gibraltar 48, 53-59,
62-64, 70, 79, 86, 166
Suspiro del Moro 98
Syria 11, 14, 17

T

Tablate 114-115
Taifa of Granada 23, 31
Taifas 21-22
Tangier 57-58
Tapial (rammed earth) walls
29
Tarifa 48, 55-58, 64
Tariq bin Ziyad 12
Tarragona 8
Tercios 116
Theodosius, Emperor 9
Tin Mal Mosque 38
Tlemcen 41, 56, 58-59, 68
Toledo 10, 13, 15, 22, 34-35,
41, 58, 90-92, 99, 120
Torre de Comares 169-171
Torre de Isma'il 197, 200
Torre de la Cautiva 193
Torre del Agua 51, 143,
150-151
Torre de la Pólvora 157, 160
Torre de las Armas 157
Torre de las Damas, 189-190
Torre de las Infantas 193
Torre de la Vela 141, 157,
160-161
Torre del Cabo de la Carrera
194
Torre del Cubo 157, 161
Torre del Homenaje 157, 161
Torre del Moral 89

Torre de los Picos 191-192
Torre del Qadí 191, 193
Torre de Machuca 163
Torre Quebrada 156-157, 160
Torres Bermejas 141, 160
Tortosa 22
Tripoli 38
Tunis 68
Tunisia 12, 124
Turks 112, 116, 124

U

Úbeda 19
Umar Ibn Hafsun 18-19
Umayyads 14, 15, 16, 17, 18,
19, 21, 34, 42, 59

V

Valencia 7, 22, 36, 41, 112,
120-123
Valle de Lecrín 113
Vase of the Gazelles 127
Vatican 121-122
Vega of Granada 8, 17, 24, 40,
51, 60-61, 79-80, 87,
91, 95, 99, 120, 131,
133, 141, 194, 200
Vejer de la Frontera 13, 53
Vélez-Málaga 91
Venice 183
Visigoths 9, 10, 12, 13, 15, 17
Viznar 32, 131

W

Weiditz, Christoph 111-112,
125
Wellington, Duke of 139

Y

Yusuf I 63- 66, 74, 103-104,
143, 166, 171, 190,
193
Yusuf II 73
Yusuf III 76, 78
Yusuf IV 80

Z

Zahara 76-77, 87
Zaragoza 15, 22, 36, 41
Zawi bin Ziri 23
Zayyanids 41, 56, 58-59, 68
Zirids 23-24, 27-29, 31-33,
36, 48-49, 51-52, 76,
133, 156
Ziri ibn Manad 23
Zoraya 82, 88

208